W9-CDM-700

THE BEER
TRIALS

SEAMUS CAMPBELL & ROBIN GOLDSTEIN

Fearless Critic Media New York
www.fearlesscritic.com

First Edition

ISBN 978-1-6081600-9-9

10 9 8 7 6 5 4 3 2 1

Authors

Seamus Campbell is one of just 96 beer experts to have passed the rigorous Certified Cicerone exam. An experienced homebrewer, Seamus happens to share a birthday with legendary Beer Hunter Michael Jackson. He lives in Portland, Oregon, where he writes the beer blog *The Daily Wort* and is a contributor to the *Fearless Critic Portland Restaurant Guide*.

Robin Goldstein is the author of *The Wine Trials*, co-author of *The Wine Trials 2010*, and founder and editor-in-chief of the Fearless Critic restaurant guide series. Robin is a graduate of Harvard University and the Yale Law School. He has a certificate in cooking from the French Culinary Institute in New York and a WSET advanced wine and spirits certificate.

Associate Editors

Alexis Herschkowitsch is a co-author of *The Wine Trials 2010* and editor of six Fearless Critic restaurant guides. Alexis has written for the *Fodor's* travel guides to Mexico, Central America, and Thailand. She is a graduate of the University of Texas at Austin, and has a WSET advanced wine and spirits certificate.

Andrea Armeni is a San Francisco-based reporter for *Emerging Markets* magazine. He is a graduate of Columbia University and the Yale Law School, has practiced wine law in Napa Valley, and has contributed to many Fearless Critic books. He was an associate editor of *The Wine Trials* and *The Wine Trials 2010*.

This book is dedicated to Bruce Campbell, whose countless hours on the road between breweries made this—and other achievements large and small—possible.

Blind tasting panel

The following people, listed alphabetically, served along with the authors on the blind tasting panel for this book. The opinions set forth in the reviews do not necessarily reflect the views of any one of these individuals or their affiliated institutions. Any errors are ours alone.

Suzy Choate is a professional beer server at Portland, Oregon's Hop and Vine. She has also cooked professionally at restaurants in Portland. **Rick Freed** is an avid homebrewer and a chef with degree from the Western Culinary institute. **Jeff Ganong** is a BJCP-trained beer enthusiast and a process engineer for a semiconductor manufacturer. **Niki Ganong** is BJCP-trained and writes about beer for portlandfoodanddrink.com under the pen name "Suds Sister." **Adam Gaydosh** has been hombrewing for 10 years. He works in the technology industry and is a travel addict. **Tim Hanrahan** is a homebrewer and creative director who has worked with major breweries on their graphical materials. **Bruce Kinzey** is a homebrewer who left the East Coast for Portland in 2006 and hasn't been seen since. **Marc Ledbetter** chose to live in Portland because of its beer. He has also lived in the Czech Republic. Do you sense a trend here? **Dan May** is a brewer and runs the beer blog *A Pint For Dionysus*. **Morgan Miller** has worked in and around the Portland, Oregon craft brewing industry since 1985. He currently works for Ninkasi Brewing in Portland. **Mellie Pullman** is the Willamette Industries professor of Supply Chain Management at Portland State University. She was the brewmaster and co-founder of Wasatch Beers in Park City, Utah, after brewing at Pyramid in Kalama, Washington. **Ben Salzberg** has been brewing since 1993. **Matthew Schuler** is an adjunct member of the Oregon Bartenders' Guild with a background in homebrewing. **Sam Sugar** wears the exquisitely appropriate title of "Beer Gazelle" at Rogue's Green Dragon Brewpub in Portland, where she is in charge of beer selection for a remarkable 50 taps. **Seth Vores** is a certified BJCP (Beer Judge Certification Program) judge, a proud member of the Oregon Brew Crew, and an award-winning homebrewer of eight years. **Guest blind tasters:** Aaron Furmanek, Reiko Hillyer, Brian Smith, Danielle Tarpley.

Special thanks to **Laurel Hoyt** for her work as the behind-the-scenes engineer who enabled much of this book's creation.

Other editorial contributors

Johan Almenberg, Anna Dreber Almenberg, Aaron Furmanek, Laurel Hoyt, Christiane Kurcius, Mellie Pullman

Tasting stewards and assistants

Martin Chase, Jenn Dolan, Rick Freed, Shawn Furst, Laurel Hoyt, Christiane Kurcius, Megan Manley, Carrie Padian, Phil Sano, Megan Savage, Matthew Schuler, Meghan Sinnott, Luiz Sudbrack
Catering: Martin Chase, Margo Dobberton

Sample procurement

David Carter, Martin Chase, David Manley, Carrie Padian

Tasting experiment participants

Derek Abe, Aaron Abrams, Benjamin Adrian, Jev Asher, Ben Barber, Alyssa Beers, Brian L. Bloom, Erik Blumenthal, Terra Brown, Michael Brown, Craig Brozefsky, Sierra Callahan, Anna Capacci, Camille Castaneda, Stephanie D. Caulley, Cindy Chambers, Jonathan Andrew Cox, Chris M. Chambers, Bill Dameron, Diana Dameron, Clint DeNyse, Jed Dolbeer, Chris Dunlap, Benedikt Feuerecker, Russ Fortney, J. Freelove, Jeffrey Fuller, Julia Gammons, Sergio Garcia, Paul Glahn, Kathleen Grinager, Cory Hain, Grant Harman , Dave Haskins, Matthew Hickey, Jeff Howard, Kimmy Howland, Adrian Hutapea, Frank D. James, Wilson Johns, Stephen Judkins, Stefan Kaiser, Edward Kasch, Lori Kruse, Astrid Kurcius, Daniel Lerch, Sophia Luchini-Dexter, Michelle Magura, Michele Maloney, Luisa Mastroberardino, Dan May, Nils McCutcheon, Ronald McElroy, Patricia McElroy, Lyle McNaughton, Elizabeth U. Meiners, Morgan Miller, Christina Mullin, R.F. Mullin, Brennan Novak, Kathleen O'Malley, Nicole Olson, Siri Osis, Kristina Pants, Lauren Pedersen, Matthew P. Picio, Ira Pollack, Catherine Poole, Joshua Ray, Brandy Ray, Paula Rowan, Sabrina Santos, Brian Schultz, Molly Schultz, Sherry Schwenderlauf, Jake Sepulveda, Richard Seymour, Patrick Shearer, Jaya Skinner-Maginnis, Justin Slone, Rachel Slone,

Tasting experiment participants (continued)

Oliver Smith, Amanda Rae Soares, Ken Southerland, Tim Speth, Don Stearns, John Stupak, Michael Sugarbaker, Jess Suter, Shane Swilley, Angela Szegedi, Tobias Szegedi, Dwayne Tallmadge, Jennifer Tallmadge, Gerry Thefish, Jesse Todhunter, Barbara Trott, Isabella Trott, David van Hook Jr., Diana van Hook, Lea Vanlue, Rev. William D. Vanlue, Andrew Veen, Larry Walters, Kami White, Amy Williams, Travis Wonders, Frank Yrle, Ellen Zientek, Keith Zientek. *This list is not exhaustive; some tasting experiment participants choose to remain anonymous.*

Photo credits

AleSmith Anvil ESB, AleSmith IPA, AleSmith X, Arrogant Bastard, Stone IPA, and Stone Levitation Ale images courtesy of StudioSchulz.com. Beer images courtesy of their respective breweries. Photos also contributed by Seamus Campbell.

Tasting event hosts:

Green Dragon Brewpub, Portland, Oregon

We would like to thank **Russ Menegat, Sam Sugar,** and the entire staff of the Green Dragon for their generous support and collaboration in hosting our blind-tasting beer experiment.

Mary Ann Hoyt and Jody Hoyt, Portland, Oregon

We would like to thank the Hoyts for generously hosting the entire series of panel tastings for our beer ratings and reviews.

The Cicerone Certification Program (www.cicerone.org), founded by Ray Daniels, president of the Craft Beer Institute, is the industry's only formal beer sommelier certification. The Cicerone Certification program has licensed 1,000 certified beer servers and 96 higher-level Certified Cicerones, who passed rigorous brewing and blind tasting examinations. *"Certified Cicerone" and "Cicerone Certification Program" are registered trademarks of the Craft Beer Institute.*

Contents

Fearless Critic
restaurant guides

Brutally honest reviews. By undercover chefs and food nerds.
No restaurant ads. In print and online at **fearlesscritic.com.**

fearlesscritic.com

Preface

This is a book about beer in the twenty-first century.

We believe that beer needs a new book for this new age, because we are in the midst of a beer renaissance. This renaissance is happening not just in the world of craft brewing, which has reached unprecedented heights of sophistication, but also at industrial-scale breweries, which, driven by increasing interest in beer at the ground consumer level, are slowly broadening their horizons and improving their products, too. Within these pages, we hope to highlight the unprecedented skill, creativity, and depth of experience of brewers working in every corner of the industry.

Beyond the changing nature of what's brewing, beer's distribution has been extending its reach at a breakneck pace. Diverse, well-rounded beer programs are popping up with increasing frequency—not just at the trendy beer bars that have grown up in urban areas, but also at small-town supermarkets and back-road neighborhood bars where, for decades, the only choice was between the "domestic" (Bud) and the "import" (Heineken).

As craft IPAs and Trappist ales work their way onto even those dusty shelves and grungy chalkboards, selecting beer has suddenly gotten a lot more exciting. But it has also become bewildering, and that's where we think we can help. We believe that a ratings guide covering a broad swath of today's beer landscape, from craft beers to macro-lagers, is more necessary than ever.

Not all beer is worthy of your attention—far from it—but the unprintable joke about American beer and sex in canoes (you'll have to look it up) is still a reflection of too much popular opinion. For that stereotype ignores the truth of the matter: North America's west coast is the now perhaps the world's most dynamic beer region. It is a place where beer appreciation is more than a cult movement; it is a new social norm, whether in California, where US microbrewing was born; in the craft-beer petri dishes of Oregon and Washington, home to Cascade hops; or in Canada's British Columbia, where there are now more than 50 craft breweries. Yes, there's sometimes snobbery involved—too many Portlanders these days dismiss noble European pale lagers as beneath them—but mostly, it's just unbridled enthusiasm for the nuances of interesting local beer, even where you'd least expect it, amongst corporate drones and underage slackers, in strip-mall chain restaurants and run-down package stores.

At the risk of sounding like Howard Dean, it's taking hold everywhere from Texas to Alaska, Massachusetts to Maine, Montana to Québec. The seeds of a new beer order are being sown in Singapore and Riga, La Paz and Reykjavik, Perth and San Pedro Sula. (All of these cities have had recent entries in beer festival competitions.) A craft-brewing culture has even spread from the towns of El Bolsón and Bariloche across Argentine Patagonia.

But don't be fooled into thinking that the mass-market conglomerates are all bad. While that position may have geopolitical merit, it's narrow-minded from a gustatory perspective. The modern machinery, technical expertise, and marketing resources of big companies can often help smaller breweries impose better quality controls on their beer, and to get it out to a lot more people. And as you'll see in Part II of this book, in which our tasting panel reviews 250 of the world's most popular beers—including a lot of globalized brands—the best of these are able to industrialize production without industrializing the style.

In short, the state of the beer union is strong, and this book aims to help you navigate it. Part I of *The Beer Trials* are devoted to the exploration of the modern beer landscape, from the way our palates and brains experience beer to the ins and outs of the world's beer styles, ingredients, and flavors. In Part II, we aim to impose some structure on the vast landscape of modern beer by rating a broad range of the world's most widely available craft and macro-brews, based on a series of blind tastings conducted by our panel of beer experts over the better part of a year.

That these beers were rated and reviewed blind was of paramount importance to this project. We believe this to be the only way to avoid perceptual bias and give each beer an equal chance to succeed, regardless of its prestige or price in the marketplace. While the beer world does not yet suffer from the sort of arbitrary pricing that plagues the wine industry, there are certainly beers whose reputation outstrips reality. The world of beer, alas, is in danger of following that of wine into becoming the basin for pretentious, unscientific, fuzzy beer talk by newly proclaimed pundits, and endless strings of obnoxious adjectives.

To meditate on beer—to use your imagination to coax more flavors, images, and emotions from the experience—can be a lot of fun, but to claim those sensory free-associations as objective facts is to poison the dialogue. Don't fall into the trap of believing that because a beer wins a competition or gets a high rating on a website—or even in this book—that you should like it. Don't convince yourself that you don't have a sophisticated palate just because you don't have a taste for strong Belgian ale (a phenomenon that we'll discuss again in chapter 2, "Beer goggles").

We do hope that our beer tasting panel's collective palate, and the rigor of our blind tastings, will help narrow your choices when you're faced with beers that you haven't yet had the chance to taste yourself and highlight some interesting beers available in your region that you might not have known about.

The world of beer is vast, and even people with a lot of experience with beer can easily settle into complacency and become set in their ways. (We know this because we're constantly fighting that instinct in ourselves.) So if you're a connoisseur of obscure Belgian ales with verticals of Westvleteren in your cellar, then we hope that this book might point you as well to some of the more subtle pleasures of the world's great pale lagers. If, instead, you're just a casual beer drinker wedded to a ritual of Stella every Friday night at your local pub, then we hope this book might persuade you to branch out into an exploration of beers with more pronounced hop or malt characters than you're used to.

If this is a book with an agenda, then that agenda is simple: to broaden your horizons, and narrow your search, by arming you with better information about beer. If we can help you find a new beer to love, then our purpose is met.

Part I: Chapter 1 Selling you beer

What motivates us to argue that people need to know more about the beer they're drinking, or that our approach of blind tasting is a good idea for beer appreciation? Let's look at some of the science behind beer tasting.

In 1964, two scientists working for the Carling Beer Company, Ralph Allison and Kenneth Uhl, ran the following experiment: first, they chose five beer brands that were verified by expert tasters as containing objective perceptual differences. Next, they sent a free six-pack of beer to more than 300 regular beer drinkers. Out of the five brands, a taster was sent two bottles each of three different brands. If a drinker had indicated beforehand that one of the five brands was his or her regular brand, the drinker would receive two bottles of that brand as part of the six-pack.

Each beer came with a neck tag for simple ratings of the beer. However, some of the six-packs had beers with labels, while some of the six-packs had unmarked beers.

When participants received the six-packs with the beer labels intact, their ratings showed clear differentiation between the various beers. As expected, they rated their favorites higher than other beers.

But when participants received the six-packs with the bottles' labels removed and their caps wire-scrubbed to render their brands unidentifiable, they showed virtually no preferences for certain beers over others. On the characteristics, there were no statistically significant differences between any of the beers, with the exception of carbonation level (one beer had a better "Just Enough" carbonation score than the other four). No beer was judged by its regular drinkers to be significantly better than the other samples.[1]

The scientists concluded that "product distinctions or differences...arose primarily through [participants'] receptiveness to the various firms' marketing efforts rather than through perceived physical product differences," and they recommended that Carling should work harder at defining their brand image through marketing. It is telling that the strongest appeals to marketing and the strongest instances of brand loyalty in the beer world appear in the market segment that features the most subtle differences between brands: pale lager, the world's most popular style of beer.

In late 2009, we conducted an experiment at the Green Dragon Pub in Portland, Oregon, with the goal of building upon Allison and Uhl's work to investigate the ability of modern American beer consumers to distinguish between pale lager beers. Our experiment employed a setup known as a "triangle test," similar to the setup used by Roman Weil, a University of Chicago business school professor, in a fascinating series of blind-tasting wine experiments that we discuss at length in our wine book, *The Wine Trials*.[2]

Our experiment set out to test whether regular beer drinkers in the United States could distinguish between major brands of similarly styled European pale lager. Brands from Northern and Central Europe, where the pale lager and pilsner styles originated, are considered to be archetypes of the style.

We served three different major brands of European pale lager from three different countries to a sample of 138 regular beer drinkers: Czechvar from the Czech Republic, Heineken from the Netherlands, and Stella Artois from Belgium. (All three of these beers are also reviewed in Part II of this book, classified as "Continental lagers" in the pale lager category.)

Each subject in our experiment received three tasting-sized samples of pale lager beer, of which two were identical and the third was different. Subjects were asked to identify which of the two beers were the same. The order of samples was randomized, and brands were rotated through in equal proportions.

The result? Tasters performed no better than chance at identifying the two identical beers.[3] We concluded that the differences between major European pale lager brands from different countries are too subtle to be detected by regular beer drinkers, even under controlled conditions.

Interestingly, in an experiment we conducted in Bavaria with the help of Christiane Kurcius of the University of Regensburg, a small sample of college students from the Munich area performed dramatically (and statistically significantly) better than chance in identifying, blind, the major brands of Munich helles lager (Augustiner, Hacker-Pschorr, Höfbrau, Löwenbräu, Paulaner, and Spaten). Unlike Allison and Uhl's subjects, most of the subjects in this study also ranked their favorite brand (usually Augustiner) as the best beer in the blind tasting.

Bavaria's lager culture is perhaps unparalleled anywhere else in the world. We attribute this result partly to the fact that Bavarians grow up with so much exposure to the local beer brands, from their early teens onward, that their palates become extremely sensitive to the differences between them (compelling evidence, as if we needed any more, for the repeal of America's preposterously Puritanical and irresponsibly counterproductive minimum drinking age of 21). Another important factor, though, is the fact that Bavarian helles lagers, although made in the same basic style, are more nuanced and thus distinctive than the mass-market European pale lager brands we served in our Portland experiment. But the Bavarian experiment is also a reminder of the danger of overgeneralizing about the world's beer drinkers.

Unfortunately, it's incredibly difficult to find Augustiner—or young Bavarian beer consumers—outside Bavaria, and our finding that beer consumers cannot perceive the taste differences between the more generic mass-market pale lager brands suggests that those brands must rely largely on means other than taste differentiation to win customer loyalty in the beer market.

This conclusion is consistent with the prodigious advertising expenditures of pale lager producers. Compared with the producers of other comestibles, an extraordinarily high proportion of the cost base of mass pale lager brands goes toward advertising.

In 2009, according to *Advertising Age*, Anheuser-Busch—a company that seems to have gotten the Allison and Uhl memo— pumped more than $1.5 billion into domestic advertising. Bud Light commercials have become as indispensible a part of the Super Bowl as the Vince Lombardi trophy. SABMiller pitched in a little less than a billion dollars. (By comparison, McDonald's spent $1.2 billion; Nike spent $790 million; and luxury-products giant LVMH Moet Hennessy Louis Vuitton spent a mere $687 million.)

Perhaps, on some level, we already know that when we choose a mass-market lager beer, we're buying more into a brand image than into a taste profile. It has become an inescapable fact of modernity that we often rely on brands to define ourselves, both to ourselves and to others. Whether we're buying limited-edition shoes, local organic yams, or frugal military surplus jackets, most of us are influenced—consciously or otherwise—by the pitch and story associated with the products we consume. We believe, in a very real way, that some of that story we liked will rub off on us.

In the wine world, lifestyle marketing seems to regularly convince people to spend extra money on premium wine whose superiority they can't actually detect. In an experiment we conducted for *The Wine Trials*, we actually found an *inverse* correlation between the price of a wine and its rating in blind tastings by everyday wine drinkers. Many tasters—particularly those without formal training in wine—*preferred* the flavor profile of less expensive wines to wines that, in some cases, cost 10 times as much.[4]

Happily, beer does not yet approach the stratospheric cost of well-marketed or well-regarded wine. If someone really wants to believe that his or her $1 Heineken is clearly superior to his or her friend's $1 Stella—even if a blind tasting wouldn't support that hypothesis—the impact is still relatively low. But we like to think that there is ultimately a greater pleasure to be found in veridical experiences of beer than in imagined ones—that the Bavarians' ability to recognize, blind, the properties they so admire in Augustiner unlocks a pleasure deeper than the placebo effect that's sparked by mere admiration itself.

And it's not necessary for Americans to travel to Germany to find beers that the average consumer can tell apart. The Carling study was conducted in 1964, a time representative of the post-Prohibition struggle to keep beer relevant. From the beginning of the 20th century until the early 1980s, beer in North America suffered a steady progression of brewery closures and consolidation, with the result that the public impression of beer was of a uniformly pale, fizzy lager—an environment in which European lagers like the ones we tested were seen as exotic, high-end products. By 1983, there were just 80 breweries left in the US, down from a peak of over 4,000 a century earlier.

But in 1978, just as the American commercial beer scene was on the verge of hitting rock bottom, something interesting happened: with the passage of House Resolution 1337, Congress legalized homebrewing for the first time since before Prohibition. This legitimized the sort of grassroots experimentation with beer that would evolve into a cottage trade and ultimately a full-fledged microbrewing industry in America in a remarkably short span of time.

A few short decades later, our grocery shelves are stocked with dozens of styles of beer, many of which were nearly extinct a generation ago. This dramatic reversal has brought about its own challenges—a subject we address in the next chapter—but for the curious drinker, it's a welcome change from the generic "BEER" products of the 1970s.

Not all of the side effects of a maturing industry are positive. One of the main traditional differences between the beer and wine industries is the way that lifestyle marketing has come to dominate the luxury end of the market in wine (e.g. associating Veuve Clicquot in consumers' minds with a jet-setting lifestyle), while it has historically surrounded everyday beers (the lifestyle in this case: kicking back with a Corona on the beach, or pairing Bud Light with NFL football). As such, most beer prices have long reflected, and still, to a large extent, tend to reflect a cost-plus-reasonable-profit model of pricing. The power grab in beer has been for share in what amounts to a commodity market.

But that is starting to change. In chapter 2, we'll reflect on the impact of craft beer's growing role as a product that can offer the consumer prestige and sophistication, particularly in the form of high-cost, low-production beers that mirror a model we've frequently seen in high-end wine. There are a lot of good consumerist reasons to fight against any kind of perceptual prestige bubble, and a lot of good personal reasons to strive to understand a constellation of goods and their relationships in terms of their intrinsic properties. Ultimately, there is only one really good defense against the excessive influence of marketing, branding, and expectation: a rigorous understanding of what you like and why you like it. Your preferences should be your own, but until they're freed from the placebo effect—which we'll discuss more in chapter 2—you don't really own them.

Chapter 2 Beer goggles

If your job as a consumer is to look beyond all categories of lifestyle marketing, that doesn't just mean skepticism of Anheuser-Busch's Super Bowl ads. It also means skepticism of the well-intentioned but ultimately narrow and unscientific opinions of the beer snob who insists that all great beer must be Belgian and cost at least $10. That enthusiastic beer geek may turn out to be even less aware of lifestyle marketing than your average Bud Light drinker.

As craft beer has moved into the mainstream and growth has slowed, producers have shifted from marketing craft beer as a concept to marketing their specific brands. One fashionable approach in the last decade has seen smaller breweries calling attention to themselves by brewing expensive, limited-production beers with huge ingredient bills, big flavors, and high alcohol.

These Imperial-strength beers and barleywines tend to have modest sales but attract disproportionate amounts of press time and beer hobbyist attention, thus boosting their producers' reputations. The alcohol of these beers usually falls between 8% and 11%—double that of mainstream beers. Sometimes—with beers like Dogfish Head World Wide Stout, Samuel Adams Utopias (one of the world's most expensive beers), BrewDog's Tactical Nuclear Penguin, and Sink the Bismarck!—it's even higher.

These beers are impressive, they make good conversation pieces, and beer enthusiasts' excitement over their complexity and intensity is completely legitimate. But the human brain is better tuned to contrast than to absolutes, and there may be a habituation effect in play here, too: as the enthusiast tastes more and more complex and intense beers, his or her baseline begins to move, and he or she seeks out beers with even greater complexity and intensity. As enthusiasts ourselves, although we do our best to keep this effect in check, we're hardly immune from it. If these beers are generally enjoyed only by beer drinkers who have been habituated to high alcohol levels and extremely concentrated aromatics, should they really be held up as the pinnacle of the brewing world?

Certainly it would be overly relativistic to claim that every beer style has equal pleasure potential. However much some people might enjoy a bottle of 55-calorie light lager, we can't defend, even theoretically, the flavor profile for which it aims.

But even if not all beer styles are created equal, we don't think the super-strong style that's currently in vogue should be elevated above the rest of the world's noble beer traditions. Lighter beers serve a completely different purpose. They go with different foods and different seasons, and the best of them gain in balance and harmony what they lose in strength and complexity, and the best-executed versions of, say, pilsner, German hefeweizen, or good old normal-strength West Coast IPA deserve every bit as much renown as the top examples of the Imperial or Trappist styles.

As such, we find it fairly meaningless to compare Imperial stouts to pale lagers using a single numerical scale, and we do not believe that the highest beer ratings should be reserved exclusively for the highest-alcohol beers. In part II of this book, beers are rated on a 10-point scale that's relative only to the other beers we've reviewed and placed in the same "family" of beers—that is, beers whose styles are similar enough to warrant a fair comparison.

There is a clever subtlety in the ways that the most successful small producers are able to manipulate a sophisticated set of emotional levers to get us to feel a certain way about their products. Yes, we often love artisanal beers just because they're good; but sometimes, we love them just because they're artisanal, and in the process of loving them for that reason, we *convince* ourselves that they're good. It is important, in short, to keep in mind that just because someone isn't a conniving capitalist pig doesn't mean he or she hasn't been captured by lifestyle marketing.

Enthusiasm for a product is an ineffable, fleeting, emotion-driven thing, and it can often be driven as much by an intentional supply shortage than by its intrinsic qualities. In 2006, Portland's Deschutes Brewery hit a minor PR jackpot with their release of the limited-production, vintage-dated Abyss Imperial Stout—an 11% ABV beer brewed with licorice and molasses—which sold for $10. As the first in Deschutes' "Reserve Series," it sold out quickly. By the time most consumers heard about the 2006 Abyss, it was long gone from stores.

This lesson was apparently not forgotten the following year. The West Coast accounts that had landed the first few cases publicized that their small quantities required them to limit sales to a few bottles per customer, and it became clear that consumers would have to act quickly if they wanted any at all. Prices went haywire; bottles on Craigslist within a week of release went for $20, $30, or even $40. The 2007 Abyss was the must-have beer of the winter.

Abyss, which we've consumed on several occasions, is rich, complex, and deserves much of the acclaim it receives. But why, in the years since, has it been abandoned by the enthusiasts that once coveted the beer? While the 2007 production rapidly sold through its reported 350BBL production, stocks of the 2009—with a moderately higher reported production of 600BBL—are still readily available in Portland at the original retail price, four months after the beer's introduction.[5] The hype seems to have vanished.

Is this because the more recent beer is of lower quality? It's unlikely; our own experience tasting the beer is that it's still essentially the same fine product, with modest year-to-year variation in flavor profile. The Abyss is a fine, perhaps even a great, beer, and given the resources required to produce it—large volumes of grain and adjunct ingredients, oak barrels to store the beer, the cost of storage space, and so on—$10 is probably an entirely reasonable cost for a 22-ounce bottle.

Abyss defenders might perhaps point to the economy, or changing tastes, to explain the sudden drop in demand. But a more compelling explanation, we think, is the simple fact that the Abyss is no longer playing hard to get—and that it's no longer the "it" beer. (Pliny the Younger is the subject of the latest wave of panic buying in the beer world, while Westvleteren seems to have the lifetime achievement award for supply-shortage pricing.[6])

When an industry falls into that sort of "it" trap, and prices begin to break free from their original relationships to the cost of production, it risks going down the disturbing path of first-growth Bordeaux, where prices have spiraled into absurdity.

As the craft beer industry continues to mature, we should be wary of falling into that pattern. In the wine industry, an opaque network of barriers to entry have risen for small producers who can't afford, or don't want, to participate in the persuasion or artificial scarcity game. Pay-to-play schemes disguised as "criticism" are now legion in the wine world[7]—a fact that should sound a warning bell to beer enthusiasts everywhere. When the "customers" of wineries are not consumers but rather media intermediaries, the aromatic and sensory properties of the drink become a secondary factor, with persuasion the primary one— much as it is in the world that Budweiser and Corona inhabit.

The core mission of what is now a *Trials* series of two is to empower consumers—to bring them back into this equation. This is why we make such a big deal about tasting blind, which removes perceptual bias and the placebo effects of marketing and prestige from the process of reviewing.

The placebo effect is as powerful in the world of taste as it is in the world of medicine. Nobody can beat it; nobody can even hope to contain it, other than through blind tasting. It is now more or less accepted as scientific fact that if a consumer—whether an expert or a novice—believes a product to be expensive, he or she actually appreciates it more, on a basic sensory level, than if he or she believes the same product to be cheap.

The proof of this effect has come from an increasingly broad body of evidence from neuroscience and behavioral economics. One of the landmark papers in the field was an fMRI (functional MRI, a brain-scanning technology) study by Hilke Plassmann, Antonio Rangel, and their colleagues at Stanford Business School and Cal Tech. The study showed that activity in the brain's left medial orbitofrontal cortex—an area commonly associated with pleasure—was correlated with how much subjects had been *told* a wine was worth, and not with the *actual* price of that wine.[8]

An earlier experiment by Shane Frederick and Dan Ariely at MIT and Leonard Lee of Columbia Business School offers another interesting bit of evidence on the power of perceptual bias and expectation. Their experiment, which involved adding vinegar to beer, was aimed at tracking when exactly in the tasting process it is that a consumer forms a sensory preference.[9]

Every subject was given one taste of regular beer and one taste of beer with balsamic vinegar added, and every taster was asked to compare two beers and pick a favorite.

Tasters were divided into three groups. Group 1 was asked to compare the two beers without ever being told that either of the beers contained vinegar. As it turned out, that group actually *preferred* the vinegared beer. Group 2 was told about the vinegar in one of the beers, and that group—grossed out by the idea of it, perhaps—dramatically preferred the non-vinegared beer.

The most counterintuitive result, though, came from group 3. Like group 1, they tasted the two beers without knowledge of the vinegar. But then, after tasting but before rating, they were told about the vinegar. Interestingly, this group's results mimicked group 1's more than group 2's—that is, the vinegar didn't bother them much. Knowing about the vinegar when they were *rating* the beer did not have the negative effect on that group's preference that knowing about it when they were *experiencing* the beer did. The perceptual bias of expectation, that is, affected the *sensory experience itself*, not the *judgment* of that experience.

This is a long way of saying that if you believe, before taking your first sip, that Corona will refresh you—as you sunbathe by the pool, thinking of happy, successful people in the shadow of coconut palms—you may actually be more refreshed by that beer than you would by Pacífico, even if a blind tasting under controlled conditions might reveal the liquid inside the Pacífico bottle to be the more refreshing of the two. You prefer Corona for reasons *extrinsic*, not intrinsic, to the liquid inside the bottle.

Although extrinsic factors can enhance pleasure—there's no reason to brown-bag your beer at dinner—we believe that extrinsic factors should be removed from the objective assessment and judgment of beer. Unless beer is judged blind, it's impossible to tell which of its pleasures come from the physical properties of the drink, and which come from one's associations with the brand—whether those associations are positive or negative.

Experimentation through blind tasting is also the best way to learn your own palate. As a beer drinker and consumer, understanding your own palate is more important than reading any amount of literature, however trustworthy, about how much other people might have liked a particular beer. If you just hate extremely bitter IPAs, or smoke beers, no amount of salesmanship might suffice to convince you otherwise. Only experience can do that.

So, as much pleasure as there is in just kicking back and sipping a pint from a bottle or can, take time, too, to learn your palate through blind tasting, focusing, and even meditating on beer.

The world of flavor and aroma chemistry is dazzlingly complex. The human brain—especially the olfactory system—has the capability to register a huge number of aromatic chemical compounds as distinct flavors. Yet we rarely experience even a small fraction of those compounds on their own (or even as a primary flavor). The sense of smell is far more nuanced than the sense of taste; humans have perhaps 100 times as many detectors for different aromas than different tastes. As a consequence, flavor memory is highly associative and rarely as specific as we would wish. A particular organization of carbon and hydrogen may bring back fleeting childhood memories of place and time, or it may conjure a specific dish, with immediately recognizable ingredients.

Whether you're part of a large blind tasting or just taking a moment at the pub to really savor a pint, don't try to force yourself to label or identify everything you smell and taste. The more time you spend tasting different beers and allowing associations to bubble up to the surface, the more readily you'll be able to make those connections. In the meantime, look for the parts you can easily spot, and enjoy the fact that you're drinking beer!

For less experienced tasters, we suggest starting with basic flavors. Get in the habit of asking yourself simple questions every time you taste a beer: is it sweet? Is it bitter? Is the aroma floral? Citrusy? Grainy? We find that yes-or-no questions are an excellent way to start the process; identifying intensity can come later.

You'll notice that for beers with bold flavors, the answers to the set of questions will vary from beer to beer. Even if you can't identify or put a name to most of what you're tasting, the unique set of answers will start to give you a frame of reference for that beer, which will help you remember beers by taste and start to give your brain the freedom to look for more subtle flavors.

Some people use lists of flavors to remind them what they might look for: esters, banana, and clove, for example. Others relax and let the flavors come to them. But if you smell, taste, and think about the beers you drink, you'll develop an approach—and a vocabulary—that works for you.

There are countless approaches to beer drinking. There's Michael Jackson—the late, great beer writer, not the late, great pop singer—and his world travels in search of interesting or novel local styles. Then there's the guy who drinks whatever he finds in the neighbor's fridge without paying much attention. So the advice and suggestions in this chapter should be taken only as advice and suggestion; in the words of homebrewing author and advocate Charlie Papazian, "Relax, don't worry, have a homebrew."

Another thing to be aware of as you figure out what you like is that preferences definitely evolve over time, and it can be very rewarding to periodically go back and taste styles or beers that you've avoided for a while. You may find flavors and nuances that you didn't notice on previous forays, or you may simply find that your preferences have evolved to a place where the whole package has become more appealing.

When I (Seamus) discovered in the early days of my beer drinking that I enjoyed intense, hoppy ales (often wildly bitter), I wrote off lagers almost categorically for a long time. It's only in the last few years that I've come back around to the opinion that a well-balanced, carefully made pale lager can be every bit as satisfying as a vibrant IPA, and I'm still in the process of discovering the full, beautiful range of German lagers. On the other hand, I'm still rarely interested in American wheat beer. But who knows? That may still change.

There's also a place and time for each style of beer. If you are sitting on the beach on a nice sunny day, the best doppelbock in the world is unlikely to quench your thirst, even if it's your professed beer preference. And even within styles, the world of beer is big enough that it's not reasonable to expect anyone to like all of the well-made examples out there.

This all points at an important decision you can make as you taste: do you go to the beer, or look for the beer to come to you? You can evaluate a beer strictly on the success it has at pleasing your palate at a particular moment in time, but you can also choose to taste a beer and try to figure out what the brewer was trying to accomplish and how well they did at that. Both approaches are useful, but in our experience it's tough to do both at once.

In the end, there are three keys to developing your palate for beer: drink many different beers and styles; be aware of what you're drinking; and, of course, enjoy yourself.

Let's turn, then, to the more technical portion of this book: a discussion of the world's beer styles and flavors. If you're just an occasional beer drinker, we hope you find the next few chapters educational. If you're already an enthusiast, we hope that they might serve as a good reference guide.

Chapter 3 A beer primer

When used in a historical context, the word "beer" refers to any fermented-grain beverage. In modern usage, it's the collection of drinks known as lagers and ales—terms that are defined later in this chapter. The world of beer, sweepingly broad and millennia old, has a dizzying array of styles and categories, laws and deviations, terms and descriptions, many of which are hard to reconcile with the beverages to which they are attached. English bitter may not be particularly bitter, and pale ales can be a rich red-brown color.

This is a book about beer appreciation, but knowing something about beer's taxonomy, its physical properties, and the basic brewing process is important. Understanding a bit about why beer looks, smells, and tastes the way it does will enable you to get more out of the next few chapters on the world's beer styles and flavors.

The brewing process in a nutshell

The primary ingredient of beer—aside from water (see "water flavors" in chapter 5 for more on the water used in beer)—is barley, although it can sometimes also be wheat, as in wheat beers, or other grains such as rye. Barley use in beer ranges from about two ounces of dry grain per pint in the lightest pale lager to about 10 ounces per pint for the heaviest barleywine.

The first major step in beermaking is the malting of the barley, during which raw grain is soaked in water, causing it to sprout. The sprouted barley is then dried in a kiln (see "malt flavors" in chapter 5 for more on the malting process). The second major step is known as "mashing"—heating a mixture of water and crushed malted barley (called "malt") to very specific temperatures. During mashing, proteins called diastatic enzymes (produced during the malting process) are activated and split the barley's starches into different sugars. The sugary mixture is then drained in a variety of ways to extract the sweet liquid called "wort"—unfermented beer.

Some of these sugars are easily fermentable ("fermentable," by the way, is a fancy word for "usable as a food source for microorganisms"); some are moderately fermentable, meaning that yeasts can consume them given enough time; and some are unfermentable by normal brewing organisms. Those unfermentable sugars later stick around to give different flavors to the beer.

The wort is then mixed with hops and boiled in a kettle. The boiled, hopped wort is then cooled and transferred to a fermentation tank, where carefully selected yeasts (see "yeast flavors" in chapter 5 for more on yeasts) are added to begin the process of fermentation, which converts the sugar to alcohol and produces byproducts of heat and carbon dioxide. Fermentation can last days or weeks or months, and it can be done at warmer temperatures (for ales) or colder temperatures (for lagers).

When the yeasts finish consuming the sugars, they settle out of the liquid, and the beer is nearly finished. Brewers employ a number of techniques to ensure that carbonation of the beer and clarity are appropriate for the type of beer (and type of package), but the yeasts have done most of the hard work of transforming a sugary cereal mixture into the fascinating beverage we call beer.

About beer styles

Unlike wine, beer is made with a set of consistent ingredients—water, hops, barley, yeast—and isn't at the whim of climate. This makes consistency easy for industrial-strength brewers. By blending to mask any minor batch-to-batch differences, Anheuser-Busch can make the Bud experience almost identical from Seattle to Miami.

The production of beer in a specific region is a different thing. evolves slowly, with gradual improvements to better suit the qualities of the local water and ingredients: selecting amongst available hops, modifying the acidity of the grain through roasting, picking suitable yeast strains.

While commercial brewing operations worldwide now have access to the tools, technologies, and ingredients necessary to brew virtually any style of beer, most of what we know as classic, iconic beer styles have evolved to fit a particular set of local variables. The chalky, hard water of northern England accentuated the bitterness of beer-preserving hops, leading to the high-alcohol, long-shelf-life India Pale Ale. On the other side of Europe, the soft water of Plzen, in what is now the Czech Republic, made it impractical to brew hoppy, bitter beers, resulting in the world's most dominant single beer style: the pale lager called pilsner.

Over time, local brewers produced fermented grain products that share surprisingly few flavor characteristics with their cousins from around the world. Even blindfolded, only the most damaged palate would be challenged to distinguish between a dry Irish stout, a sour Flemish farmhouse ale, and a Czech pilsner.

Specific styles—whether provincial or world-renowned— flourished. And while many of these are now shadows of their former glory, it's still possible to appreciate that the world of beer is still one in which the pale kölsch, the traditional beer of Cologne, Germany, is almost totally eschewed in Düsseldorf, a mere 25 miles away, where the locals drink the amber altbier.

Today's brewers are free to brew traditional beers or invent their own styles. Many work from style guidelines published by organizations that run beer competitions, which provide extremely technical reference ranges for the evaluation of each beer. In the Great American Beer Festival, judges deduct points if they notice even a slight deviation in specific gravity, IBUs (bitterness), or color.

Because of the widespread use of these rules, there is a fair degree of consistency between beers within one style. The more obscure the style, the more likely one beer is to be similar to other beers in that style. On the other hand, some brewers find these style guidelines stifling, and you may, too. You should trust a bottle's contents more than its name, but to keep in mind, too, that the labels applied to beers are a way of building relationships to a style and its history. When you find one you like, it can be a great ticket to guided exploration.

A few essential beer terms
These basic beer terms can vary regionally, but these explanations should prepare you for the discussions in later chapters.

Ale is the family of beers fermented with warm-temperature yeast (usually fermented between 55°F–70°F). These yeast strains are often called "top-fermenting," because they are suspended throughout the fermenting beer, and create a big layer of foam on top of the ferment called "kreuzen." Ale brewing is a much older tradition than its Germanic brother, lager. To say that ales tend to be maltier, sweeter, fruitier, or fuller-bodied than lagers is a vast overgeneralization—but there's certainly a strong correlation.

Lager is the family of beers fermented with cold-temperature yeast (40°F–48°F, typically). The word "lager" comes from the German verb "to store"; German beers were traditionally cold-conditioned in ice caves. Over time, brewers selected yeast strains that developed the ability to ferment at much lower temperatures than ale yeasts. These yeasts, which don't create the layer of kreuzen, are known as "bottom-fermenting."

Barleywine is a style of high-alcohol ale originating in England but currently enjoying a broad renaissance around the beer world. Barleywines are typically 8–12% alcohol by volume, thick and malty, though some American barleywines make an effort to balance the sweetness with bitterness. They can generally be aged for some years before drinking.

ABV is an abbreviation for "alcohol by volume," a measure of the alcoholic strength of beer, expressed as the percentage of the beer's volume that is comprised by ethanol. Most beers fall between 4% and 7% ABV. The average for this book is 5.84%, and the median is 5.4%, but these are above average for beer worldwide, since we have included a large selection of high-alcohol West Coast IPAs, Imperial IPAs, Belgian ales, and barleywines.

Pale should have a straightforward use in brewing circles—except that it doesn't. It does mean roughly what one would expect (light in color), but the reference point for "pale ale," historically, wasn't where you'd expect it to be—English brewers began using the phrase to refer to beers that were less dark than porter, which is pretty much as dark as it gets. Given the wide range of pale in ales, the colors are commonly broken out into "pale ales" and "amber ales," if somewhat inconsistently, in American usage.

Light is perhaps the most ambiguous word in the brewer's arsenal. With respect to the aspect of a beer, it is used to mean "pale-colored," particularly in the case of golden- or straw-colored beers. It can also mean "low in gravity or density," and refer to beers that were made with a modest amount of grain. In a commercial context, especially in North America, "light beer" generally applies to low-calorie beer, and we use that term to define that style within the pale lager family (see chapter 4 for the full definition). Otherwise, we use the adjective "light" to mean "low in gravity or density."

Mellie Pullman: **What's brewing with sustainability?**

From purchasing ingredients to packaging and storing beer, brewers are faced with numerous decisions that affect the environment. Many craft brewers now consider sustainability a personal value. Those at the forefront of sustainability initiatives are pushing the envelope to reduce the damaging effects of commodity agricultural practices and the waste of resources.

As a vital part of beer production, fresh water use and waste water reduction are clear targets. While inefficient operations consume as much as 20 gallons of water for each gallon of beer (GW/GB) produced, both the **New Belgium** and **Full Sail** Breweries use less than four gallons GW/GB. They achieve this by reusing sanitation water, and with redesigned bottle and keg washing systems that use less water than conventional systems.

Some brewing byproducts (e.g. spent grain, hops) find second lives as animal feed, but other waste packaging materials end up in landfills. Conscious breweries measure and monitor their recycling or repurposing rates of products like paper, cardboard, glass, stretch wrap, pallets, and hop burlap.

In an ideal world, every neighborhood would have its own brewery, and packaging waste would be virtually eliminated by people drinking draft beer or taking beer away in refillable containers like growlers instead of single-use glass bottles. Bottle deposit states with glass production typically recycled glass content around 50% (vs. 10% in non-deposit states).

Any brewer who's serious about sustainability will look at the upstream impacts of ingredients. The Climate Conservancy calculated that for a 6-pack of New Belgium's Fat Tire ale, barley production comprised 12.6% of greenhouse gas emissions. To reduce barley growing's impact, some brewers are looking for local, low-impact sources. The "direct-seed" system uses a drill to plant barley seeds into the stubble left from the previous crop, increasing water retention and reducing soil erosion, runoff, and associated greenhouse gas emissions by over 80%. Custom micro-malting facilities now support these smaller growers, and breweries like Oregon's **Rogue Brewing** are beginning to differentiate themselves by purchasing their malts.

Mellie Pullman is the Willamette Industries professor of Supply Chain Management at Portland State University. She was brewmaster and co-founder of Wasatch Beers in Park City, Utah, after brewing at Pyramid.

Chapter 4 The world's beer styles

This chapter is our attempt—an imperfect one, no doubt—to simplify the odd, overlapping, and often contradictory world of beer styles into something more systematic and helpful to readers. We will divide the world of beer—and the reviews in Part II of this book—into 11 broad groups of beer styles, which we call "families." We then divide most families into subcategories, which we call "styles." For example, Stout and Porter are two styles within the Dark Ale family. These style categories often appear somewhere on the label of a beer.

In what follows, we'll list describe each of the 11 families and their substyles, and we'll point you to the *Beer Trials* reviews of a few good examples of each (generally rated 7 or above). Our descriptions sometimes use beer terms like "esters"; if these are unfamiliar, you may want to refer to the definitions in chapter 5.

The beer families are listed below in alphabetical order: Amber Lager, Belgian Ale, Brown Ale, Dark Ale, India Pale Ale, Pale Ale, Pale Lager, Smoke Beer, Sour Beer, Strong Beer, and Wheat Beer.

Family: Amber Lager
Prior to the development of pilsner (a style in the pale lager family, described below), amber was the default color for lagers. Amber lagers take their color and flavors from two distinctive elements: malts that are kilned longer than modern pale malts, and a long boil, which reduces water content and caramelizes sugar, darkening

the final product. The traditional brown beer of Munich, hard to find in North America, is now known as dunkel, German for "dark." The most famous modern amber lagers—Oktoberfest beer—are at least seasonally available in North America.

Style: American Amber Lager. This isn't a style that beer taxonomists have really embraced yet, but we have seen it suggested, and it strikes us as an excellent idea. There are a handful of lagers—the wildly successful Samuel Adams Boston Lager being perhaps the best known—that have too dark a color and too much caramelized sugar to fit with traditional pale lager styles, yet are too hoppy and bright to fit with the canonical German amber lagers. *Beer Trials* recommendations: Brooklyn Lager (p. 107), Coney Island Lager (p. 124), Samuel Adams Boston Lager (p. 257).

Style: American Bock. This is like a hybrid between traditional bock and American pale lager, with malt character and alcohol in between the two. Smooth and fairly light in body, these beers are built for hot-weather drinking, and are popular in Texas and the south. *Beer Trials* recommendation: Shiner Bock (p. 271).

Style: Dunkel. This is the traditional dry and malty brown lager of Munich, produced long before technology allowed for the creation of the pale lagers. We haven't included any in this first edition of the book, as few are imported (you might occasionally see Beck's Dark), and those brewed in North America are typically small-production seasonal beers.

Style: German Bock. These strong, intensely malty, high-alcohol beers are darker and a little sweeter than Oktoberfest style (below). The name "bock" comes from the town of Einbeck, where the style was founded. There is a pale version, Maibock, that's traditionally consumed in the spring. The very strongest bocks, doppelbock and eisbock, are in the strong beer family instead.

Style: Oktoberfest (includes Märzen and Vienna Lager). These beer styles date to the 19th century, and golden-colored Oktoberfests (taking the name from Munich's annual beer extravaganza) are increasingly common. The traditional amber Märzen is nutty, with a particular fruity character from the malt, low hop character, and alcohol that's often a bit higher than most pale lagers. Vienna lagers use a different malt base, but are fairly similar. In our experience, commercial beers sold as Vienna lagers tend to have a more forward caramel character and less of the nutty character of the Märzen style. *Beer Trials* recommendations: Ayinger Oktoberfest (p. 76), Great Divide Hoss Rye Lager (p. 157), Spaten Oktoberfest (p. 280).

Family: Belgian Ale

Belgium has a rich brewing tradition that extends far beyond the production of Stella Artois. More Belgian ales are exported across the Atlantic (and Pacific) every year. In Belgium, there is less of a tradition of brewing to style than in England, Germany, or even the United States, so Belgian ales are characterized more by generalities than the levels of specificity we offer for some of the other families.Belgian ales tend to be full-bodied and high in alcohol. While only extreme beers reach 8% ABV in the rest of Europe, many Belgian producers brew to this strength. Sugar is frequently used to help boost alcohol without adding weight or body.

We have divided Belgian ales into dark and pale styles. Note that Belgian witbiers are included in the Wheat Beer family, while the lambic and gueuze styles are included in the Sour Beer family.

Style: Dark Belgian Ale. Generally much more brown than black, these beers tend to take much of their color from dark sugars added to the boil, which also contribute dark caramel and molasses flavors. There's even less stylistic adherence to the dark Belgians than there is to the pale versions, but one rule seems to prevail: roast grain character should be subtle. Otherwise, brewers make use of the full spectrum of dark flavors, and while esters can be plentiful, they generally find places to hide, increasing these beers' sublety. *Beer Trials* recommendations: Chimay Blue (p. 119), Allagash Dubbel (p. 65), Maudite (p. 197).

Style: Pale Belgian Ale. The pale Belgians reviewed in this book fall on a rough line between two extremes. At one end are saisons—refreshing, dry beers fermented with yeasts that tend to contribute pepper or other spicy phenols. Saisons vary a lot—some are spiced, some are lightly tart, some are hoppy. At the opposite end of the spectrum are tripels, which tend to be more ester-focused than phenol-focused, rarely have significant hop character, and are frequently a bit sweet. The other pale Belgian ales fall somewhere in the middle; our notes should help guide you to promising selections. *Beer Trials* recommendations: Fin du Monde (p. 146), Allagash Tripel (p. 66), Delirium Tremens (p. 131).

Family: Brown Ale

Brown ales tend to have dark amber colors, but often with a clarity that makes them seem light. They are the milder cousins of dark ales (which have their own family, defined below), with more of a focus on toasty, nutty notes than dark roast flavors. They can have a wide range of flavor profiles, though, ranging from intensely malty or full of rich caramel flavors, to light, dry, and nutty beers. Hop character—both flavor and bitterness—tends to be on the low end. When done well, brown ales can be refreshing and light without coming across as thin. If you like the maltier, full-bodied instances of these beers, you may also like beers from the amber lager family (defined above). *Beer Trials* recommendations: Brooklyn Brown (p. 105), He'Brew Messiah Bold (p. 167).

Family: Dark Ale (Porter and Stout)

It's a matter of debate whether porter and stout are distinct styles—originally, they weren't. Both use dark kilned grain to give color and flavor. Roasted flavors can stand alone in low-alcohol and light-bodied beers—as in a typical dry stout—or they can be paired with and provide balance for strong malt and rich, full body.

Dark ales are noteworthy because they have some of the widest variation in alcohol content and body of all beer families. You can preview what to expect by looking for the alcohol content on the packaging; low alcohol usually portends a lighter, drier style, and the highest-alcohol varieties can be on the syrupy end of the spectrum. The strongest dark ales—Imperial porters and Imperial stouts—are included in the strong beer family (defined below).

Style: Porter. Porters tend to be less black and more brown than stouts, as they generally avoid using the harshest dark grains (black patent malt and roast barley) in significant quantities, favoring chocolate malt instead. *Beer Trials* recommendations: Boulder Planet Porter (p. 97), Deschutes Black Butte Porter (p. 132), Eel River Organic Porter (p. 144).

Style: Stout. If porters tend to avoid black patent malt or roast barley, stouts tend to embrace the. Dry stouts, such as Guinness, are built almost solely on roast barley character. Other styles use these malts but balance them with other ingredients—milk stouts, for instance, use lactose (milk sugar, which cannot be fermented by yeast) to sweeten the palate and take the edge off dark grains. Oatmeal stouts use their namesake grain to add creaminess to balance dark roast flavors. *Beer Trials* recommendations: Deschutes Obsidian Stout (p. 135), Rogue Shakespeare Oatmeal Stout (p. 252), Bison Chocolate Stout (p. 87).

Family: India Pale Ale

India Pale Ale is technically a subcategory of the pale ale family (described below), but the massive popularity and proliferation of IPAs these days—along with IPA's distinctive profile and the aversion some drinkers have to forward hop bitterness—led us to give IPA its own family.

The IPAs sold in North America tend to be more aggressive versions of the American pale ale style—more alcoholic and more bitter, with the same focus on citrusy hops. As the alcohol goes up and so do the residual sugars that go with it, the bitterness can recede somewhat. This means that drinkers who like amber ales but not pales or IPAs may find, paradoxically, that they enjoy some Imperial IPAs (which we've grouped into the strong ale family). *Beer Trials* recommendations: Bear Republic's Hop Rod Rye (p. 175), Goose Island IPA (p. 156), Widmer Broken Halo IPA (p. 301).

Family: Pale Ale

We've mentioned this already, but it's confusing enough that we'll say it again: while "pale lager" refers to golden and straw-colored lager, "pale ale" encompasses a much broader territory that is not easily defined by color; the term was originally used by the English to imply that a beer was not as dark as porter. In American parlance, the term "pale ale" covers a similarly wide range of color, but is often used with a more descriptive color slant, breaking things into "pale ales" and "amber ales." Some brewers employ even more descriptive color words, like "copper" or "red" ale.

Style: Alt. Native to Düsseldorf, Germany, the alt style predates modern lager yeasts (altbier means "old beer"). These are amber ales that are cold-conditioned in the manner of a lager, giving them a very clean character that showcases the nutty, fruity character of German malts. Their hop bitterness is mild, often making these beers deliciously subtle. Warm the glass a bit with your hands to release more of the flavors—altbiers are often serve too cold. *Beer Trials* recommendation: Alaskan Amber (p. 60).

Style: American Amber Ale. Ambers tend to be darker and more caramel/malt-oriented than American pale ales, but hop flavor can still be forward. Amber ales are the best bet for "starter beers" in the pale ale family—Boont Amber (p. 94) is a classic example of an easy-drinking American amber. *Beer Trials* recommendations: Anchor Liberty Ale (p. 68), Bear Republic Red Rocket Ale (p. 80), Red Seal Ale (p. 242).

Style: American ESB. The American takes on ESB ("Extra Special Bitter"—see "English Pale Ale" below) are frequently indistinguishable from American ambers, but they are more likely to contain the less citrusy and more woody British hops. Hop bitterness is generally higher than in the softest ambers, but there is significant overlap between the two types. *Beer Trials* recommendations: Bridgeport ESB (p. 103), Redhook ESB (p. 244).

Style: American Pale Ale. These ales often show a strong hop flavor component, most frequently of the citrusy American hop varieties. Golden color (sometimes darker), a caramel and malt character that is light to moderate, and medium to substantial bitterness are the hallmarks. These beers move in the direction of IPAs, but stop short of that full-out hop bitterness. As noted above, however, some American breweries use "pale ale" to describe ales in the same broad ballpark of color and intensity as English pale ales, but many differentiate between pales, ambers, and ESBs. *Beer Trials* recommendations: Bear Republic XP Pale Ale (p. 81), Kona Fire Rock Pale Ale (p. 182), Stone Levitation Ale (p. 289).

Style: English Bitter. This style isn't often seen in North America, both because these beers don't tend to suit the palates of American drinkers and because their low alcohol and hops give them a shorter shelf life than is necessary for transatlantic travel.

Bitters—which, in England, are traditionally poured from the cask, at room temperature, with little carbonation—dominated the English domestic beer industry for much of the 20th century, although they've since been overtaken by lagers. The focus on malt complexity can make these wonderful beers, but the challenge of getting good, well-stored examples in other countries can be maddening. Frequently, the export versions of "ordinary bitter" and "best bitter" are bulked up in alcoholic strength to increase their lifespan. This makes good sense, but it also changes the character of the beer, and not always positively. Increased interest in cask ale means that drinkers are now more likely to run into locally produced examples of these beers, but they're still on the rare side. *Beer Trials* recommendation: Goose Island Honker's Ale (p. 155).

Style: English Pale Ale (also known as Extra Special Bitter). This is the strongest sort of English bitter. These beers, which are plentiful in North America, have assertive malt character but range between strongly malt-focused and fairly bitter and hoppy. Their malt character tends to be more complex and less overtly caramel than in their North American counterparts. *Beer Trials* recommendations: AleSmith Anvil ESB (p. 62), Pike Pale (p. 237), Old Speckled Hen (p. 222).

Style: Scottish Ale. Scottish ales are malty, in the fashion of English ales. Being brewed farther from the production of delicate and perishable hops, however, they tend to sacrifice bitterness in favor of more malty sweetness. In some cases, the water can impart peaty phenolic flavors. In the same tradition as the English hierarchy of bitter (Ordinary/Best/Extra Special), Scottish ales have a sequencing that corresponds to strength: 60/- (read as "60 shilling," which once represented the barrel price of the beer; and also called "Light"), 70/- (or "Heavy"), and 80/- (or "Export"). By North American standards, heavy isn't very—only Export reaches the standard alcoholic strength of today's full-strength lagers; Belhaven is the most common example in North America. *Beer Trials* recommendations: Oskar Blues Old Chub (p. 227), Belhaven Scottish Ale (p. 83), Pale Kilt Lifter (p. 236).

Style: Scotch Ale. The strongest pale ales from Scotland are called Scotch ales, setting them apart, if confusingly, from Scottish ales. "Wee Heavy" is another name for them, and, like Scottish ales, they often employ the shilling system, finding beers labeled as 90/- or even 100/-. These potent, heavy ales push into barleywine territory, and tend to have significant residual sweetness.

Family: Pale Lager

The history of pale lager starts in a small town in the Czech Republic, from where the style has gradually expanded to its current state of near total domination of the beer world. It's tough to apply style labels to these beers, because the differences are often subtle, and a lot of brewers throw around terms like "pilsner" with little regard for the actual characteristics of the beer.

If we accept, for instance, the premise that American Budweiser is a pilsner, and that Paulaner Pils is also a pilsner, we'd have emptied the concept of meaning. If a curious drinker could walk into a beer bar, ask for a pilsner, and receive either a Paulaner or a Bud, then the label would be useless. Easier, by far, is to call all of these beers "pale lagers" and use the sub-styles to tease out their similarities and differences. (In this book, we categorize the Paulaner as Pilsner and the Budweiser as American Lager.)

Style: Continental Lager. More than a true style, this is a catch-all for the most generic form of pale lager—e.g. Heineken, Stella Artois, Beck's—that has less hop character and bitterness than you'll find in a true pilsner (pilsner has its own style below), but more bitterness and body than North American lagers have. This is the sort of crisp, refreshing, light-bodied, frothy lager that proliferates at informal bars across Southern Europe—Italy, Spain, France—but it's also popular across Asia. Interestingly, this style is also sometimes known as "Premium American Lager." Since most of the best-known examples are European but not British, we think

"Continental Lager" makes more sense. *Beer Trials* recommendations: Victory Prima Pils (p. 296), Czechvar (p. 129), Spaten Premium (p. 282).

Style: Cream Ale. Confused as to why this is in the pale lager family? Well, cream ales are either ales produced to approximate a pale lager taste profile, or a blend of a very light ale and a pale lager. Either way, they have more in common with pale lagers than with pale ales. They're not very common anymore; we've reviewed just one (the classic Genesee Cream Ale). *Beer Trials* recommendation: Genessee Cream Ale (p. 154).

Style: Japanese Lager. The Japanese version of pale lager is even lighter in body than American lager. The vogue for the last two decades has been for fermenting as much body out of the beer as possible, so it tends to be both lighter and less sweet. The better examples find some malt character and use a light but evident addition of hops to avoid coming across as watery in the way that light lagers can. *Beer Trials* recommendation: Kirin Ichiban (p. 180).

Style: Kölsch. Similar to cream ale is kölsch, a style native to Cologne (Köln in German, hence the name). It's a pale, light-bodied ale, low on bitterness and cold-aged like a lager, and like cream ale, it has more in common with pale lagers than it does with other ales. It is increasingly common to see these as summer seasonal beers from craft breweries—Goose Island's Summertime Ale is a well-known example.

Style: Light Beer. Low-calorie beers have been known as "light beers" since Miller released Miller Lite, the first commercially successful lo-cal beer. If you're wondering why "light," and not "lite," is now the generally accepted spelling for the term, it's because SABMiller (producers of Miller Lite) has a trademark on "Lite." These beers generally undergo an enzymatic process that reduces unfermentable sugars to fermentable ones, leaving them with a bit more alcohol and a bit less of everything else. Light beers come in a number of flavor profiles, but they generally are even thinner than American lagers and have little beer character. There's a fine line to walk between watered-down flavor and clean non-flavor; achieving the right balance is a tall order, and these beers are technically demanding to produce. *Beer Trials* recommendations: Sam Adams Light (p. 256), Amstel Light (p. 67), Bud Light (p. 109).

Style: Malt Liquor. "Malt liquor" isn't really a style so much as a legal term for high-alcohol fermented beverages made from malted barley—one of the cheapest of all delivery mechanisms for alcohol in North America. These high-alcohol beers typically target the approximate flavor profile of pale lagers, which is why we've classified Mickey's and Olde English 800, for instance, under this style, while high-alcohol Stone Arrogant Bastard and Rogue Old Crustacean are instead classified as Strong Pale Ales. *Beer Trials* recommendations: Steel Reserve 211 High Gravity (p. 285).

Style: Non-alcoholic Beer. It's not actually non-alcoholic, but this style (sometimes known as "near beer") has a very low alcohol content, usually less than 0.5% ABV. There are multiple methods of production. Some non-alcoholic lagers are fermented and the alcohol is then removed, while in others, the fermentation is arrested almost immediately, before most of alcohol is produced. They can range from tasting very clean, similar to light beer, to intensely grainy. *Beer Trials* recommendation: O'Doul's (p. 221).

Style: North American Lager. These beers were developed by large North American breweries employing corn, rice, or sugar, leaving the very light, slightly sweet beer that dominates the mainstream United States, Canadian, and Mexican markets. These beers tend to have a significantly lighter body and less hop character than other lagers from around the world. Note that in our reviews, some beers from other countries (e.g. Australia and New Zealand) are included in this category because of their adherence to the style. *Beer Trials* recommendations: Bohemia (p. 93), Kokanee Glacier Beer (p. 181), Molson Canadian (p. 209).

Style: Pilsner. The original pale lagers came out of Plzen ("Urquell" is Czech for "original source"), characterized by substantial hop character and ample bitterness. German pilsners tend to come from areas where water with higher mineral content gives them much more pronounced, focused bitterness than the soft Czech water gives Czech pilsners. Many beers claim to be pilsners, but most don't have the bitterness for us to consider them part of that family. *Beer Trials* recommendations: Lagunitas Pils (p. 188), Bitburger Pilsner (p. 89), Trumer Pils (p. 293).

Family: Smoke Beer

Intentionally smoky beer might strike you as an unusual idea, but it was once the norm for much of the brewing world. Drying malts over open fires, which for a long time was the only option in many regions, imparted a smoky signature that simply reflected the cooking fuel used. For the most part, these beers died out when indirect-heat kilning technology was developed. Still, the city of Bamberg in the northern part of Bavaria retains a proud tradition of producing beer with beechwood-smoked malt, called rauchbier, and a number of craft breweries brew the occasional beer with commercially produced smoked malt. These beers have little that unites them except the (generally prominent) use of smoke flavors; Bamberg breweries make rauchbier versions of most of the traditional Bavarian lager styles. *Beer Trials* recommendation: Alaskan Smoked Porter (p. 61).

Family: Sour Beer

The world of intentionally soured beers is a fairly foreign one to most of North America, but it is a fascinating glimpse into a world of unusual, often fruity, and sometimes bizarre flavors. Sour beers are brewed with microorganisms such as Brettanomyces, Acetobacter, and Lactobacilli. (For more on these, see chapter 5, "Beer flavors and ingredients.") Generally blended and frequently aged, these beers are far less amenable to the consistency of mass production that characterizes most of the world's commercial brewing. Some styles have nevertheless managed to become quite popular even outside of Belgium, where they're most common.

  Style: Flanders Red Ale. One of the major areas of sour brewing in Belgium is in Flanders, a region in the north of the country. Flanders red ales are aged in large oak casks, used repeatedly so that they pick up the full complement of fermentation microorganisms. Acetobacter gives these beers a distinct vinegar twang, and the mild, slow oxidation afforded by the wooden casks can push them toward the flavor profiles of Balsamic vinegar or sherry. Rodenbach and Duchesse de Bourgogne are the best-known examples of this style, and both are reviewed in this book. Flanders Oud Bruin (old brown) ales are done in a related style, but not aged in wood, and get their sour character from inoculation with Lactobacilli. These ales are very rarely seen on our shores. *Beer Trials* recommendations: Duchesse de Bourgogne (p. 141), Rodenbach Grand Cru (p. 249).

  Style: Lambic. The tart, dry lambic beer, produced in Brussels and the region just to the south, is the product of spontaneous fermentation. After the wort is boiled, it is exposed to the outside air through the use of special slatted roofs. Various bacteria take residence and go to work. The blend of microorganisms, and the resulting character of the beer, is said to depend on the time of year. Much of the fermentation happens slowly in wooden barrels. The dry lambic can be intensely sour, and increasingly so with age. Unblended lambic is relatively rare (particularly as an export product). More common is gueuze, a blend of aged and young lambic; or a fruited lambic beer, with sour cherries, known as kriek, being the most popular addition. The fruit eases the sharpness of sour notes and the character of Brettanomyces. Even fruited lambic is relatively rare outside of Belgium, although the Lindemans brand enjoys widespread distribution. Lindemans' fruited lambics are produced with a sweeter, more accessible profile than most, so they provide a gentle introduction to the style. *Beer Trials* recommendation: **Lindemans Cassis** (p. 190).

Family: Strong Beer

While strong beers are enjoying something of a renaissance these days, they have been around for a long time. Every major beer culture has its own take on strong beer. This family covers high-alcohol pale ales made in the English tradition, along with several styles of strong dark beer, including the doppelbocks of Munich, the Russian Imperial stouts of the English-speaking world, and the dark abbey ales of Belgium.

Style: Baltic Porter. A unique variation on porter brewed with lager yeasts, Baltic porters were an export from Great Britain that took hold in northeastern Europe and Russia in the 19th century. These beers tend to be malty and sweet, but also show some roast character, as well as the dark fruits and spices common to malty, dark beers with high alcohol. *Beer Trials* recommendations: **Boss Black Porter** (p. 95).

Style: Barleywine. One of the challenges of making strong beers is convincing the yeast to consume enough of the sugar in the wort (unfermented beer) that the beer is not painfully sweet. Alcohol inhibits fermentation, and the process of boiling thick, sugary wort produces caramelized sugars that can't be fermented. Barleywines embrace this, to a degree; nearly every barleywine is somewhat sweet. This sweetness is offset, to varying degrees, by hop bitterness; as with all styles, but perhaps more importantly than in any other, finding the right balance is crucial to the success of the beer. American barleywines tend to have much more overt hop aroma and flavor than their English counterparts, although if these beers are aged—as they frequently are—the hop aroma is one of the first things to go. *Beer Trials* recommendations: Anchor Old Foghorn (p. 69), Rogue Old Crustacean (p. 251).

Style: Doppelbock. One of the world's oldest styles of beer still in significant production, this intensely malty style of lager was originally brewed for consumption during Lent fasting. Doppelbocks derive most of their color and dark flavor from boiling, and the flavors show the rich interplay of alcohol and dark caramels. There's little hop bitterness in these beers. *Beer Trials* recommendations: Ayinger Celebrator (p. 75), Paulaner Salvator (p. 234), Spaten Optimator (p. 281).

Style: Imperial IPA. This is the supersized version of the classic IPA, characterized by high alcohol, a strong body, and even higher levels of hop bitterness. The tendency toward residual sugars in strong beers makes hop bitterness seem milder. Some examples of Imperial IPA, like Dogfish Head's 90 Minute, don't up the hopping nearly enough to compensate for the increased sweetness, and come off as less bitter than regular-strength IPAs. *Beer Trials* recommendations: Russian River Pliny the Elder (p. 254), Dogfish Head 90 Minute IPA (p. 137), Sierra Nevada Torpedo (p. 275).

Style: Imperial Porter. A fairly recent style development, this is basically a strong version of the standard porter. As with Imperial stouts, it's not uncommon for breweries to age these beers in oak, or add dark-flavored, nontraditional ingredients (The Abyss from Deschutes, for example, is brewed with licorice and molasses). *Beer Trials* recommendation: Flying Dog Gonzo Porter (p. 147).

Style: Imperial Stout. The use of the word "Imperial" to describe strong versions of existing styles is a back-formation from the Russian Imperial stout style. The earliest of these were brewed for the court of Catherine the Great, and high alcohol was necessary to keep the beer from freezing as it was shipped across the Baltic Sea. The end result is a full-bodied, rich beer that has more roast character than a doppelbock, but enough alcohol and residual sugar to keep dark grain bitterness down. *Beer Trials* recommendations: Great Divide Yeti (p. 158), North Coast Old Rasputin (p. 219), Victory Storm King (p. 297).

Style: Strong Ale. Strong ales are the less intense cousins of barleywines. These beers frequently aim for a lower alcohol content than barleywines in order to ensure a dry fermentation. *Beer Trials* recommendations: Arrogant Bastard Ale (p. 71), Fuller's 1845 (p. 153), North Coast Old Stock Ale (p. 220).

Family: Wheat Beer

The wheat beers in this category are ales that tend to use roughly equal portions of wheat and barley. Most of them come from a Bavarian tradition, with the exception of the Belgian witbiers and some obscure German styles (the nearly extinct Gose and the less-obscure Berliner Weisse). Wheat's high protein content gives these beers a full mouthfeel while keeping flavors light and easygoing, and a fruity ester called isoamyl acetate endows many wheat beers, especially Bavarians, with a prominent banana character.

Style: American Wheat Beer. The American take on hefeweizen is very similar to the German with respect to recipes, but distinguishes itself by using clean, neutral yeasts, rather than the classic Bavarian yeasts. The end result is a product that has a very light overall flavor palate, with no harsh edges, and usually some apparent grainy flavors from the protein-rich wheat. *Beer Trials* recommendations: Pyramid Haywire (p. 239).

Style: Bavarian Hefeweizen. This is German for "yeasty white beer"; these cloudy beers, which originated in Bavaria, are the most popular in the family of German wheat beers. Bavarian hefeweizen use a form of top-fermenting yeast that produces bright, spicy flavors and intense esters. The classic aromas are clove and banana. Hop character is generally low, and high carbonation and big, fluffy heads are a hallmark of the style, which presents some variation in body weight. Sometimes there's a hint of fresh, sour tang, which can help keep these beers light and refreshing. *Beer Trials* recommendations: Paulaner Hefe-Weizen (p. 231), Franziskaner Hefe-Weisse (p. 150), Sierra Nevada Kellerweis (p. 272).

Style: Dunkelweisse, Kristalweisse. There are several standard variations on the basic hefeweizen made by the traditional Munich breweries. Dunkelweisse is darker and a little fuller of body, with flavors that can come from all over the darker grain spectrum (medium or dark caramels, toasted grains, roast character, etc). Kristalweisse is filtered wheat beer (as opposed to the unfiltered hefeweizen), with smoother, less grainy taste. There are also lighter, low-alcohol and low-calorie versions of hefeweizen that are sold (in Germany) as health-restoring beverages. We haven't reviewed any for this book, given their very limited availability.

Style: Weizenbock. These are wheat beers brewed to the malty darkness and alcoholic intensity of bock and doppelbock beers. They're strong, rich, and intense, and because they use Bavarian weissbier yeast, they give off banana and clove aromas similar to those in Bavarian hefeweizens. *Beer Trials* recommendation: Aventinus Weizenbock (p. 73).

Style: Witbier. The Belgian cousin of weissbier, witbier is traditionally spiced, usually with coriander and often with bitter orange peel or grains of paradise. The esters that one expects from Belgian yeast are often noticeable. These beers are light by Belgian standards. *Beer Trials* recommendation: Hoegaarden (p. 173).

Chapter 5 Beer flavors and ingredients

In this chapter, we take you on a tour through the range of flavors that compose the world's beers, and we discuss where they come from. This is the most technical chapter in *The Beer Trials*, but, we hope, also one of the most helpful to those who want to delve more seriously into beer tasting.

Water flavors
The history of beer is largely the history of water. While water does not generally turn up as a major flavor element directly, we would be remiss not to touch on its contribution to the brewing of beer.

For the most part, water, largely through its chemistry, guides the development of beer styles more than it directly influences taste. The process of converting grain starches to sugars requires a particular pH range. Although they wouldn't have phrased it in terms of pH, brewers long ago discovered that certain kinds of grains suited some water supplies more than others. Classic examples are Dublin, whose intensely alkaline water required the equally intense acidity of dark roasted grains; and Plzen, birthplace of the world's pale lagers and home to water that has so few minerals as to mimic distilled water.

Some minerals contribute directly to the flavor of beer. **Iron** is detectable in beer in very low concentrations in the form of undesirable bloody or metallic flavors. **Sulfates** accentuate hop bitterness. Generally, beer brewed with water that has high mineral content can carry some of the flavors of that water through to the finished product. As a general rule of thumb, though, water that tastes good enough to drink is good enough to brew with—provided that the brewer is aware of the impact that dissolved minerals will have on the chemistry of the beer, of course.

Hop flavors

Hops are the most divisive element of beer flavor. It is rare to find a serious drinker who doesn't have a strong opinion about hops. Hops play several roles in beer; imparting flavor is just one of those. There are intensely bitter beers that have little hop character, and there are wonderfully hoppy beers that are hardly bitter at all.

Hops combat the two main causes of beer going bad: oxidation and bacterial spoilage. In fact, hops were historically boiled in beer for the protective effect of the bitter hop oils. These oils, called isohumulones, inhibit bacterial growth, thereby preventing beer from going sour with lactic acid or vinegar. As an important source of antioxidants, hops also stave off the cardboard-like flavors of stale, oxidized beer.

The use of hops is a relatively recent phenomenon in the timeline of beer, dating back only 1,000 years. The first record of hop use dates to late 11th-century Germany, and the use of hops in beer has been widespread for the last five or six hundred years. The hop vine arrived in England, via the Netherlands, in the 15th century.

For centuries, "ale" in England referred to unhopped (and generally unboiled) beers, while "beer" meant ale boiled with hops prior to fermentation. The difference between unboiled, unhopped beer and the new style was drastic. Judith Bennett, in her book on medieval beer brewing, notes a 1446 law in Worcestershire prohibiting the sale of ale more than four days old; hopped beer, with its relatively long lifespan, was not subject to the rule.

The oils that provide the protective effect in beer are the same compounds that make beer bitter, and for many drinkers, the word "hoppy" is a synonym for "bitter." And indeed, boiled hops are perhaps as definitive an ingredient in beer today as malted barley: while it is possible to make a beverage that is recognizably beer without malted barley or without bittering hops, it happens so rarely as to be a footnote in the modern brewing discussion.

Not all bitterness is the same when it comes to beer, however. The bitter lupulin glands of the hop cone come in varying intensities and styles. Some hop bitterness is crisp and dry, and some is resinous and lingering. The careful brewer selects bittering hop varieties to suit a particular shape of bitterness, and then polishes that bitterness with water chemistry and malt profile. Try a Czech pilsner like Pilsner Urquell next to a German pilsner like Spaten Pils to notice the different interplays of water chemistry with hop bitterness. The German beer has a longer, lingering bitterness, brought out by the mineral content of the water, while a Czech pilsner, brewed with famously soft water, exhibits up-front hop bite that quickly fades away on the finish.

In addition to bitterness, brewers use hops to provide a range of flavors and aromas to beer. There are dozens of varieties of hops, each with a unique flavor profile, and weather differences in the various centers of hop cultivation produce further nuances in the contribution a given hop makes to the finished product.

While the bitter components of hops require boiling to become water-soluble, flavor and aroma molecules in hops are more delicate, and tend to either vaporize or denature under the strain of a long boil. So brewers add hops at various points in the brewing process to manipulate the contribution they make to the beer, from the initial addition of bittering hops at the start of the boil (which usually lasts 60–90 minutes) to the use of the hop randall, a device that runs draft beer through a sealed container of hops on the way to a customer's glass. (The original example, invented at the Dogfish Head brewery, is known as "Randall the Enamel Animal.")

There are three major historical hop cultivation regions in the world, each producing hops with a distinct character.

Germany and Eastern Europe (the Czech Republic, Poland, Slovenia) produce the family of hops known as **noble hops**: the famous pilsner hop **Saaz**, plus **Hallertauer**, **Tettnanger**, and **Spalt**. These have refined herbal aromas, floral, pungent, and sometimes spicy. These aromatic hops are the gold standard for pale lagers, although European lager producers can be fairly stingy with them by modern North American craft beer standards. For a full-volume rendition of noble hops, try a Victory Prima Pils.

England produces hops with earthier, woodsy character—most famously **Goldings** and **Fuggles**, named for the farmers who first propagated them widely, according to beer guru Michael Jackson. These hops support the malty character of many English ales.

North American hops come mainly from the Yakima valley in Washington and the Willamette valley in Oregon. Most of the acreage there is devoted to the specialized, high-bitterness hops used in large-volume lager production; despite the low bitterness of most of these beers, their sheer quantities demand the bulk of the hop crop. There are also several notable aroma and flavor hop varieties that are staples of American craft beer. The **Cascade** cultivar, with its intense, resinous citrus and pine qualities, is the most famous among them. Cascade hops are the iconic symbol of hoppy, aggressive West Coast pale ales and IPAs, although in recent years some brewers have traded them for **Simcoe** and **Amarillo**—more recently developed hops featuring similar profiles with even higher bittering potential. Bitterness is generally measured in **IBUs** ("international bitterness units").

Incidentally, the third largest country for hop production, behind Germany and the United States, is China, a country not yet noted for the production of great beer but currently seeing a growing internal market for beer and wine.

Malt flavors

The second main axis of beer taste is "maltiness." To understand what maltiness is, and how it fits into the flavor profile of beer, we need to look briefly into the malting process.

To prepare barley for brewing—a process called malting—raw kernels of the grain are soaked in water until they begin to sprout. The kernels are then are heated and dried in a kiln (a thermally insulated oven), which stops the sprouting process. The temperature at which the sprouted kernels are kilned determines a lot about the character of the malt, particularly the different types and amounts of unfermentable sugars that wind up in the mash.

Each of these unfermentable sugars has a distinct set of perceptual characteristics that affect the way the beer smells, tastes, looks, and feels in your mouth.

Pale malted barley forms the bulk of most modern beer recipes, including dark beers, and comes in several forms. Most Continental pale malts and North American pale malts are similar—the product is kilned just enough to dry the grain, resulting in minimal coloring. The flavors produced by these malts are subtle, dry grain flavors, often difficult to detect in beers with significant hopping or adjunct grain use. In well-made pale lagers and very light-bodied ales, they can come across as cracker-like or just somewhat grainy.

English pale malts are similar, although a touch darker, with very lightly caramelized flavors. These caramelized sugars provide the classic English pale ale malt character (English pale ales frequently have a color and malt profile that would be labeled as "amber" in the US). The best known of the English barleys is Maris

Otter, which is also used by many American craft breweries. Serious brewers also use such varieties as Halcyon, Optic, Golden Promise, or Pearl. There is a focus on malt flavors in many English and Scottish beers. The character derived from English malts and fermentation techniques often resembles the maltiness of malt vinegar, but without the acidity—a strikingly different flavor than the maltiness of German or North American beers, which tend toward crisper, baked grain flavors.

Crystal malts, also called caramel malts, are malted barley "stewed" with water before being dried. This treatment is similar to the mash procedure that brewers use later to convert starches to sugars, but here, it takes place inside the intact grain. When the grain cools before kilning, the sugar crystallizes, and then caramelizes under the dry kilning. These malts contribute nearly no fermentables to a beer.

Crystal malts come in a wide range of flavors. The lightest are similar in color to a pale malt or pilsner malt, and contribute insignificant flavor and color to a beer. Despite their lack of flavor and color, they are used by brewers because of their dextrins, which are sugars contained in these malts that add to the body of the beer, resulting in a richer, thicker mouthfeel to the beer.

Slightly darker versions of crystal malt also add color depth and mildly sweet caramel flavor. As color deepens, so does the intensity of caramel flavor, although it may retreat from registering as sweet and begin to take on dark, dried fruit flavors. **Medium crystal malt** is the primary coloring ingredient for most American pale and amber ales, although caramel flavors may hide behind the hops.

Most beer drinkers associate the word "lager" with pale, light-bodied beers like pilsner, but German brewers have long used a wide range of colored malts in their bottom-fermented beers, from pale Helles to viscous, opaqué doppelbock. One of the key grains for these brews is **Munich malt**, an amber malt used in the original brown Munich lagers, and still used regularly in Oktoberfest, märzen, and doppelbock beers (along with the related **Vienna malt**). Munich malt adds a distinctive toasty note and a malt sweetness that can have a bit of a light fruit character to it.

Dark grain flavors

Hidden among the acres of golden-colored lagers, only one dark ale is truly a part of the world's most mainstream beer culture: Guinness Stout. Whether this is a testament to the effectiveness of the Irish cultural lobby, the low hopping rate of the dry Irish stout style, the toucan they use as a mascot, or simple tradition, we don't know. One result of this ubiquity is that nobody will accuse you of being a beer elitist when you order a Guinness. There are many fine dark beers beyond Guinness, though, and this is a fertile territory for those who aren't wild about hop bitterness.

Dark, opaque beers, like porters and stouts, are typically made with a base of pale malted barley, with a careful selection of dark grains to add color and flavor. **Dark malts** vary widely in character. Grain selection for dark beers is generally more significant to the final product than hop selection or mash technique.

Some crystal malts can get pretty dark. The dark end of the crystal malt spectrum is full of rich sugar flavors that tend toward fruit flavors rather than the sweet caramel flavors of lighter malts. The touch of dark crystal malts is easily recognizable in big dark beers that aim for darkness through density of flavor and ingredient, rather than by roasting the grains within an inch of their lives. This means beers like barleywines or dark Belgian abbey ales like dubbels, where the concentration of dark rich caramel sugars frequently suggests prune or plum notes. In the case of dubbels, there's a particular strain of Belgian crystal malt called "Special B" that can add raisin-like notes.

The confusingly named **chocolate malt** is the first of the three major dark malts. The color of the grain is a rich, deep brown, which we imagine is the source of the name. The flavor of chocolate malt is smooth, rich, and roasty, without sharp or burnt flavors. A deep nuttiness characterizes the flavor of this grain, frequently used in porters and stouts, and sometimes used in small quantities for coloring in beers with a lighter flavor profile.

Black malt is barley that has been kilned until the grain has carbonized. This grain wasn't available to brewers until one Daniel Wheeler invented a device that sprayed water on the grain as it was kilned, allowing it to cook well past the time when traditional maltsters would have had a grain fire on their hands. He patented the device and, consequently, this grain is also known as patent malt or black patent malt. It's sharply bitter, sometimes described as "ashy," and generally used with a light hand. There's little question that, in a beer made with black malt, you're drinking something that's basically burnt.

Roasted barley, and its darker sibling **black barley**, are unusual in the brewer's array of ingredients because they're not malted (that is, they aren't allowed to start sprouting before the kilning process). Roasted barley has a distinctive dry bitterness to it that is similar to coffee. The dominant flavor note of the traditional dry Irish stout, such as Guinness, is roasted barley.

A not-precisely-dark flavor that one encounters here and there is **smoke**. Smoke was a ubiquitous beer flavor in cooler beer-producing regions for many centuries, as toasting the malt frequently meant burning wood or other smoky sources. These direct-fired kilning systems also put a practical upper limit on how dark malt could be toasted before burning to a crisp, and a practical limit on just how pale a malt could be without leaving some of it untoasted.

By the end of the 1600s, maltsters had already developed indirect heating systems, making even, pale malts with a near absence of smoke flavor possible. Smoke as an interesting flavor shows up in Bavarian rauchbier ("smoke beer"), which is still brewed to this day, especially in the city of Bamberg. In the Islay region of Scotland, whiskey producers have long used peat in the kilning of malt for its distinctive flavors; it is possible to find Scotch ales here and there that use a touch of peated malt. A few American brewers have also taken up smoked-malt beers.

Yeast flavors

Ah, yeast. Our favorite microbial fungus, without a doubt. These little guys put the bubbles in our bread and the booze in our beer. They also contribute a host of flavors to both bread and beer.

The basic job of yeast is to convert sugars to alcohol and carbon dioxide. Humans have been employing yeast for this end for thousands of years, so it's remarkable that it wasn't until 1857 that it was shown—by Louis Pasteur, who was awfully interested in beer for a Frenchman—that yeast was a living organism, and fermentation was not a simple chemical reaction.

Yeast generally likes the same temperatures that we do. Most yeast strains are inert below about 60°F, most active at temperatures in the mid-80's, and die when the temperature hits 100°F or so. When yeasts really get going in the mostly anaerobic conditions of beer fermentation, they produce some fairly intense and striking flavors, most prominently a non-specific fruitiness.

Yeasts commonly produce **diacetyl**, a substance with a pronounced butter flavor. To limit this result, brewers warm up the beer during the aging process, causing the yeast to reabsorb the diacetyl. In well-made lager beers (or ales produced at low fermentation temperatures, like German kölsch), yeasts produce almost no flavor or aroma (aside from ethanol, of course).

At typical ale fermentation, some yeast character is almost inevitable, though there is considerable variability by yeast strain. The flavors of English ale yeasts tend to show through more than American varieties. It is not uncommon, however, for US craft brewers to use English ale yeasts, particularly for darker beers. English yeasts (and fermentations) tend to leave more malt character and more diacetyl. English beers, as a result, are frequently described as maltier and fruitier than their American counterparts.

The brewers of the world who have really embraced yeast character, though, are the Belgians. To experience the full measure of yeast's flavor contribution to beer, look to the high-alcohol Trappist or Abbey beers. These beers employ yeast blends that produce strong fruit character, known as **esters** in the beer world. Yeast esters are the same aromatic compounds that give fruits their characteristic flavors. There is a huge array of esters; every yeast strain will produce a different balance of these compounds, given the right ambient conditions, and it's possible in some cases for expert tasters to identify the producer of a beer they've never tasted before by recognizing the yeast through its fruity signature.

In addition to esters, yeast can produce potent, striking flavors—for better or worse—called **phenols**. Phenolic flavors from yeast can include smoke, clove, plastic, and (if there are chlorine compounds in the brewing water) the delicate flavor of Chloraseptic. As you might expect, the latter flavors are generally undesirable, but Bavarian wheat beers are brewed with yeast selected to give the clove flavors. Phenols are hard to miss, compared to many of the flavors you'll find in beer, and clove and smoke are both flavors that drinkers tend to either love or hate.

The other type of yeast flavor you may run across is more literal: a time-honored technique for carbonating bottled beer involves adding sugar to the beer (beers that follow the ancient Reinheitsgebot—German purity law, which forbids the addition of any ingredient other than water, barley, and hops—actually add fresh, unfermented wort instead) just before bottling, so that the yeast will get in a bit more fermentation time, producing the carbon dioxide to make the beer bubbly inside the bottle. (This process is called **secondary fermentation**.) When the beer is refrigerated, the yeast sediment settles to the bottom of the bottle in a thin layer. The result, if it ends up in your beer, is a yeasty taste that's similar to nutritional yeast. It may also remind you of the smell of fresh baked bread.

This layer of yeast is harmless; it even contains B-complex vitamins that may help fight off a hangover. But it's a matter of cultural style and personal preference whether you want it in your glass or not. Traditionally, Belgians prefer to let sleeping yeasts lie, while Germans make a show of stirring up the sediment and topping off the glass with it, particularly with hefeweizens. But in the end, it's up to you.

Adjuncts, additives, and unusual flavors

Adjunct is a catch-all term for just about anything that gets added to a beer recipe aside from water, hops, yeast, and the primary grain for the recipe (generally called "base malt").

There are a number of grains used to make beer in addition to malted barley. In fact, nearly every grain produced has been used to make beer, somewhere. But there are a few that you are likely to run into regularly as you peruse the shelves. There are also a few other ingredients used in beers here and there worth talking about.

Many beer recipes include adjunct grains, giving color and providing a range of flavors not obtainable from lightly kilned base malts; the term is also used—sometimes derisively—to refer to ingredients like corn, rice, or sugar that are used to add alcohol to beer without adding much body or flavor. Adjunct ingredients make up a lot recipe of most North-American-styled lager recipes.

Wheat is a common adjunct. It's often used in small portions to help with head retention, containing proteins that promote firm, long-lasting head. The amount of wheat added for that purpose does not typically add a discernible flavor.

In Germany, however, wheat plays a more prominent role in brewing. Wheat beers, while not nearly as popular as Pilsners or other clean pale lagers, are easy to find, and since Widmer created the American wheat beer style in the mid-1980s, they're increasingly easy to find in North America. Much of the flavor of these beers comes from the choice of yeast (which is why German weissbiers have typical clove and banana flavors, and American examples generally don't), but open a Widmer Hefeweizen and you'll get at the essential character of wheat in beer—a grainy, bready, full-bodied, and absolutely unmistakable flavor.

Wheat is also a key ingredient in Belgian white ales (witbier) and sour ales like lambics, although the character of these beers tends to be dominated by other elements—spices, in the case of witbier, and a wide variety of secondary fermentation characteristics, the most prominent of which is tart lactic acid, in lambics.

Oats are another popular addition, most commonly in the hearty oatmeal stout. Oats fill out the body with high protein content and fat, creating a smooth, rich mouthfeel. Brewers must strike a balance, however, as oily additions tend to inhibit head retention.

Rye was a popular brewing grain in Bavaria until the Reinheitsgebot, or purity law, made it the exclusive domain of Bavarian bakers. The Bavarian style of cloudy rye beer—called roggenbier and made in much the same way as hefeweizen—was revived in the late 1980s, and produces a dark bready ale. American brewers have also begun to use the grain in smaller amounts to make hoppy, spicy beers closely related to IPAs (Bear Republic's Hop Rod Rye, brewed in this mold and reviewed in this book, is an outstanding example). In these smaller quantities, rye adds light, spicy flavors that accentuate crisp hop bitterness.

Oak aging is a traditional part of some Belgian styles, like the sour Flanders red ale, and has also seen a recent vogue among American brewers of high-alcohol beers, particularly porters and stouts. The oak barrel serves much the same purpose as it does in winemaking, contributing toasted-wood flavors along with vanilla, chocolate, or coffee notes (barrels are traditionally lightly charred on the inside before use), and in newer oak barrels, tannins.

These flavors can be rough and dominant when the beer is fresh, and many of these beers require time in bottle to show their best. Some brewers choose barrels that have been used in the production of other beverages, like whiskey or sherry, which usually renders the wood itself somewhat more neutral, but imparts some character from the wine or spirit that previously occupied the cask.

Corn, rice, and sugar are all used to add alcohol to a beer without bulking up the flavor, particularly in American-styled lagers and their descendants. Japanese brewers have taken this approach even further than the Americans. These sugar sources are almost completely fermentable, leaving behind very little trace, although it's possible occasionally to taste a hint of corn or rice in beer. If brewers use too much of these adjuncts in their beer, yeast can produce cidery flavors.

Not everyone uses sugar as a way of lightening flavors, though. Belgian brewers use a range of sugars, from light to dark, to contribute caramel and molasses-type flavors to their strong beers; **molasses** itself has a long history as a brewing ingredient (perhaps most famously in a beer recipe by George Washington).

The brewers of Belgium also use a variety of **spices**—coriander, grains of paradise, cumin, and the dried peel of bitter Curaçao oranges, for instance. These are usually employed in combination, most often in witbiers such as Hoegaarden. The resulting flavor is complex and challenging to describe. The addition of coriander can contribute a mildly soapy flavor.

You'll also find a range of spices employed in beers brewed as winter specials. These spices are also usually blended for subtlety, but you may notice cinnamon, clove, nutmeg, or ginger in your winter warmer.

These are the most common additives to beers in the early 21st century, but the list is by no means exhaustive. You will generally find other additions listed in the name of the beer (coffee stouts, chocolate porters, and so on) or prominently mentioned on the beer's label, so it's not generally a surprise. Whether it's spices, herbs, fruits, or even vegetables, chances are some enterprising brewer has tried adding it at some point, and while some of these beers are every bit as odd as you'd expect, there are some surprising and eye-opening recipes out there.

Finally, the last major source of unusual flavors out there in the beer world is **non-yeast fermentation**. We'll touch on some of these flavors, especially since intentionally soured beers seem to be undergoing a new vogue lately, and there has been a resurgence of interest in Brettanomyces.

Lactobacillus—the same family of bugs that make yogurt and sauerkraut tangy—consumes residual sugars and dextrins in the beer and produce tart lactic acid. **Acetobacter** can convert the alcohol in beer into vinegar (acetic acid). Either way, the end result is a puckery pint.

Sometimes these secondary fermentations are part of the style. In Belgium, several beer traditions expose the beer to... well, to just about everything—in some cases, the beer is brewed in spaces where it is left open to the sky. Flanders red ale, like Rodenbach or Duchess de Bourgogne, is a soured beer often aged in oak, giving it a tannic, tart profile.

Lambic beers, meanwhile, are fermented with a wild, anything-goes attitude, leaving beers that are intensely sour. These beers often have fruit added after fermentation for palatability, but the straight lambic—or gueuze, which blends old and new lambic to moderate the sourness a bit—can be a treat, if an acquired one. Tourists in Berlin may have encountered Berliner Weisse, a lightly soured ale frequently served with a splash of brightly colored flavored syrup—red for raspberry or green for woodruff. A German style named Gose, brewed with coriander and salt, has been making a comeback in the last couple years from the brink of extinction.

Brettanomyces (sometimes shortened to "Brett"), a type of yeast, is best known today as a source of controversy in the wine world, where some consider it a flaw and others find it essential to the wines of regions like South Africa and France's southern Rhône valley. Brett has a long history, however—not as a part of the beer tradition as much as just the way beer used to be. It's an organism that makes a comfortable home in wood barrels, and feeds on sugars that normal beer yeast has a hard time digesting, so brewers who stored their beer in barrels for aging were prone to ending up with some Brett character in their beer.

Brett produces acetic acid, particularly in the presence of simple sugars like glucose, but it is more notable for producing a variety of phenolic compounds. The sensory experience of these compounds varies significantly by the amounts and the ratios of the different phenols. The most desirable of these is closely related to the clove-flavored phenol produced by weizen yeasts, and can come across as meaty (like bacon), smoky, or spicy (like cloves); or some mixture of those.

The other phenols can remind people of barnyards, plastic, or band-aids, but in low amounts aren't necessarily offensive. "Old leather" is the classic British description of Bretty beer—intriguing enough to inspire the recreation of 19th-century British beers, with authentic Brett flavors. Brett also plays a role in several Belgian styles, including lambics and Flanders ales. The Trappist ale Orval has Brett added at bottling; the character develops slowly as the bottled beer ages.

Off-flavors
Occasionally, you'll reach for a freshly poured pint and get a mouthful of "BLECCCHHH." Since that terms doesn't get you very far, it's useful to have a vocabulary for identifying flaws in beers, both so you can explain to your friends or your waiter why you need a different beer, and in some cases, so you know whether the potentially off-putting flavor is meant to be there or not.

In the wine world, there are a variety of flavors that are "flaws" for one taster and "features" for another. The same is true—though perhaps not to the same degree—with beer. Bitterness, for instance, is a fairly central beer flavor, but many people don't enjoy more than a modest dollop of it; some—notably the so-called "supertasters," who have double the number of taste buds as most people—find even small amounts of bitterness to be off-putting. They don't tend to drink much beer.

Serious beer tasters, including professional brewers, work to develop acute sensitivity to these flavors and flaws so that they can recognize them early and eliminate the causes. They doctor samples of beer with small amounts of flavor and aroma chemicals to see how close they can get to an ideal.

Pale lagers are particularly sensitive to flaws, because they often have little in the way of strong elements to mask the offending flavor or aroma. This is part of the reason that these beers are often served colder than ales or full-bodied lagers like Oktoberfests or German bocks—as we noted earlier, aromas, for better or worse, are less conspicuous at lower temperature.

Other flavors are just not meant to turn up in beer, period. Here are some common or notable flavors and aromas to look for the next time you taste a beer and think that something is just not right.

Distinct **tart or sour flavors** are frequently a sign that a beer's defenses have failed and a secondary fermentation has occurred. One of the most important pieces of beermaking is sanitation: keeping the beer as free of undesired bacteria and yeasts as possible. But making beer is not like making computer chips. It's not done in a dust-free, hermetic environment. Short of pasteurizing the beer to sterilize it, there will nearly always be some spoilage organisms. Pasteurization is effective at preserving beer against souring, but it comes at the cost of some measure of flavor and character, so it tends to be the domain of very large-scale brewers, who value consistency over maximizing flavor.

As we've noted in the previous chapter, there exists a whole category of sour beers that are soured very much intentionally.

Soapiness is a common flaw, and the cause is usually rather straightforward: soap. Good bars use a careful process for cleaning glassware to ensure that customers don't get soapy off-flavors or residual oils that can knock the head right off a beer. Less attentive pubs may use conventional dishwashing processes, leading to glasses that are not "beer clean." Don't put up with it.

We do occasionally find soapy flavors in witbiers, Belgian white ales brewed with yeast and spices, that are not due to a poorly washed glass. The coriander that is sometimes added can leave a soapy taste. If you have a strong aversion to cilantro, there's a decent chance that you won't find a strong love for beers like Hoegaarden.

Buttery or **butterscotch** aromas and flavors, caused by diacetyl, are a normal byproduct of yeast fermentation. In typical conditions, the yeast will reprocess the diacetyl into neutral-tasting compounds, which happens most easily at warm temperatures. To avoid excessive diacetyl, it's typical for lager brewers to raise the temperature of the beer after fermentation and before the cold lagering rest, or to have the last part of the lager fermentation occur at higher temperatures. This flavor is considered a significant flaw in lagers, where it sticks out like a sore thumb, but in some English and Belgian styles, a little bit is considered acceptable. These flavors may develop in English beers because many English yeast strains are quite flocculent: as fermentation nears completion, the yeasts form little clumps that float to the top. Since they have very little surface area (relative to the amount of yeast), these floating clumps contribute little to the final stages of fermentation, including the processing of diacetyl.

Historically, diacetyl was much more common in beer than it is now. It wasn't until the 1950s that the compound was recognized as the source of buttery flavor and techniques were developed for measuring it. Through better sanitation processes (particularly in yeast propagation and to avoid extraneous organisms in the beer, which can also bring about diacetyl) and better yeast selection, typical diacetyl levels are a fifth to a tenth of what they were in commercial beers sixty years ago. Diacetyl is also interesting because approximately 20% of the population is unable to taste or smell it until the concentration is very high.

Skunkiness and post-brewing quality flaws

Skunky aromas may be the off-flavor that American consumers are most familiar with. These arise when a beer is **lightstruck** thanks to the prevalence of clear or green glass bottles on ostensibly premium (don't worry, it's just a marketing term) lagers, like Heineken and Corona, and widespread use of fluorescent lighting in stores and beer coolers. When hop oils are exposed to ultraviolet light, they break apart into highly reactive charged particles. These particles interact with sulfur compounds to produce an end product, called a thiol, structurally very similar to the smelly stuff produced by skunks.

It turns out that we are exceptionally sensitive to these odors: a few parts per trillion is enough for most people to detect. And a few parts more will quickly turn a beer into a reeking mess. This is a good reason to avoid beer that's bottled in green and clear glass.

There are ways to fight light. Brown glass will filter the offending rays and mitigate the effect. And some breweries using clear glass—Miller, most notably—employ a process that eliminates the particularly vulnerable compounds from their beer before it has a chance to go skunky.

The beers most at risk for failure are filtered or, worse, pasteurized. Pasteurization is good for the short-term freshness of a beer, but it guarantees staling of the beer over the long run. Bottle-conditioned beers, with live yeast cultures providing carbonation, have protection against both bacterial spoilage and oxidation. Higher alcohol levels also provide some additional protection against spoilage. Belgian beers frequently combine both of these preservative traits and tend to be relatively hardy. Many of these beers, stored properly, can remain fresh and interesting for years. Still, multiple bottles we sampled from the revered Trappist producer Rochefort were badly spoiled.

German and English beers are a mixed bag. Frequently these beers are not bottle-conditioned, and in the case of British beers, there's often less alcohol to protect the beer than there is in comparable American styles. In our opinion, consumers interested in these import beers would do well to choose beers with explicit freshness labeling, particularly for British beers. Too many of them showed signs of spoilage—ranging from subtle to painfully obvious—for us to be happy with things as they are.

One of the main things you can do to avoid skunked or flawed beers is to keep an eye out for proper storage in stores. Beer should be kept cool and away from fluorescent lighting, and, especially, direct sunlight, which can cause beers in clear or green glass to become skunky in a matter of minutes.

Every beer market is different, and you may be fortunate enough to live in a region where your preferred imports are always fresh. Or they may languish on the shelves, waiting forlornly for the annual visit from The One Guy In Town Who Drinks Weizenbocks. Getting to know the beer buyer at your local market can help you find the beers most likely to be fresh and representative. And if your first foray into an unusual style seems unpleasant and wrong, it may not be the fault of the brewer or the style. It is also noteworthy that there seem to be plenty of drinkers who don't notice or don't mind skunky notes in beer.

Notes to part I

1. Allison and Uhl, "Influence of beer brand identification on taste perception," *Journal of Marketing Research* 1 (1964). Perversely, regular drinkers of two of the beers scored *other* beers better by a statistically significant margin.

2. Roman Weil, "Parker v. Prial: The Death of the Vintage Chart," *Chance* 14:4 (Fall 2001); Weil, 2007, "Debunking Critics' Wine Words: Can Amateurs Distinguish the Smell of Asphalt from the Taste of Cherries?" *Journal of Wine Economics* 2:2 (Fall 2007). Both of these papers are required reading for anyone interested in the influence of perceptual bias on taste experience.

3. n=138, coefficient=.370, standard error=.041, 95% confidence interval=0.288 to 0.451. Robin Goldstein, Seamus Campbell, Johan Almenberg, and Anna Dreber Almenberg, "Can people tell the difference between European pale lager beers?" Working paper, 2010.

4. Robin Goldstein, Johan Almenberg, Anna Dreber, Jay Emerson, Alexis Herschkowitsch, and Jacob Katz, "Do More Expensive Wines Taste Better? Evidence From a Large Sample of US Blind Tastings." *Journal of Wine Economics*, Vol. 3, No. 1 (Spring 2008); see also Goldstein and Herschkowitsch, *The Wine Trials* (Fearless Critic Media, 2008).

5. BBL, or barrel, of beer is 31 gallons; 350 BBL is approximately 11,000 gallons or 5,200 cases; 600 BBL is approximately 9,000 cases. Figures published at beeradvocate.com and attributed to Deschutes Brewery.

6. The legendary beers of Westvleteren are best known for being next to impossible to obtain: would-be buyers must call the abbey in rural Flanders to reserve beer before collecting it at the abbey; any person or car is limited to a single case of the beer each month. With minuscule production, it's no surprise to us that this is frequently identified as "the best beer in the world."

7. For the co-author's exposé of one such pay-to-play scheme, the *Wine Spectator* Awards of Excellence program, see Robin Goldstein, Blind Taste blog, "What Does It Take To Get a Wine Spectator Award of Excellence," http://blindtaste.com/2008/08/15/what-does-it-take-to-get-a-wine-spectator-award-of-excellence (August 15, 2008).

8. Hilke Plassmann, John O'Doherty, Baba Shiv, and Antonio Rangel, "Marketing Actions Can Modulate Neural Representations of Experienced Pleasantness," *Proceedings of the National Academy of Sciences* (January 14, 2008).

9. Leonard Lee, Shane Frederick, and Dan Ariely. "Try It, You'll Like It: The Influence of Expectation, Consumption, and Revelation on Preferences for Beer." *Psychological Science*, Vol. 17, No. 12 (December 2006).

Part II The beer trials

We take a scientific approach to our blind tastings, and we aim to be unbiased and fair. Our philosophy is predicated on openness, and we feel that much is to be gained on all sides if we are transparent with our reviewing process. Here, in this spirit, we first disclose the inner workings of the blind beer tastings that we conducted for this book. After that, we explain what our ratings and reviews mean; we present a list of our ratings, organized by beer family; and finally, we offer our full-page reviews of all 250 beers. As always, we welcome feedback at fearlesscritic.com/beer.

Selection process

Our first task was building a list of 250 widely available beers to review. We aimed for a balanced selection of beers from around the United States, Canada, and overseas, from breweries both large and relatively small. We also wanted to make sure that readers anywhere would be able to find a good portion of the beers.

As such, all 250 beers in the book are distributed in at least a dozen or so US states, and the significant majority of the beers are available much more widely across the US, Canada, and abroad. We also set as a rough rule that half the beers should be "large production" beers and half "smaller production," and that roughly a third should be imports from outside the US and Canada.

Many craft breweries that met our qualifications produce a number of noteworthy beers. (For beer lovers, this is a wonderful problem to have.) We limited ourselves to two to four beers from each craft brewery and, with a couple of exceptions, chose a brewery's flagship, year-round beers—unfortunately, there just wasn't space in this edition to include seasonally available beers.

We purchased beers, when available, at local retailers. Portland is a great city for finding beers, and local retailer Belmont Station is well known for treating beers well—all beer is stored away from UV light sources at appropriate temperature, and stocks are monitored for sell-through so that older beers can be pulled. For certain beers not sold in Oregon and Washington, we either obtained samples directly from breweries or purchased beers in other states and transported them to Oregon.

One can always hope that a book could include a higher number of reviews without losing the overall relevance. But we feel that we've covered a broad swath of important, relevant beers across all price ranges and styles that are available for sale in non-specialty stores and markets around North America and abroad.

Methodology

We held our tastings in a private, unoccupied apartment—as close to perfect for the job as it gets. We had bright lighting; a quiet working space, free from cooking smells and distractions; a clean dishwasher used exclusively for our tasting glasses; and a cool basement space in which to store the beer samples.

Each beer was tasted by a rotating subset of the larger tasting panel. At each tasting, we had a steward, who was responsible for selecting beers for each evening's panel of three to six tasters. Unlike our tasters, the stewards were generally not beer experts. Beers were grouped with other beers from the same family—and the same style, when possible—and served in flights of three, six, or (occasionally) nine beers. Tasters were informed of the family or style of beer they were served. When we served multiple styles, we generally served them in increasing order of flavor intensity.

A significant factor in many of the judgments we've made about beers is the manner in which they are served. Drinking beer too cold hides the differences between beers, as does drinking beer from a container that doesn't allow you to access the aromas of a beer, like a bottle or can. We swirled and tasted beers in special tasting glasses at temperatures that accentuated their differences—that is to say, much warmer than you'd generally get them at a bar.

Each taster had to rate and complete a tasting form on each beer. We provided a few scales to help break down flavor profiles, and we left a large area for free-flow notes. (You can download the blank rating/review forms at fearlesscritic.com/beer.) At the end of each flight, the steward collected the forms; after that, we had a brief discussion of the beers—what stood out, what we particularly liked, any flaws. Finally, the steward revealed the beers.

Notes on quality

Some beers that we tasted had suffered in their transit from the brewery to our glasses. This happens more than most beer producers—or consumers, for that matter—are willing to admit. Predictably, it was imported beers that were affected the most. A significant portion of the lagers in clear or green glass (e.g. Corona, Steinlager, Heineken) were lightstruck to one degree or another, while some imported ales from Europe—particularly the United Kingdom—showed various signs of oxidation and bacterial spoilage. We replaced and re-tasted every one of these beers, but if multiple samples were lightstruck or flawed, we noted this in the review while still attempting to give a clear picture of the rest of the beer's qualities. We feel that it's important for consumers to be aware that beer is perishable, and that it's worth patronizing businesses that properly care for the beers they sell.

About the beer reviews and ratings

Beer name, rating, and family: at the top of each review, we include each beer's most commonly used **name** and **rating** on our 10-point scale. For more on the rating system, see below. The beer's **family** appears immediately beneath the name. For more on what "family" means, see chapter 4.

Basic beer information: Beneath the name, rating, and family, each review page includes other information as well. The first line indicates the beer's **country** of origin (and state or province in the US or Canada); the beer's **style**, a subcategory of family (for a full explanation of the family-style distinction, and a definition of each family and style, see chapter 4); and the beer's **ABV** (alcohol by volume). The second line includes the **producer** (brewery), **group** (only if the brewery is part of a larger conglomerate or holding company), and **price.** For more on price categories, see below. The third line includes **packaging**, a list of the sizes and formats (bottles, cans, etc.) currently available in North America. The fourth line lists one or more of the following basic **characteristics** of the beer, in alphabetical order (characteristics are explained in more detail in chapter 5): bitter, hoppy, malty, roasty, sour, strong, refreshing, unusual, yeasty. "Bland" indicates the absence of other notable characteristics.

The rating system: *The Beer Trials* uses a 10-point whole-number rating scale. The average is 6.5, and the median is 7. Beers are judged against other beers in the same family, and thus are evaluated mainly on how successfully they achieve their particular aims, whatever those aims are. The numerical ratings aggregate the panel's normalized opinions. Here's how to interpret the numbers:

1–2: deeply flawed; virtually undrinkable.
3–4: moderately flawed; not pleasant; a beer to be avoided.
5–6: either an acceptable but unexceptional beer, or a beer that has interesting character but is diminished by some flaws or imbalances.
7–8: an interesting, enjoyable beer we'd be happy to find in a bar.
9–10: an exceptional beer, worth taking the time to appreciate.

Price categories: The price of beer varies around the country, and from store to store within a city. We've examined the typical prices of the beers reviewed and divided them into five categories of approximate cost at a retail store, and categorized them based on the price per 12-ounce bottle or can. When that format does not exist, we've calculated the price per 12-ounce equivalent. Categories are as follows:

$: Less than $1.33 per 12oz bottle (less than $8 for a six-pack).
$$: $1.33–$1.66 per 12oz bottle ($8–$10 for a six-pack).
$$$: $1.66–$2.50 per 12oz bottle ($10–15 for a six-pack).
$$$$: $2.50–$5 per 12oz bottle ($5–10 for a 22oz bottle).
$$$$$: $5+ per 12oz bottle, ($10+ for a 22oz bottle)

Beer review: each review is split into three parts. First, there's an **introduction** to each beer that discusses the brewery, the style, the history, and/or the culture surrounding the beer. Next, there's a description of the **flavors and aromas** of the beer, based on the blind tasting notes from our panel. Finally, there's our take on the **design** of the bottle or can. Accompanying each review is an **image** of the bottle or can, so you can easily locate it in a store.

Beer reference list by family, rating, and style

Each of the 250 beers reviewed in The Beer Trials *is listed below with its page number, country of origin, price, and rating. Beers are grouped first into our 11 families, which appear in alphabetical order. Within each family, beers are ordered by rating; ties are ordered alphabetically.*

To look up beers by style (a subcategory of family), see chapter 5, where each style description is followed by a list of beers in that style reviewed in The Beer Trials.

Family: Amber Lager	Page	Country	Price	Rating
Ayinger Oktoberfest	76	Germany	$$$	9
Brooklyn Lager	107	USA	$$	8
Great Divide Hoss Rye Lager	157	USA	$$$	8
Spaten Oktoberfest	280	Germany	$$	8
Coney Island Lager	124	USA	$$$$	7
Samuel Adams Boston Lager	257	USA	$$	7
Shiner Bock	271	USA	$	7
Michelob AmberBock	199	USA	$	6
Paulaner Oktoberfest	232	Germany	$$	6
Yuengling Traditional Lager	309	USA	$	6
Negra Modelo	214	Mexico	$$	5

Family: Belgian Ale	Page	Country	Price	Rating
Chimay Blue (Grande Réserve)	119	Belgium	$$$$$	9
Fin du Monde	146	Canada	$$$$	9
Saison Dupont	255	Belgium	$$$$	9
Allagash Dubbel	65	USA	$$$$	8
Allagash Tripel	66	USA	$$$$	8
Chimay Red (Première)	120	Belgium	$$$$$	8
Delirium Tremens	131	Belgium	$$$$	8
Don de Dieu	139	Canada	$$$$	8
Duvel	142	Belgium	$$$$	8
La Chouffe	184	Belgium	$$$$	8
Maredsous Tripel	196	Belgium	$$$$	8
Maudite	197	Canada	$$$$	8
Three Philosophers	291	USA	$$$$	8
Chimay White (Cinq Cents)	121	Belgium	$$$$$	7
Hennepin	169	USA	$$$	7
New Belgium Abbey Ale	216	USA	$$	7
Ommegang Abbey Ale	225	USA	$$$	7
Rochefort 6	246	Belgium	$$$$$	7
Westmalle Tripel	300	Belgium	$$$$$	7
Leffe Blonde	189	Belgium	$$$	6
Maredsous Brune	195	Belgium	$$$$	6
New Belgium 1554	215	USA	$$	6
Rochefort 8	247	Belgium	$$$$$	6

Family: Brown Ale

	Page	Country	Price	Rating
Brooklyn Brown	105	USA	$$	8
He'Brew Messiah Bold	167	USA	$$	8
He'Brew Genesis Ale	166	USA	$$	7
Big Sky Moose Drool	86	USA	$$	6
Newcastle Brown Ale	218	England	$$	6

Family: Dark Ale (Porter and Stout)

	Page	Country	Price	Rating
Boulder Planet Porter	97	USA	$$	9
Deschutes Obsidian Stout	135	USA	$$	9
Deschutes Black Butte Porter	132	USA	$$	8
Rogue Shakespeare Oatmeal Stout	252	USA	$$$$	8
Bison Chocolate Stout	87	USA	$$$	7
Eel River Organic Porter	144	USA	$$$	7
Sierra Nevada Porter	274	USA	$$	7
Yuengling Original Black and Tan	308	USA	$	7
Breckenridge Vanilla Porter	102	USA	$$	6
Samuel Smith Oatmeal Stout	260	England	$$$$	6
Young's Double Chocolate Stout	306	England	$$$$	6
Guinness Draught	160	Ireland	$$$	5
Guinness Extra Stout	161	Ireland	$$	5
Murphy's Stout	211	Ireland	$$	4
Sheaf Stout	270	Australia/NZ	$$$	4

Family: India Pale Ale

	Page	Country	Price	Rating
Goose Island IPA	156	USA	$$	9
Hop Rod Rye	175	USA	$$$$	9
Victory Hop Devil Ale	295	USA	$$$	9
Widmer Broken Halo IPA	301	USA	$$	9
AleSmith IPA	63	USA	$$$$	8
Bear Republic Racer 5 IPA	79	USA	$$$$	8
Big Sky IPA	85	USA	$$	8
Bison IPA	88	USA	$$$	8
Dogfish Head 60 Minute IPA	136	USA	$$$	8
Lagunitas IPA	187	USA	$$	8
Saranac IPA	264	USA	$	8
Avery IPA	74	USA	$$	7
Big Daddy IPA	84	USA	$$$	7
Blind Pig IPA	90	USA	$$$$	7
Bridgeport IPA	104	USA	$$	7
Brooklyn East India Pale Ale	106	USA	$$	7
Caldera IPA	117	USA	$$$	7
Redhook Long Hammer IPA	245	USA	$$	7
Samuel Smith India Ale	259	England	$$$$	7
Titan IPA	292	USA	$$$	7
Breckenridge Lucky U IPA	101	USA	$$	6
Flying Dog Snake Dog IPA	148	USA	$$	6
Pyramid Thunderhead IPA	240	USA	$$	6

Family: India Pale Ale (continued)	Page	Country	Price	Rating
Stone IPA	288	USA	$$	6
Wolaver's Organic IPA	305	USA	$$	6
Eel River Organic IPA	143	USA	$$$	5
Harpoon IPA	165	USA	$$	5
Hop Ottin' IPA	174	USA	$$$	5

Family: Pale Ale

	Page	Country	Price	Rating
Alaskan Amber	60	USA	$$	8
AleSmith Anvil ESB	62	USA	$$$$	8
Anchor Liberty Ale	68	USA	$$	8
Bear Republic Red Rocket Ale	80	USA	$$$$	8
Bear Republic XP Pale Ale	81	USA	$$$$	8
Boont Amber	94	USA	$$$	8
Deschutes Green Lake Organic Ale	133	USA	$$	8
Kona Fire Rock Pale Ale	182	USA	$$	8
Oskar Blues Old Chub	227	USA	$$	8
Pike Pale	237	USA	$$	8
Red Seal Ale	242	USA	$$$	8
Stone Levitation Ale	289	USA	$$	8
Widmer Drifter Pale Ale	302	USA	$$	8
Anchor Steam	70	USA	$$	7
Belhaven Scottish Ale	83	Scotland	$$$$	7
Bridgeport ESB	103	USA	$$	7
Caldera Amber	116	USA	$$$	7
Dale's Pale Ale	130	USA	$$	7
Deschutes Mirror Pond Pale Ale	134	USA	$$	7
Goose Island Honker's Ale	155	USA	$$	7
Lagunitas Censored Copper Ale	186	USA	$$	7
Mendocino Red Tail Ale	198	USA	$$	7
Old Speckled Hen	222	England	$$	7
Pike Kilt Lifter	236	USA	$$	7
Redhook ESB	244	USA	$$	7
Rogue Dead Guy	250	USA	$$$	7
Sierra Nevada Pale Ale	273	USA	$$	7
Smithwick's Red Ale	278	Ireland	$$	7
AleSmith X	64	USA	$$$	6
Bass Ale	78	England	$$	6
Boulevard Pale Ale	98	USA	$$	6
Budweiser American Ale	112	USA	$$	6
Full Sail Amber	151	USA	$$	6
Full Sail Pale Ale	152	USA	$$	6
Speakeasy Prohibition Ale	283	USA	$$$	6
Widmer Drop Top Amber	303	USA	$$	6
Boulder Hazed and Infused	96	USA	$$	5
Henry Weinhard's Blue Boar	170	USA	$$	5
Magic Hat #9	194	USA	$$	5
Otter Creek Copper Ale	228	USA	$$	5

Family: Pale Ale (continued)	Page	Country	Price	Rating
Samuel Smith Pale Ale	261	England	$$$$	5
Saranac Pale Ale	265	USA	$	5
New Belgium Fat Tire	217	USA	$$	4
Boddington's Cream Ale	92	England	$$	3

Family: Pale Lager

	Page	Country	Price	Rating
Lagunitas Pils	188	USA	$$	9
Victory Prima Pils	296	USA	$$$	9
Bitburger Pilsner	89	Germany	$$	8
Czechvar	129	Czech Republic	$$$	8
Paulaner Premium Pils	233	Germany	$$	8
Singha	276	Thailand	$$	8
Spaten Premium	282	Germany	$$	8
Trumer Pils	293	USA	$$	8
Beck's	82	Germany	$$	7
Bohemia	93	Mexico	$$	7
Boulevard Pilsner	99	USA	$$	7
Carlsberg Lager	118	Denmark	$$	7
Genesee Cream Ale	154	USA	$	7
Grolsch Premium Lager	159	Netherlands	$$	7
Kirin Ichiban	180	Japan	$$	7
Kokanee Glacier Beer	181	Canada	$	7
Löwenbräu Original	193	Germany	$$	7
Molson Canadian	209	Canada	$	7
Moretti	210	Italy	$$	7
Oskar Blues Mama's Little Yella	226	USA	$$	7
St. Pauli Girl	284	Germany	$	7
Stella Artois	287	Belgium	$$	7
Tecate	290	Mexico	$	7
Foster's Lager	149	Australia/NZ	$$	6
Harp Lager	164	Ireland	$	6
Heineken	168	Netherlands	$$	6
Henry Weinhard's Private Reserve	172	USA	$$	6
Iron City Beer	177	USA	$	6
Kingfisher Premium	179	India	$$	6
Michelob Original Lager	201	USA	$	6
Miller Genuine Draft	205	USA	$	6
Pabst Blue Ribbon	229	USA	$	6
Pacifico	230	Mexico	$$	6
Pilsner Urquell	238	Czech Republic	$$	6
Rainier Beer	241	USA	$	6
Rolling Rock	253	USA	$$	6
Sam Adams Light	256	USA	$$	6
Sapporo Premium	262	Japan	$$	6
Saranac Adirondack Lager	263	USA	$	6
Steel Reserve 211 High Gravity	285	USA	$	6
Warsteiner Premium	298	Germany	$$	6

Family: Pale Lager (continued)	Page	Country	Price	Rating
Amstel Light	67	Netherlands	$$	5
Bud Ice	108	USA	$	5
Bud Light	109	USA	$	5
Bud Light Lime	110	USA	$	5
Coors	125	USA	$	5
Coors Light	126	USA	$	5
Dos Equis Special Lager	140	Mexico	$$	5
Kona Longboard Lager	183	USA	$$	5
Labatt Blue	185	Canada	$	5
Mickey's	203	USA	$	5
Miller High Life	206	USA	$	5
Modelo Especial	208	Mexico	$	5
Natural Light	213	USA	$	5
O'Doul's	221	USA	$	5
Olde English 800	223	USA	$	5
Olympia	224	USA	$	5
Peroni Nastro Azzurro	235	Italy	$$	5
Red Stripe	243	Jamaica	$	5
Session Premium Lager	269	USA	$	5
Sol	279	Mexico	$$	5
Steinlager Classic	286	New Zealand	$$	5
Asahi Super Dry	72	Japan	$$	4
Budweiser	111	USA	$	4
Busch	114	USA	$	4
Busch Light	115	USA	$	4
Colt 45	123	USA	$	4
Corona Extra	127	Mexico	$$	4
Corona Light	128	Mexico	$	4
Hamm's	163	USA	$	4
Icehouse	176	USA	$	4
Keystone Light	178	USA	$	4
Michelob Light	200	USA	$	4
Michelob Ultra	202	USA	$	4
Miller Chill	204	USA	$	4
Miller Lite	207	USA	$	4
Natural Ice	212	USA	$	4
Yuengling Light Beer	307	USA	$	4
Budweiser Select 55	113	USA	$	3
Tsingtao	294	China	$	3
Clausthaler N/A	122	Germany	$$	NR

Family: Smoke beer

	Page	Country	Price	Rating
Alaskan Smoked Porter	61	USA	$$$	9
Schlenkerla Rauchbier Märzen	267	Germany	$$$$	7
Schlenkerla Helles	266	Germany	$$$$	6

Family: Sour beer

	Page	Country	Price	Rating
Duchesse de Bourgogne	141	Belgium	$$$$	9
Rodenbach Grand Cru	249	Belgium	$$$$	9
Lindemans Cassis	190	Belgium	$$$$	7
Rodenbach	248	Belgium	$$$$	7
Lindemans Framboise	191	Belgium	$$$$	6
Lindemans Kriek	192	Belgium	$$$$	4

Family: Strong beer

	Page	Country	Price	Rating
Ayinger Celebrator	75	Germany	$$$$	9
Great Divide Yeti	158	USA	$$$$	9
North Coast Old Rasputin	219	USA	$$$	9
Russian River Pliny the Elder	254	USA	$$$$	9
Anchor Old Foghorn	69	USA	$$$	8
Arrogant Bastard Ale	71	USA	$$$$	8
Fuller's 1845	153	England	$$$$	8
Paulaner Salvator	234	Germany	$$$	8
Rogue Old Crustacean	251	USA	$$$$$	8
Victory Storm King	297	USA	$$$	8
Dogfish Head 90 Minute IPA	137	USA	$$$$	7
Flying Dog Gonzo Porter	147	USA	$$$	7
North Coast Old Stock Ale	220	USA	$$$$	7
Sierra Nevada Torpedo	275	USA	$$	7
Spaten Optimator	281	Germany	$$	7
Boss Black Porter	95	Poland	$$$	6
Skull Splitter	277	Scotland	$$$$	6
Baltika #6	77	Russia	$$	5
Dogfish Head World Wide Stout	138	USA	$$$$$	3

Family: Wheat beer

	Page	Country	Price	Rating
Aventinus Weizenbock	73	Germany	$$$$	9
Paulaner Hefe-Weizen	231	Germany	$$$	9
Franziskaner Hefe-Weisse	150	Germany	$$	8
Hacker-Pschorr Weisse	162	Germany	$$$	8
Hoegaarden	173	Belgium	$$$	8
Sierra Nevada Kellerweis	272	USA	$$	8
Weihenstephaner Hefe	299	Germany	$$$	8
Boulevard Unfiltered Wheat Beer	100	USA	$$	7
Schneider Weisse	268	Germany	$$$$	7
Blue Moon Belgian White	91	USA	$$	6
Pyramid Haywire	239	USA	$$	6
Erdinger Hefe-Weizen	145	Germany	$$$	5
Henry Weinhard's Hefeweizen	171	USA	$$	5
Widmer Hefeweizen	304	USA	$$	5
Samuel Adams Cherry Wheat	258	USA	$$	3

Alaskan Amber

rating
8

Pale Ale

Country USA (AK) **Style** Alt **ABV** 5.3%
Producer Alaskan Brewing Company **Price** $$
Packaging 12oz/355ml bottle
Characteristics Malty, refreshing

Founded in 1986, Alaskan is the largest brewery in Alaska and is one of the larger American craft breweries, despite distributing only as far east as the Rockies. That success rests largely on their amber, a malt alt-style beer.

Flavors and aromas Mild hops are dominated by the strikingly malty nose, which has some fruity Munich malt character and a hint of cinnamon adding complexity. The palate features dark caramel notes and toasted malt that is very well complemented by light, crisp bitterness. A nice mouthfeel completes the package. Our team was very happy with this beer.

Design The clean lines of this eye-catchingly red label are nice partners for the crisp malt flavors of the beer.

Alaskan Smoked Porter

Smoke Beer

Country USA (AK) **ABV** 6.5%
Producer Alaskan Brewing Company **Price** $$$
Packaging 12oz/355ml, 22oz/650ml bottle
Characteristics Bitter, malty, roasty, unusual

We will have to get in line to praise Alaskan Smoked Porter—according to the brewery, it's the most decorated beer in Great American Beer Festival history, with 18 medals. Many beer fans might be hard put to name another smoke beer, but that doesn't change the fact that we found it delicious.

Flavors and aromas Alaskan's Smoked Porter has a bit of a reputation for being over the top with smoke character, but our tasters didn't find that to be the case at all. A rich, roasty nose has smoke notes that are more subtle than overt, and the palate is roasty, slightly ashy, with full body, cola notes, and some acidity from the dark roasts. Ample malt eases the tension of the smoke and roast flavors, and the end result is delightfully complete.

Design There's a jumble of fonts here that's somewhat amateurish, but the imagery and use of color suits the beer well.

AleSmith Anvil ESB

Pale Ale

Country USA (CA) **Style** English Pale Ale **ABV** 5.5%
Producer AleSmith Brewing Company **Price** $$$$
Packaging 22oz/650ml bottle
Characteristics Bitter, hoppy, refreshing, unusual

San Diego's AleSmith prides itself in hiring exclusively from the ranks of homebrewers, and founder Peter Zien is a grandmaster-level homebrew competition judge. This may explain, in part, why AleSmith's beers have little text on the bottles—competition beers are always submitted in unlabeled bottles.

Flavors and aromas This beer polarized our tasters. The nose has complex citrusy aromas that reminded one taster of Campari. The palate, with traditionally English carbonation, balances malt with potent bitter elements that suggest both hops and the massive mineral content of the brewing water. You will likely find this adorable or intolerable; we think it's worth a shot.

Design More text—that's an extra two letters—bring the volume down on the Anvil package from the slightly shouty AleSmith IPA bottle and the extremely shouty AleSmith X bottle.

AleSmith IPA

rating 8

India Pale Ale

Country USA (CA) **ABV** 7.8%
Producer AleSmith Brewing Company **Price** $$$$
Packaging 22oz/650ml bottle
Characteristics Bitter, hoppy, strong, yeasty

AleSmith is a small but significant player in the current bigger-and-badder craft beer trend. Their Belgian- and English-styled beers are almost uniformly high in alcohol and flavor, and they're among the most popular breweries at the various online ratings websites.

Flavors and aromas This potent beer poured with a huge head, which along with some fruity esters, reminded our tasters of some fine Belgian-style ales. This is definitely an IPA, though, with complex pine, citrus, and floral hop character, and a sprightly palate that is crisply bitter. The dry finish has elegant lemon peel and a hint of coriander.

Design Big and bold is the bottle of AleSmith IPA. Simple, clean, direct, and effective. Like the A-Team.

AleSmith X

Pale Ale

Country USA (CA) **Style** American Pale Ale **ABV** 5.5%
Producer AleSmith Brewing Company **Price** $$$
Packaging 22oz/650ml bottle
Characteristics Bitter, hoppy, unusual, yeasty

About half of Alesmith's beers have straightforward names, like Wee Heavy and IPA, but the other half have interesting, enigmatic names, like X, Horny Devil, and My Bloody Valentine.

Flavors and aromas This is a challenging beer that feels somewhat thin and unbalanced, but there are intriguing flavors nonetheless. Lemon and citrus hops are focused and precise in the nose, perhaps a bit aggressive. There's also a hint of soap, and as this warms in the glass, the soap/lemon pairing gets more intense. The palate is very bright and lemony, showing a bit of estery fruit. Hop bitterness isn't terribly high in absolute terms, but there's not much malt character here, and the bitterness comes off as herbal or medicinal.

Design Why is there a large X on the bottle of AleSmith's pale ale? Maybe because X marks the spot where your bottle is. Peace of mind is a wonderful thing.

Allagash Dubbel

Belgian Ale

Country USA (ME) **Style** Dark Belgian Ale **ABV** 7.0%
Producer Allagash Brewing Company **Price** $$$$
Packaging 12oz/355ml, 25.4oz/750ml bottle
Characteristics Strong, yeasty

20 years ago, Belgian-style beers in North America were the exclusive provenance of Belgian importers. Nowadays, Allagash Brewing Company, in Portland, Maine, is certainly one of the major parties responsible for the wide availability of American-produced Belgian-style beers.

Flavors and aromas Pepper, allspice, and banana notes bring the nose into bright harmony, and the palate has faint roast grain notes, light caramels, and an interplay of alcohol, sweet malt, and spices that suggests dark rum and wood. The finish is clean with a slight alcoholic bitterness; there's enough alcohol here to produce a pronounced warming effect, and a nice mix of bright and darker flavors.

Design The label depicts a scene of a square forest, which probably ties into the background's white-to-red fade in some way that is too clever and subtle for us to fathom.

Allagash Tripel

Belgian Ale

Country USA (ME) **Style** Pale Belgian Ale **ABV** 9.0%
Producer Allagash Brewing Company **Price** $$$$
Packaging 12oz/355ml, 25.4oz/750ml bottle
Characteristics Malty, strong, unusual, yeasty

In the beer world, there's plenty of railing against the use of adjuncts (mostly corn, rice, and sugar) to lighten the body of a beer, but the tripel style is a fairly persuasive counterargument. Sugar is used to bring alcohol into balance with intense yeast flavors without leaving the body heavy and sweet.

Flavors and aromas Traditionally bright, fruity esters make up the prominent part of the nose, but there's also a hint of darker sugars. The palate is, for the most part, a conventional tripel, with esters, yeasty spices, and light residual sweetness, but there's also a pleasant, mild hop bitterness that is unusual for the style. The overall impression is of a deft, charming beer.

Design It's nice that the brown glass of this bottle-conditioned beer is clear enough to make it easy to keep an eye on yeast sediment as you pour.

Amstel Light

Pale Lager

Country Netherlands **Style** Light Beer **ABV** 3.5%
Producer Amstel Brewery **Group** Heineken **Price** $$
Packaging 12oz/355ml bottle
Characteristics Refreshing

Amsterdam's Amstel makes several pale lagers, but only Amstel Light is currently distributed in the United States. It's absolutely iconic, especially at hotel bars and velvet-rope nightclubs, where it's particularly popular amongst skinny-and-wanting-to-stay-that-way women. It's the low-calorie alternative to the Cosmo—seemingly more sophisticated than Corona or Bud Light.

Flavors and aromas A creamy, softly malty nose and a bare touch of hop character lead into a light, thin palate. There's not a lot here, but there is a modicum of bitterness, which is a pleasant surprise. One taster called this an ideal pairing for chicken strips and a football game, while another thought it lacked "beerness."

Design The round beer label is an intriguing variation on the tried-and-true oval, and conveys its information in anefficient manner, although it feels a bit cheap. But, then, so do the club girls.

Anchor Liberty Ale

rating
8

Pale Ale

Country USA (CA) **Style** American Pale Ale **ABV** 6.0%
Producer Anchor Brewing Company **Price** $$
Packaging 12oz/355ml, 22oz/650ml bottle
Characteristics Bitter, hoppy

Anchor Liberty Ale is the easiest beer in the Anchor stable to overlook, without the ubiquity of Anchor Steam, the heft of Old Foghorn, or the annual hype of Anchor Christmas Ale. But Liberty might just be the most balanced of the lot. It's been a regular production since the mid-1970s.

Flavors and aromas Liberty Ale is a bright, refreshing pale ale that straddles the line between an American-styled pale ale and an English IPA. A delightful crispness and bright carbonation are paired with flavor hops and yeast that avoid typical West Coast resin-pine character. Hop bitterness is light at first and builds over several steps to an assertive finish. This is a well-crafted ale that seems a touch nostalgic, rather like the label.

Design Anchor's labels are so retro that they're not even retro; they're more Colonial fetishist. But not in a bad way. The round label pairs well with the distinct, soft-shouldered bottle.

Anchor Old Foghorn

Strong Beer

Country USA (CA) **Style** Barleywine **ABV** 8-10%
Producer Anchor Brewing Company **Price** $$$
Packaging 12oz/355ml bottle
Characteristics Bitter, hoppy, malty, strong

Anchor's take on the English barleywine style was one of the originals in the US—first produced in 1976, it has served as the template for a distinctly American version of the style. These beers have a long shelf life; well-stored bottles can last for over a decade.

Flavors and aromas A big, thick nose of rich caramel, citrusy hops, and alcoholic sweetness introduces a straightforwardly classic American-style barleywine. An expansive fruity palate has raisiny dark notes, thick texture, loads of sweet caramel, and full citrusy hop character. There's just enough bitterness to begin to cut through the sweetness. Still, we could stand for a little more bitterness or a little less sweetness, but if you like barleywines, this is a dead-on example of the style.

Design As with all Anchor beers, the label here is classy and distinctive. But we miss the old 7oz bottles, which were positively adorable.

Anchor Steam

Pale Ale

Country USA (CA) **Style** American Pale Ale **ABV** 4.9%
Producer Anchor Brewing Company **Price** $$
Packaging 12oz/355ml, 22oz/650ml bottle
Characteristics Bitter, hoppy, malty, refreshing

There's a lot of debate about whether Anchor Steam is a true example of the historical San Francisco Steam Beer style, but there's little question that this is a classic American craft beer. The brewery dates its history to 1896, but the current incarnation goes back to 1965, when Fritz Maytag (of the appliance family) purchased the brewery and began building an icon of the modern craft beer movement.

Flavors and aromas Anchor Steam is not, technically, a pale ale—it's fermented at ale temperatures with a lager yeast—but it has much more in common with, say, Sierra Nevada Pale Ale than with Budweiser. There's some fruity yeast character, along with clean toasty malt and balanced, if slightly harsh, bitterness. Hops have a pleasantly woody character and help the beer stand out.

Design Sure, this logo, with its mottled background, is a touch busy. But it's also distinctive.

Arrogant Bastard Ale

Strong Beer

Country USA (CA) **Style** Strong Ale **ABV** 7.2%
Producer Stone Brewing Company **Price** $$$$
Packaging 22oz/650ml bottle
Characteristics Bitter, hoppy, malty, strong

Stone Brewing's most famous—
and brash—beer has perhaps the
most comprehensive and
audacious branding campaign in
the beer world. A trip through the
beer's website, or a quick reading
of the text on the bottle,
encourages drinkers to move on to
lighter, easier beers—the idea
being to dare you into drinking
this high-alcohol blockbuster.

Flavors and aromas Cinnamon-
spice and caramel malt drive the
big, attractive nose with mild
hops. The palate is big, opening
with a shock of sweetness that
quickly fades to an onslaught of
bitterness and spice. Citrusy hop
flavors mingle with mild esters in
the finish, but spice, malt, and
bitterness maintain high intensity.
Alcohol is clearly high here but
doesn't really register.

Design The lengthy screed printed
on this bottle is a fine example of
truth in advertising, which it turns
out isn't always pretty.

Asahi Super Dry

Pale Lager

Country Japan **Style** Japanese Lager **ABV** 4.9%
Producer Asahi Breweries **Price** $$
Packaging 12oz/355ml, 21.4oz/633 bottle; 12oz/355ml,
16.9oz/500ml, 33.8oz/1L can **Characteristics** Bland

Dry beer (i.e. fully fermented, leaving no residual sugar) is not a Japanese invention; in Germany, fully fermented lagers have been produced and marketed as safer for diabetics. But Asahi's Super Dry puts a marketable face on the style, and it's the brewery's flagship brand to this day.

Flavors and aromas Asahi struck our tasters as watery and devoid of flavor. There's little hop or malt character, leading one taster to think that this was a low-calorie light beer. While adding a lot of hops would quickly upset the balance, a little would go a long way to making this more palatable.

Design There are some very strange packages for this beer in its native Japan. But here, in the bottle, we get a nearly unreadable label. And we must admit to being fans of the mega-can enclosure of Asahi—and not just because it's an excuse to order two and a half beers at once.

Aventinus Weizenbock

Wheat Beer

Country Germany **Style** Weizenbock **ABV** 8.2%
Producer Schneider **Price** $$$$
Packaging 16.9oz/500ml bottle
Characteristics Malty, strong, unusual, yeasty

Weizenbock is wheat beer brewed to the strength and intensity of bock beer. And if this 8% alcohol version isn't strong enough for you, there's also an eisbock version, where the beer is frozen and chunks of ice removed, concentrating it further.

Flavors and aromas You'd be forgiven for guessing that this moderately dark beer was Belgian, given the ample esters and rich dark sugar/molasses notes. But banana and clove are your cue that this delicious beer is from the German side of the border. This is probably a good test of whether you appreciate banana esters, which carry through from start to finish. Our tasters do, and they loved this beer.

Design The text is hard to read, but you'll have no trouble spotting the shiny purple label from across the supermarket.

Avery IPA

India Pale Ale

Country USA (CO) **ABV** 6.3%
Producer Avery Brewing Company **Price** $$
Packaging 12oz/355ml bottle
Characteristics Bitter, hoppy, yeasty

One of the most adventurous breweries in a state full of left-of-center beer concerns is Boulder, Colorado's Avery, which produces a dizzying array of beers. While there are many craft brewers today working in Belgian styles, and a good few producing English-inspired beers, Avery does both.

Flavors and aromas Avery's IPA is produced with typical American hop varieties and malts, but we were struck by a pronounced estery, fruity character that—along with intense and full-bodied bitterness—made us imagine this as a Belgian-styled IPA. That seems right in accord with the brewery's goal of "producing eccentric ales and lagers that defy styles or categories."

Design This label, which depicts the trade route from England to India, is one of our absolute favorites. The graphic doesn't compromise or muddy up the rest of the visual elements, and the end result is strikingly attractive.

Ayinger Celebrator

Strong Beer

Country Germany **Style** Doppelbock **ABV** 6.7%
Producer Brauerei Aying **Price** $$$$
Packaging 11.2oz/330ml bottle
Characteristics Malty, roasty, strong, unusual

The focus of both German and English brewers on the importance of malt character as a dominant element of flavor is highlighted by a partnership that has existed for some years between Ayinger and England's Samuel Smith, which brewed a line of beers under the brand Ayingerbräu.

Flavors and aromas Of the three German doppelbock beers our tasters tried, this was the best liked. The aroma shows rich, dark fruit notes, dark caramels, some alcohol, and roasted grain notes—an unusual flavor in a style that gets its dark color from long boils. This beer fills your mouth with massive malt flavors, forming a spectrum from light sugars and caramels to rich roast notes, along with intense dark sugar and spice combinations that hint at rum with the warming alcohol.

Design Maybe it's too literal, but we think the depiction of two goats embracing a giant glass of beer is pretty sweet.

Ayinger Oktoberfest

rating 9

Amber Lager

Country Germany **Style** Oktoberfest **ABV** 5.6%
Producer Brauerei Aying **Price** $$$
Packaging 16.9oz/500ml bottle
Characteristics Malty

Official Oktoberfest celebrations are limited exclusively to the seven Munich breweries, so this Fest-style brew won't be seen there—the town of Aying sits some 15 miles outside Munich city limits. Foreigners.

Flavors and aromas Tasters delighted at the abundant and complex malt character of this Oktoberfest beer. Ample fruity Munich malt does most of the driving, giving a fresh, almost sweet character that one identified as "juicy." There's soft bitterness to balance here, and the overall impression is of a deeply drinkable, full and round beer with a clean character. Don't drink this too cold, though, or you'll miss the excitement.

Design A nice color palate is somewhat lost in a blocky, rigid design that seems more cluttered than should be possible with its simple lines.

Baltika #6

rating
5

Strong Beer

Country Russia **Style** Baltic Porter **ABV** 7.0%
Producer Baltika Brewery **Group** Carlsberg **Price** $$
Packaging 16.9oz/500ml bottle
Characteristics Malty, strong

There are 10 numbered beers produced by St. Petersburg's Baltika brewery, the second-largest brewer in Europe, behind only Heineken. In North America, this porter is distributed more widely than any of the others, making it perhaps the best known of all Russian beers.

Flavors and aromas This strong, dark-colored beer defied expectations and split opinions. There's little dark grain flavor here; we found no coffee or roast flavors, as you might expect from a porter. There are some dark spices, like cola, and modest but bubbly carbonation. There's also a lot of sugar. In some ways, this seems more like root beer than a black beer. If you have a sweet tooth and a hard time with bitterness, this may be for you.

Design An impressively weird bottle wears a cool embossed logo right where your eyes want the label to be. It's so awkward it's suave.

Bass Ale

Pale Ale

Country England **Style** English Pale Ale **ABV** 5.0%
Producer Bass Brewery **Group** InBev **Price** $$
Packaging 12oz/355ml, 16oz/473ml bottle; 16.9oz/500ml can
Characteristics Malty

Bass forms an important part of the history of British brewing as one of the first breweries from Burton upon Trent. It's also the first English beer that many a North American youth encounters. These days the Bass brand is owned by InBev, and the brewing facilities have passed into the hands of Coors' UK operations.

Flavors and aromas Our samples of Bass were a little skunky, which is odd given the brown glass packaging. Woody, spicy hops are mild. Light carbonation supports a healthy amount of smooth, mild English malt, leading into modest bitterness in the finish. Our tasters weren't crazy about Bass, but we might pin some of that on the lack of a freshness date.

Design Okay, we didn't love the beer, but the logo is pure class—and a bit of history: the Bass triangle is the oldest registered trademark in Britain. Here's to aging gracefully.

Bear Republic Racer 5 IPA

India Pale Ale

Country USA (CA) **ABV** 7.0%
Producer Bear Republic Brewing Company **Price** $$$$
Packaging 12oz/355ml, 22oz/650ml bottle
Characteristics Bitter, hoppy

The California Republic, or "Bear Flag Republic," was an attempt at secession by the people of Sonoma in the mid-19th century. There's something about northern California that has inspired many attempts to form a separate state. As long as we can still import their beer, we don't mind.

Flavors and aromas The dominant note in the nose is pine, with some sweetness. There's good mouthfeel, with nice carbonation, moderate flavor hops, and pronounced but still soft bitterness. The Racer 5 is lean and restrained for an IPA, but it doesn't lack for character. It's good for drinkers who like solid bitterness but are put off by the over-the-top West Coast hop character of many IPAs.

Design The elements here—the background flag checkerboard, the "5" logo, the '60s font—all work reasonably well as parts, and come together into a nice whole. Just like the beer.

Bear Republic Red Rocket Ale

Pale Ale

Country USA (CA) **Style** American Amber Ale **ABV** 6.8%
Producer Bear Republic Brewing Company **Price** $$$$
Packaging 12oz/355ml, 22oz/650ml bottle
Characteristics Bitter, hoppy

According to Bear Republic Brewery, Red Rocket is a "bastardized Scottish-style red ale." We're not terribly sure what they mean by that. We've dubbed it an American amber ale, but our tasters liked the big flavor and ample hops, so we won't quibble.

Flavors and aromas We wouldn't dream of calling Bear Republic's offerings "balanced," but that didn't stop our tasters from loving Red Rocket Ale. With a big hop profile that is more like an IPA than a lighter pale ale, this beer is really driven by bitterness, with a bit of malt hiding within. Plenty of hop flavor and some dark grain notes fill out the package, but we can't recommend this fine ale unless you're ready for pronounced bitterness from start to finish.

Design We like this bottle, with its whimsical children's-illustrator-meets-train-graffiti style. But which is faster—Red Rocket, Racer 5, or the Hop Rod?

Bear Republic XP Pale Ale

Pale Ale

Country USA (CA) **Style** American Pale Ale **ABV** 5.4%
Producer Bear Republic Brewing Company **Price** $$$$
Packaging 22oz/650ml bottle
Characteristics Hoppy, refreshing

"Exceptional Pale" is what the XP stands for, and it certainly stands out in the Bear Republic lineup of powerful, hoppy ales. A relative lightweight at 5.4% ABV, this might be the only Bear Republic beer that you want to drink more than one of.

Flavors and aromas A perfume of fruit blossoms, grapefruit, and honey manages to be airy, light, and intense at the same time. The palate has blossomy hop flavors, mild smooth malt, and balanced bitterness in a light-bodied package. This is a relaxed pale ale in a similar style to Widmer's Drifter, ideal for lazy spring and summer afternoons. The XP is a significant departure from Bear Republic's other offerings; it seems as effortless as the others are powerful.

Design The biggest, loudest Bear Republic label goes on the softest, most delicate beer? This makes no sense.

Beck's

Pale Lager

Country Germany **Style** Continental Lager **ABV** 5.0%
Producer Beck's Brewery **Group** InBev **Price** $$
Packaging 12oz/355ml, 24oz/710ml bottle
Characteristics Bitter, hoppy, refreshing

Beck's, which hails from Bremen in northern Germany, is the biggest-selling German export around the world. You'll see this beer everywhere, from thumping nightclubs to corporate hotel bars to the Lufthansa Senator lounges. Really, Lufthansa? Must Germany's flag carrier choose such a mediocre representative of one of its country's proudest products?

Flavors and aromas The combination of medium skunkiness (verified in bottle after bottle, from diverse storage conditions) and light lemony/floral hops make European pale lagers like Beck's fairly recognizable. We liked the soft bitterness and bright carbonation, and sweetness is minimal, which helps elevate Beck's over Heineken in our minds.

Design Beck's plays it safe with a generic oval label that prominently features the brand against that trademark green glass, which exposes the beer to sunlight and easy skunking.

Belhaven Scottish Ale

Pale Ale

Country Scotland **Style** Scottish Ale **ABV** 5.2% **Price** $$$$
Producer Belhaven Brewery Company **Group** Greene King
Packaging 12oz, 16.9oz bottle; 14.9oz/440ml nitro can
Characteristics Malty

Creamy Scottish ales, like English bitters, come in three strengths (plus a fourth, stronger style, called Scotch Ale), but only the strongest, known as "Export," are sturdy enough for long travel. To sample Belhaven's lower-strength "Light" or medium-strength "Heavy," you'll have to travel to the source.

Flavors and aromas A thick, dense head shows off the nitro can to good effect; as in a can of Guinness, a widget injects liquid nitrogen to simulate the beer's velvety draft texture. The nose has intense creamy English malt aroma, light butterscotch, and a hint of deeper fruitiness. The body has the expected low carbonation and a malty, palate-coating feel. Strong malt character is rich without being sweet, with nice complexity and depth. Hop character is low and bitterness is light. This is a fine Scottish ale.

Design The dreaded Oval Beer Logo strikes again, and this time it's on nitro.

Big Daddy IPA

India Pale Ale

rating
7

Country USA (CA) **ABV** 6.5%
Producer Speakeasy Ales and Lagers **Price** $$$
Packaging 12oz/355ml, 22oz/650ml bottle
Characteristics Bitter, hoppy

San Francisco's Speakeasy has a cool, Prohibition- and organized-crime-themed style—their mailing list members are collectively known as "The Mob," and the brewery's website refers to the staff as "The Family"—but their beers are mostly modern and West Coast in style. Big Daddy's taps can be found around the Western US, and bottled beers have been available since 2000.

Flavors and aromas Big Daddy IPA is a dry-hopped beer with a big floral-citrus nose. It's bitter, but not overwhelmingly so; the full-bodied malt balances the bitterness to a point where you may find that this comes together more like an amber ale than an IPA. We'd be happy to run into this tap at the local watering hole.

Design This is all a little bit like the world of the Tim Burton Batman films. We like the eyes on the bottleneck, but the fedora- and trenchcoat-wearing guy looks like a 6th grade doodle.

Big Sky IPA

India Pale Ale

Country USA (MT) **ABV** 6.2%
Producer Big Sky Brewing Company **Price** $$
Packaging 12oz/355ml bottle
Characteristics Bitter, hoppy

Big Sky's lineup of generally English-styled beers was apparently chosen early on as a way to avoid direct competition with Montana's other Missoula-based brewery, the German-styled Bayern Brewery. That kind of cooperation seems to be the norm among microbreweries.

Flavors and aromas An intense citrus hop character jumps from the glass here, with focused grapefruit and orange tea aromas. Big bitterness is tempered only slightly by light malt presence with big flavor hops. Balanced? Not remotely, but if you've got a taste for big hops, this IPA has a unique and impressive flavor profile.

Design You know what we like about the stag on this bottle? He's totally not drooling. At all.

Big Sky Moose Drool

Brown Ale

Country USA (MT) **ABV** 5.3%
Producer Big Sky Brewing Company **Price** $$
Packaging 12oz/355ml bottle; 12oz/355ml can
Characteristics Roasty

According to Big Sky, the name "Moose Drool" was actually inspired by the illustration that appears on the label. Apparently all of the early brews were named in the same way, starting with a painted illustration of local wildlife.

Flavors and aromas Moose Drool seems a bit self-contradictory. There are pronounced dark notes here—in particular, loads of dark roast/coffee flavors, but the light malt and low alcohol just don't manage to stand up to them, and the end result was described—repeatedly, and over multiple tastings—as "watery." There's also a hint of sourness in the finish, likely from the roast grains. In order to make this low-alcohol style work, the malt backbone has to be in place, and Moose Drool doesn't quite have it.

Design An attractive label, until you realize that the moose is, uh, drooling. To a degree that puts Tom Hanks' costar in Turner and Hooch to shame.

Bison Chocolate Stout

Dark Ale

Country USA (CA) **Style** Stout **ABV** 6.1%
Producer Bison Brewing Company **Price** $$$
Packaging 12oz/355ml, 22oz/650ml bottle
Characteristics Bitter, malty, roasty

Bison started brewing in 1989 in
Berkeley, as an early entrant into
the explosion of brewpubs across
the US. In 2003, rising rent forced
them out of the pub business, but
they've continued as a contract
brew (their beers are produced at
Mendocino Brewing's facilities).

Flavors and aromas A sweet
coffee and dark roast nose is big,
warm, and rich. Dark, complex
sweetness and roast character
gives this a nice full mouthfeel,
creamy and palate-coating. There
are mild floral undertones and
pleasant coffee or chocolate
bitterness, along with some fruity
acidity. The use of cocoa is subtle
and well-integrated. Some tasters
felt that the roast character was
too sharp, while others thought
the malt balanced it nicely.

Design We don't think there's any
comparison between this bison
and the goofy label animals of the
wine world. He just has a gravitas
that can't be matched by $7
Shiraz.

Bison IPA

India Pale Ale

Country USA (CA) **ABV** 6.8%
Producer Bison Brewing Company **Price** $$$
Packaging 12oz/355ml, 22oz/650ml bottle
Characteristics Bitter, hoppy

We've tasted fairly mainstream beers from Bison Brewing, but their all-organic lineup of beers includes the eclectic Honey Basil Ale and popular winter seasonal Gingerbread Ale.

Flavors and aromas We liked Bison's Organic IPA for its open, fresh aromas of citrusy hops and the fine balance struck between mellow bitterness and sweet grain flavors, which tilts in favor of the hops without being overwhelmed by them. Our tasters called this beer "very drinkable," and what else can you ask for, really?

Design Clean lines, readable fonts, and nice colors make this bottle design a winner. Plus there's an animal of some sort.

Bitburger Pilsner

rating 8

Pale Lager

Country Germany **Style** Pilsner **ABV** 4.8% **Price** $$
Producer Bitburger Brewery
Packaging 11.2oz/330ml, 16.9oz/500ml, 12oz/355ml bottle,
16.9oz/500ml PET bottle, 11.2oz/330ml, 16.9oz/500ml can
Characteristics Bitter, refreshing

Bitburger is nearing its second full century of operations, having opened in 1817. In Germany, several unique variations on their pale lager are sold, including a pomegranate-flavored lager and a rum-and-coke flavored lager.

Flavors and aromas A lightly malty beer with a low hop aroma, our bottles of Bitburger were slightly—but not badly—lightstruck. This beer is firmly German, with moderate but focused bitterness as the center of attention. There's bright carbonation, which helps frame the bitterness and provides a crisp finish with some lingering hops. Light bodied and very clean.

Design In the grand German tradition, Bitburger's label is essentially all text. For a label that barely communicates more than the name of the beer, this has way too many fonts.

Blind Pig IPA

India Pale Ale

Country USA (CA) **ABV** 6.0%
Producer Blind Pig Brewing Company **Group** Russian River
Price $$$$ **Packaging** 16.9oz/500ml bottle
Characteristics Bitter, hoppy

Russian River Brewing was the product of sparkling wine maker Korbel's foray into craft beer. They sold the operation shortly afterwards to brewmaster Vinny Cilurzo, who seems to be doing just fine with it.

Flavors and aromas This is an intensely hoppy and bitter beer, but it may find some favor with drinkers who normally don't like high bitterness. There's a huge explosion of hops in the nose—resinous and citrusy—and it smells sweet and full-bodied. But there's nothing cloying or syrupy about this beer in the mouth, where hop flavor and bitterness compete for attention. The latter dominates in the finish, but it doesn't linger, which is why we think it might be worth stepping outside your comfort zone to try.

Design The namesake pig on the label is not your standard cute-and-fuzzy mascot. He's a dignified pig who happens to be vision impaired. We respect that.

Blue Moon Belgian White

Wheat Beer

Country USA (CO) **Style** Witbier **ABV** 5.4%
Producer Blue Moon Brewing Company **Group** Molson Coors
Price $$ **Packaging** 12oz/355ml, 22oz/650ml bottle
Characteristics Malty, unusual, yeasty

Blue Moon is marketed as a craft beer, and given the unusual flavor profile, we can't really fault them for it. But the origin of the beer— Golden, Colorado—is a tipoff to the fact that Blue Moon is a Coors brand.

Flavors and aromas It's heartening that American drinkers have taken to Blue Moon, since it decidedly does not taste like typical American beer offerings. A moderately soapy coriander nose with slight sour notes wafts from the glass, and the palate is floral, gently malty, with light bitterness. But the flavor fades quickly, and this lacks the conviction of a true Belgian witbier like Hoegaarden, relying too much on coriander to carry it.

Design This is a nice design that reminds us—without condescension or ridicule—of a children's book. We'd buy it for a toddler nephew or niece if it weren't full of alcohol.

Boddington's Cream Ale

Pale Ale

Country England **Style** English Pale Ale **ABV** 4.7%
Producer InBev **Price** $$
Packaging 16oz/473ml can
Characteristics Malty

Boddington's is widely available in the US and Canada, but it's not quite the same product as it is in England, where alcohol character is lower and the product is known as "Draught Bitter."

Flavors and aromas An English ale nose of sweet malt with an apple-cider character to it and a thick head lead to a surprisingly flat—both for carbonation, which is less surprising, and for flavor—palate that is light, with little of the rich and complex malts that English ales promise. There's a slight bitterness, but it comes off more as medicinal than hoppy. A sickly solvent-fruit character emerges at the end as this warms.

Design The lettering on this can is so impeccably British that the red "Imported From Britain" tag seems terribly redundant.

Bohemia

Pale Lager

Country Mexico **Style** North American Lager **ABV** 5.3%
Producer Bohemia **Group** Cuauhtémoc Moctezuma **Price** $$
Packaging 12oz/355ml bottle
Characteristics Malty, refreshing

Bohemia is produced by the same Mexican group that produces Dos Equis, Sol, and Tecate, which today is owned by Heineken. The name is an homage to the Czech region that pilsner comes from.

Flavors and aromas Some of our tasters felt this was a balanced, rich version of a pale lager, while others found it heavy and lacking the crispness of the best lagers. Either way, it seems to be set more in the mold of a Bavarian Helles lager than its Czech namesake. At any rate, this is worth trying if you'd like a lager with more body than your standard domestic.

Design Arguably the most stylish of Mexican beer packages, with an old-school look that is clean and pleasant. The classy brown bottle looks like it should be resting in the foreground of a Rockwell scene of domestic tranquility. Where's our pipe?

Boont Amber

Pale Ale

Country USA (CA) **Style** American Amber Ale **ABV** 5.8%
Producer Anderson Valley Brewing Company **Price** $$$
Packaging 12oz/355ml bottle
Characteristics Malty

About a decade ago, Boont Amber was the go-to tap at many bars, both upscale and divey, in San Francisco. All too often, growing brands and evolving tastes mean that the beers of our youth don't hold up quite as we remember them. We're pleased to see that's not the case here. This beer is ubiquitous in the northern half of California; from Eureka to San Jose, it's never hard to find a bar serving Boont Amber.

Flavors and aromas The star of Anderson Valley's lineup is an appealingly malty take on on American Pale ale, which makes it easy to recommend to drinkers looking for flavor intensity without excess bitterness. There's a fruitiness that reminds us of Oktoberfest beers, but the palate is dry and balanced, with just enough bitterness to make it crisp.

Design AV's labels are detailed without being cluttered. We could live without the "Gold Medal Winner" alert, though.

Boss Black Porter

rating
6

Strong Beer

Country Poland **Style** Baltic Porter **ABV** 9.4%
Producer Browar Witnica **Price** $$$
Packaging 11.2oz/330ml, 16.9oz/500ml, 67.6/2L bottle
Characteristics Malty, strong, yeasty

The strong Baltic porter style—and this is one of the strongest—recalls a time when England exported beer, often strong beer, all over the world. This style is noteworthy in part for being fermented with lager yeasts.

Flavors and aromas If you're bothered by the smell of butterscotch, stop here—Black Boss is not for you. There are heaping helpings of diacetyl (the source of that smell in beer) in the nose of this beer. But in the mouth this is much more interesting, with a full, sweet, and intensely nutty palate. Roast character and bitterness are both low, and some drinkers may find this too sweet, but we found it to be pleasant, if not exactly a beer for a long afternoon of drinking.

Design An intimidating, tough label, with big, bold fonts, for a sweet, nutty beer. It's a little like Chuck Norris-branded wine coolers.

Boulder Hazed and Infused

Pale Ale

Country USA (CO) **Style** American Pale Ale **ABV** 4.9%
Producer Boulder Beer Company **Price** $$
Packaging 12oz/355ml bottle
Characteristics Hoppy

An experimental beer launched in 2001, Hazed and Infused demonstrates that hop character and bitterness are distinctly different. Hops are soaked in the beer post-fermentation, adding chemically delicate flavor and aroma compounds—a process that many breweries use, but few with such force as this.

Flavors and aromas Big resinous piney hop character, with wild floral notes, dominates the nose. Hops is the primary flavor in the mouth, with flavor hops overwhelming the muted malt and mild bitterness. This left our tasters wanting a little more, either in the form of crisp bitterness, malty body, or both, as the end product is a little lacking in definition. The bitterness lingers a bit, but doesn't ever really ratchet up in intensity.

Design The label here isn't tie-dye, but you'd be forgiven for thinking that it is. It's a high contrast jumble of colors that accentuates the beer's punnish name.

Boulder Planet Porter

Dark Ale

Country USA (CO) **Style** Porter **ABV** 5.5%
Producer Boulder Beer Company **Price** $$
Packaging 12oz/355ml bottle
Characteristics Hoppy, malty, roasty

While there are nearly one hundred breweries in Colorado today, most of them microbreweries. In 1979 there was just one craft brewery: Boulder Beer Company, founded by a pair of professors from the local University of Colorado at Boulder.

Flavors and aromas Like Eel River's porter, this offering gives an impression of strength and density well beyond its actual alcohol level. Big chocolate, butterscotch, and minty aroma hops fairly dance around the nose, and the palate's dark-roast cold coffee flavors are nicely rounded out by slightly sweet chocolate. A dense mouthfeel finishes pleasantly dry in a satisfying conclusion.

Design It's a little surprising that the Tax and Trade Bureau approved a label that might be construed as advocating the combination of alcohol and telescope operation.

Boulevard Pilsner

Pale Lager

Country USA (MO) **Style** North American Lager **ABV** 5.4%
Producer Boulevard Brewing Company **Price** $$
Packaging 12oz/355ml bottle
Characteristics Refreshing

Craft breweries have been slow to move into the world of lagers, which requires more equipment to produce finicky beers that are less forgiving than full-bodied ales. Boulevard's Pilsner is one of their most recent releases, dating to 2009.

Flavors and aromas The basic idea here—a malty, Continental-style lager, with distinct but modest hop character—is sound. And there's good balance in the slightly sweet palate between malt and bitterness, along with nice lift from the carbonation. But tasters disliked the aftertaste of this beer, whose lingering bitterness had a harsh flavor they didn't care for.

Design The fancy, stylized "B" and "P" are like the hybrid of the logos for the Brooklyn and Ranier breweries—both of which we adore. Hard to complain about this one, then.

Boulevard Pale Ale

rating
6

Pale Ale

Country USA (MO) **Style** American Pale Ale **ABV** 4.8%
Producer Boulevard Brewing Company **Price** $$
Packaging 12oz/355ml bottle
Characteristics Hoppy, refreshing

The largest independent brewery in Missouri, Boulevard has focused on supplying the Midwest with beer, rather than expanding its reach. But that doesn't make this a small operation; it's the 8th largest craft brewery, with capacity to move up several spots as sales grow.

Flavors and aromas Lemon and floral hop notes populate a light nose. There's up-front, forward bitterness here, but it is soft and smooth, with crackery malt in a body with appropriate weight. Carbonation is a little low for an American pale ale, which along with woody flavor hops give this a character that reminds us of an English take on Anchor Steam.

Design Noisy colors, but an otherwise simple and clean design gets the thumbs up from us. And anyway, we don't know how you'd make a mascot out of a boulevard.

Boulevard Unfiltered Wheat Beer

Wheat Beer

Country USA (MO) **Style** American Hefeweizen **ABV** 4.4%
Producer Boulevard Brewing Company **Price** $$
Packaging 12oz/355ml bottle
Characteristics Malty, refreshing, yeasty

Is the tide shifting on American wheat beers? Between this and Sierra Nevada's Kellerweis, it seems like high-profile craft brewers are looking to change American attitudes about what wheat beers taste like.

Flavors and aromas Our tasters didn't quite know what to make of this beer, stylistically—it's got elements of American and Bavarian hefeweizen as well as Belgian witbier. There are soft esters—mostly pear—on the nose, along with a floral sweetness. The palate shows grainy wheat character, pepper, and yeast, with a slightly sweet finish. We think this is a nice alternative to traditionally bland American hefeweizen, in a style that isn't exactly what you'll find anywhere else.

Design The symmetry of this label is somewhat distracting, and it's a nice enough design, but it isn't really going to pop out at you on store shelves.

Breckenridge Lucky U IPA

India Pale Ale

Country USA (CO) **ABV** 6.2%
Producer Breckenridge Brewery **Price** $$
Packaging 12oz/355ml bottle
Characteristics Bitter

Breckenridge is one of a startling number of small breweries and brewpubs in Colorado reaching out into the craft beer world with bottled offerings. Originally from the ski town of the same name, they now own three pubs and a brewing facility in Denver.

Flavors and aromas Lucky U IPA perplexed our tasters. Pale malt and a hint of skunkiness (despite brown glass and a bottle direct from the brewery) stood out in the nose, along with earthy hops. A thin, mildly bitter palate finished short, with herbal hops and chalky, mineral flavors. Several tasters guessed that this was an English beer, but none were terribly interested in finding out whether they were right.

Design Each of Breckenridge's labels could easily represent a different brewery. The Lucky U label is kind of loud, but it has a certain charm to it, and the double-B logo is nice but oddly downplayed on these beers.

Breckenridge Vanilla Porter

rating
6

Dark Ale

Country USA (CO) **Style** Porter **ABV** 4.7%
Producer Breckenridge Brewery **Price** $$
Packaging 12oz/355ml bottle
Characteristics Malty, unusual, yeasty

Ask any wine critic, and they'll agree: vanilla is a tough flavor ingredient to use in alcoholic beverages. The high intensity and perceived sweetness tend to jump all over other flavors. A light hand is key.

Flavors and aromas There's some complexity to this beer, but whether it lives up to the "remarkable" moniker is debatable. Diacetyl-butterscotch, chocolate, root beer, and vanilla all come together into a sweet, synthetic scratch-and-sniff aroma. The finish is dry, though, probably assisted by some well-hidden hop bitterness. The overall effect is perplexing enough that it might rise to the level of "remarkable" after all.

Design Old-timey and cute, but a little more of a soda label than a beer label, in our estimation. But an attractive soda label.

Bridgeport ESB

Pale Ale

Country USA (OR) **Style** American ESB **ABV** 6.1%
Producer Bridgeport Brewing Company **Price** $$
Packaging 12oz/355ml bottle
Characteristics Malty, refreshing

In England, "pale ale" and "extra special bitter" denote basically the same style. On this side of the pond, brewers frequently use "ESB" to imply a beer with a more restrained hop character than their standard pale ale.

Flavors and aromas English-styled beers are a challenge for American palates; the flavor and aroma hops are by nature more subtle, and the malt/bitterness balance and low carbonation both tend to come off as flat and lacking in intensity. And this American ESB lived up to that expectation, with light aromatics. Our tasters split on whether the palate was nicely balanced, or too delicate and soft. This might be a crossover choice for drinkers who don't normally like the bitterness of American pale ales.

Design Traditional, simple, and not particularly eye-catching, Bridgeport's labels do benefit from a nice rendition of Portland's famous St. John's bridge.

Bridgeport IPA

India Pale Ale

Country USA (OR) **ABV** 5.5%
Producer Bridgeport Brewing Company **Price** $$
Packaging 12oz/355ml bottle
Characteristics Bitter

Portland's Bridgeport Brewing may have been the first modern craft brewery in Oregon. Founded in 1984 by Willamette Valley wine makers, the operation has grown from a 600-barrel annual capacity to 100,000 barrels, making it the fourth largest brewery in Oregon.

Flavors and aromas Of all the IPAs we tasted, Bridgeport's had one of the least hoppy aromas—though the earthy quality suggests that this may be due to the use of English hop varieties, which are generally less assertive than American hops—but the nose filled out with toasty, sweet malt. There's a moderate bitterness and a somewhat clipped finish, making this a quaffable IPA that, for better or worse, does little to stand out.

Design The basic style here—round and busy, with text around the edges, through the middle, and everywhere else—is cliched, but this is a boring, rather than unattractive, bottle of suds.

Brooklyn Brown

Brown Ale

Country USA (NY) **ABV** 5.6%
Producer Brooklyn Brewery **Price** $$
Packaging 12oz/355ml bottle
Characteristics Malty, refreshing, roasty

Brown ales are tough to do well: the delicate flavor profile doesn't leave a lot of places to hide flaws, and any beer that is "delicate" runs the risk of coming off as watery. Brooklyn does an admirable job of avoiding all of these pitfalls.

Flavors and aromas Dark, smooth malt, cinnamon, and clove weave through the nose with hop floral aromas and a hint of roast character. The palate is a nice blend of pale malt, light caramel, darker grains, and fruity acidity. Our tasters expected a sweetness or heaviness that never materialized. The medium carbonation supports a vibrancy to the palate and a brightness that is atypical for an ale of this color.

Design This classic logo gives us the warm fuzzies, conjuring alternating images of the Brooklyn Dodgers of Ebbets Field and a torn T-shirt clinging to the concave chest of an indie emo wannabe-poet strutting down Bedford Ave.

Brooklyn East India Pale Ale

India Pale Ale

Country USA (NY) **ABV** 6.8%
Producer Brooklyn Brewery **Price** $$
Packaging 12oz/355ml bottle
Characteristics Bitter, hoppy

Calling this beer "East India Pale Ale" rather than "India Pale Ale" or just "IPA" seems to be intended to help us notice that it's built with English hops. There's nationwide distribution of this IPA, but you'll still see it a lot more in the Northeast than in other parts of the country.

Flavors and aromas Woody, lemon-and-citrus hops form the nose here with low malt character. The palate has brightly bitter hops, with citrusy flavor, spicy and suggestive of lemon rind. The finish, in addition to rich, fruity hop flavor, has a grippy, astringent quality to the bitterness that detracts somewhat from an otherwise excellent and lively IPA.

Design Red-and-green color schemes are dangerous in their potential to look like Christmas advertisements, but this package avoids that through deft color selection while maintaining the major league look.

Brooklyn Lager

Amber Lager

Country USA (NY) **Style** American Amber Lager **ABV** 5.2%
Producer Brooklyn Brewery **Price** $$
Packaging 12oz/355ml bottle
Characteristics Bitter, hoppy, refreshing

Much has been made of the fact that the Brooklyn Brewery has revived brewing in Williamsburg— the borough's hottest hipster neighborhood. But they seem to be victims of their own success: they don't have the capacity to brew all of their beer in the 'Burg. Much of the production takes place at F.X. Matt, in Utica. The Lager is by far Brooklyn's widest-distributed beer

Flavors and aromas Woody, lemony hops with some floral character contribute to a nose that is light but pleasant. An intensely creamy mouthfeel presents a good pile of flavor hops, unobtrusive malt, and good bitterness. This beer is significantly more dry than most lagers of comparable flavor intensity. The finish shows more hops, and soft bitterness, totally devoid of hard edges.

Design This might be our least-favorite color palette for the formidable Brooklyn Brewery logo. They can't all be the best.

Bud Ice

Pale Lager

Country USA (MO) **Style** North American Lager **ABV** 5.5%
Producer Budweiser **Group** Anheuser-Busch **Price** $
Packaging 12oz/355ml, 22oz/650ml,24oz/710ml, 32oz/946ml
bottle, 12oz/355ml; 16oz/473ml, 24oz/710ml, 40oz/1.18L can
Characteristics Refreshing

Ice filtration—trapping fine particles in ice crystals that are easier to comb out—allegedly makes lagers "smoother," but in our opinion, the problem with beers like Budweiser is not that they are insufficiently smooth. It's that they have insufficient personality. Although "ice" is just a code word for higher alcohol, the rise of craft ales in America has made even the most alcoholic of Buds seem like a party pooper on that front, too.

Flavors and aromas The aroma of this beer is sweet, with some soft floral notes that reminded one taster of white wine. The palate is also sweet, but there's a light, tart kick (possibly from the very high carbonation) along with neutral, bready malt. The clearest indication of hop character is found in the clean finish.

Design This might be the least attractive label in the Anheuser-Busch portfolio. Why is the AB eagle logo whooshing along?

Bud Light

Pale Lager

Country USA (MO) **Style** Light Beer **ABV** 4.2%
Producer Budweiser **Group** Anheuser-Busch **Price** $
Packaging 7oz/207ml, 12oz/355ml, 16oz/473ml, 22oz/650ml,
24oz/710ml, 32oz/946ml bottle; 16oz/473ml aluminum bottle; 8oz,
10oz, 12oz, 16oz, 24oz, 40oz can **Characteristics** Refreshing

Bud Light is the best-selling beer in the United States. It's also the best-selling beer in the world, despite only being sold in a handful of countries. It's hard to say anything about this beer that hasn't been said before. But the beer is the way it is by design, and it serves a market that wants it.

Flavors and aromas This is an excellent example of the light-beer style. It's got light body, light flavor, and no perceptible bitterness; but it's a clean emptiness rather than a watered-down beery flavor. From a brewing perspective, this is a technically impressive beer. But this won't do much for beer lovers.

Design We prefer the traditional Budweiser labels—the swoosh stuff screams "Nike focus group rejects"—but not nearly as much as we prefer drinking full-bodied beers.

Bud Light Lime

Pale Lager

Country USA (MO) **Style** Light Beer **ABV** 4.2%
Producer Budweiser **Group** Anheuser-Busch **Price** $
Packaging 7oz/207ml, 12oz/355ml, 22oz/650ml bottle;
12oz/355ml, 24oz/710ml can **Characteristics** Refreshing, unusual

Bud Light Lime, which features "natural lime flavor," quickly became a hot seller after its inception in 2008, with an industry exec calling it "the atomic bomb in the marketplace." It's not hard to see why—like Yellowtail in the wine world, this beer plays to America's taste for sweet drinks.

Flavors and aromas This beverage isn't much like beer. But it is refreshing, in a flavored-club-soda kind of way. It's also sweet. Our tasters split fairly evenly on whether Bud Light Lime was awful or okay, with the balance coming down on the side of okay. But it does have some strange qualities. Every taster mentioned soap (mostly citrusy, lemony dish soap) in the nose. And nobody loved it. But as alcoholic, candy-flavored club soda goes, this is okay.

Design Normally we would rail against the clear glass, but it's unclear whether this beer even has any hops that could become skunky.

Budweiser

rating
4

Pale Lager

Country USA (MO) **Style** North American Lager **ABV** 5.0%
Producer Budweiser **Group** Anheuser-Busch **Price** $
Packaging 7oz/207ml, 12oz/355ml, 16oz/473ml, 24oz/710ml
bottle; 16oz/473ml aluminum bottle; 8oz, 10oz, 12oz, 16oz, 24oz,
40oz can **Characteristics** Bland

Arguably the world's best-known beer, both for better and for worse, the King of Beers is also the King of Beer Advertising. The face of Bud has evolved constantly, while the brewery claims that the beer hasn't changed in over a century. Is there any other brand that inspires so much interest in their ads from people who don't consume their product?

Flavors and aromas We tasted Budweiser out of both can and bottle, and the results were impressively consistent: the beer is flat and thin, with a palate dominated by weak, bready malt ("watery cornflakes," in the words of one taster). We found no evidence of the promised "choicest hops." There's also no aftertaste, which may be the reason for this beer's popularity: all the alcohol of beer with none of those pesky beer flavors.

Design We take comfort in the never-changing nature of this logo.

Budweiser American Ale

Pale Ale

Country USA (MO) **Style** American Pale Ale **ABV** 5.3%
Producer Budweiser **Group** Anheuser-Busch **Price** $$
Packaging 12oz/355ml, 22oz/650ml bottle; 12oz/355ml can
Characteristics Refreshing

When it was introduced in 2008, Budweiser American Ale raised some eyebrows for its upmarket positioning. But it's been a relatively quiet presence since, with Bud Light Lime and Michelob Ultra representing the flashy, ad-driven side of Anheuser-Busch.

Flavors and aromas Light crystal malt, clean bread, and fresh citrus notes compose the nose. There's a bit of sweet malt, balanced with a bit of bitterness, and the hop character in the mouth is low. This is a very low-intensity take on an amber ale, sort of My-First-Amber, but it has no rough edges or off-flavors, and it's decently refreshing, if a little bland.

Design The choice of the Budweiser brand rather than Michelob (Anheuser-Busch's higher-level brand) is interesting, though it's almost academic—the brand name nearly disappears in the design.

Budweiser Select 55

Pale Lager

Country USA (MO) **Style** Light Beer **ABV** 2.4%
Producer Budweiser **Group** Anheuser-Busch **Price** $
Packaging 12oz/355ml bottle; 12oz/355ml can
Characteristics Refreshing

Typical light beers have about 100 calories per 12-ounce bottle, and weigh in at 4% to 4.5% alcohol. Select 55 has just over half the calorie count and just over half the alcohol. Any guesses on how they get there? Buying regular light beer and cutting it with water would be much cheaper—you'd get two beers for the price of one.

Flavors and aromas Watching people drink this beer is fascinating. It's so light and thin as to beggar belief. Lightstruck notes from the clear bottle (consistent across multiple tastings) are modest, but still overwhelm all else. Our biggest question is how it's possible to brew a beer with this little flavor (aside from the skunky notes). If there's a market for "vitamin water", then might there be a market for "alcohol water"?

Design Minimal label reinforces the low-calorie concept and maximizes light-collection area for optimal skunkiness.

Busch

Pale Lager

Country USA (MO) **Style** North American Lager **ABV** 4.6%
Producer Busch **Group** Anheuser-Busch **Price** $
Packaging 12oz/355ml, 22oz/650ml, 32oz/946ml bottle; 12oz,
16oz, 24oz, 40oz can **Characteristics** Bland

Anheuser-Busch's most prominent
budget label was launched in
1955 as Busch Bavarian Beer. The
brand today includes Light and Ice
versions of this light lager.

Flavors and aromas It takes all
kinds to make up the world of
beer drinkers; our experts and
brewers rarely agreed unanimously
on anything. But we were of one
mind on the question of Busch: it's
a poor excuse for a lager. The sole
redeeming point was a hint of hop
aroma. But then, how much time
do you plan to spend smelling
your pint of Busch? On the palate,
this beer was flat, bready, and
insipid. Even at the bottom of the
price ladder, you've got better
options.

Design Big, snowy mountains are
the workhorse of the domestic
lager label. Here, they're not
particularly attractive, but they do
remind you not to drink this until
it's cold enough that you can't
taste it.

Busch Light

Pale Lager

Country USA (MO) **Style** Light Beer **ABV** 4.2%
Producer Busch **Group** Anheuser-Busch **Price** $
Packaging 12oz/355ml, 22oz/650ml, 32oz/946ml bottle; 12oz,
16oz, 24oz, 40oz can **Characteristics** Bland

According to beer author Stan
Hieronymus, Busch Light is the
second-best selling sub-premium
("cheap") beer in the United
States, trailing only its older
brother Natural Light.

Flavors and aromas A faint
yeasty smell—as of sourdough
starter—is about all there is to be
found in the nose. The palate,
wrote one taster, is "more mineral
water than beer," with
effervescent fizz, and no real malt
or hop character. The finish is very
dry, and while most of the parts
here are common for light beer,
there's less character than there
was in our samples of Anheuser-
Busch stablemate Natural Light.

Design Sideways text running the
length of the can is the current
vogue in cheap labels. This one
has the obligatory speedy italic
font, which must be a dog-whistle
for "shotgun me."

Caldera Amber

Pale Ale

Country USA (OR) **Style** American Amber Ale **ABV** 5.4%
Producer Caldera Brewing Company **Price** $$$
Packaging 12oz/355ml can
Characteristics Bitter, hoppy, refreshing

Tiny Ashland, Oregon is home to the Shakespeare festival and to Caldera Brewing Company, which has made a name for itself among craft beer drinkers and fishermen by producing quality microbrews in aluminum cans—the first craft brewery in Oregon to do so.

Flavors and aromas This is a no-frills pale ale with a bright flavor palette of citrusy hops and a clean, crisp mouth of toasted malt and balanced but bright bitterness. Citrus character, including grapefruit, lingers into the finish. All of those high-toned notes left some tasters feeling like the beer lacked punch, but this seems like a drink for warm summer days, when the lack of heft is refreshing.

Design It's a bright muddle of clashing colors; this can definitely stands out, but it's hard to look at.

Caldera IPA

India Pale Ale

Country USA (OR) **ABV** 6.1%
Producer Caldera Brewing Company **Price** $$$
Packaging 12oz/355ml can
Characteristics Bitter, hoppy

It only takes a glance at its website to see that Caldera is a small operation. But these beers pop up in beer discussions regularly—it's clear that the brewery has hit upon something with its unique canning operation.

Flavors and aromas Caldera's IPA starts off strong, with potent grapefruit and resiny hops in the nose, along with a caramel quality that one taster likened to maple syrup. In the mouth, mild sweetness and fruity esters are quickly replaced with an intense bitterness that grabs the tongue and refuses to let go. This was tasty, but we found the bitterness hard-edged and tough to clear for the next tasting.

Design Craft beer in a can? Get used to it. Caldera is on the leading edge of a trend that only seems to be accelerating.

Carlsberg Lager

Pale Lager

Country Denmark **Style** Continental Lager **ABV** 5.0%
Producer Carlsberg **Price** $$
Packaging 12oz/355ml bottle
Characteristics Hoppy, refreshing

Carlsberg established a laboratory for brewing research in 1875 which isolated lager yeast for the first time and invented the pH scale. That strikes us as a profoundly Scandinavian approach to beer. Nowadays, Tuborg battles Carlsberg for dominance in Denmark, but in the rest of the world, it's no contest.

Flavors and aromas The noble hop-skunk combo that characterizes imported Carlsberg tipped our tasters off to the fact that this is a Continental lager from a green glass bottle. The skunk is mild, though, and the light, sweet malt supports a soft bitterness and medium mouthfeel with some nice hop character.

Design The green color scheme of Carlsberg mirrors its peers—Heineken, Becks, Stella, and so on. European name plus green package has become the consumer signal, perhaps, for noble hops and skunks.

Chimay Blue (Grande Réserve)

Belgian Ale

Country Belgium **Style** Dark Belgian Ale **ABV** 9.0%
Producer Chimay Brewery **Price** $$$$$
Packaging 11.2oz/330ml, 25.4oz/750ml bottle
Characteristics Malty, strong, unusual, yeasty

The monks of Scourmont Abbey have been producing beers and cheeses since the mid-19th century. As the most readily available Trappist ale outside Belgium, Chimay is many world beer drinkers' introduction to the style. Chimay Blue (the 750ml version is called Grande Réserve) is the most expensive of the brand's three main beers, with the highest alcohol content. It's often cellared and aged; Antwerp's Kulminator beer bar has verticals of the Blue going back to the 1970s.

Flavors and aromas The nose is restrained and mild, carrying dark sugars, alcohol, and raisins, but the palate really blossoms, with deliciously rich flavors brought out by lively carbonation, with mild esters and low bitterness. There's a spicy hint of alcohol in the finish.

Design If the rich blue robes of Chimay Grande Réserve give it a regal, noble appearance, then the rich blue robes of the Chimay Blue make it a spunky, regal sidekick.

Chimay Red (Première)

Belgian Ale

Country Belgium **Style** Dark Belgian Ale **ABV** 7.0%
Producer Chimay Brewery **Price** $$$$$
Packaging 11.2oz/330ml, 25.4oz/750ml
Characteristics Malty, strong, unusual, yeasty

Chimay Red (called Première in the 750ml packaging) is only slightly less strong, and slightly less widely available, than the Blue. Neither has quite the snob appeal of the smaller-production Trappist beers, but they held their own in our tastings, and better recognition and sell-through decreases the chances of getting bad bottles.

Flavors and aromas This beer lacks the extremes found in some Belgian ales, but it more than makes up for that with complexity. There are the expected fruity esters, a variety of medium- and dark-sugar flavors, hints of cinnamon and allspice, and just enough sweetness and alcohol to give it a warm, full body. The carbonation is less forceful, which works with these darker, more restrained flavors.

Design The custom glass bottles used for the 330ml size are interesting, but the larger 750ml package really carries an understated elegance.

Chimay White (Cinq Cents)

Belgian Ale

Country Belgium **Style** Pale Belgian Ale **ABV** 8.0%
Producer Chimay Brewery **Price** $$$$$
Packaging 11.2/330ml, 25.4oz/750ml bottle
Characteristics Strong, yeasty

White (also called Tripel, and Cinq Cents in the 750ml packaging) is the most restrained, hoppiest, and spiciest of the three main Chimay labels. If you don't enjoy the Trappist style, this is the Chimay you're most likely to enjoy. But it's also the hardest of the three to find.

Flavors and aromas Our tasters would have sworn that this beer has traditional Belgian brewing spices—coriander, bitter orange peel, and the like—which seemed apparent in the nose and as a source of bitterness in the slightly medicinal finish. But the ample body and well-hidden alcohol are nice, and if the complex spices are actually the product of yeast action, we can't complain.

Design Despite all being essentially the same, the various Chimay labels all manage to retain a nice sense of personality. Like the liquid within, Chimay White is the restrained, quiet one.

Clausthaler Non-alcoholic

Pale Lager

Country Germany **Style** Non-alcoholic **ABV** 0.5%
Producer Binding-Brauerei **Price** $$
Packaging 12oz/355ml bottle
Characteristics Malty, unusual

There are different ways to produce near-beer. O'Doul's, for instance, is fermented and then has the alcohol removed, while Clausthaler mashes the grain using a process that produces only a small amount of fermentable sugars.

Flavors and aromas A touch skunky, this near-beer smells of nuts and sweet corn; it's an interesting nose but one which isn't much like beer. The palate is slightly sweet, with low hop character and a touch of bitterness, and a strange mouthfeel that's alternately grainy and chalky. Given the lack of beer character, we've chosen not to rate this, but that doesn't mean it was flawed.

Design There's not much going on with the label here. It's built to blend in, perhaps because most non-alcoholic beer drinkers aren't really interested in calling attention to their bottles.

Colt 45

Pale Lager

rating
4

Country USA (IL) **Style** North American Lager **ABV** 6.0%
Producer Pabst Brewing Company **Price** $
Packaging 12oz/355ml, 25.7oz/760ml, 40oz/1.18L
bottle;12oz/355ml, 16oz/473ml can
Characteristics Bland

Colt 45, dubbed "malt liquor" for
its strength, is generally drunk in a
goal-oriented manner, sometimes
brown-bagged (for different
purposes than ours). Ironically, its
alcohol content is actually lower
than that of many craft IPAs. We
tasted the 6.1% ABV version
available in the US, but Canadian
readers will find an 8% product.

Flavors and aromas There's nearly
no aroma to Colt 45, and the
palate is flat, with strong
carbonation that fails to make
things lively. The finish is sweet
and slightly tangy, and you'll be
hard-pressed to find any hops or
bitterness. But if you're looking to
get drunk, this gets the job done.
But then, so do 247 of the other
249 beers in this book (Clausthaler
and O'Doul's don't).

Design Colt 45's label doesn't
appear to have been updated in
the last quarter-century, nor do the
proportions appear to have been
altered for any semblance of grace
on a 40-ounce bottle.

Coney Island Lager

rating 7

Amber Lager

Country USA (NY) **Style** American Amber Lager **ABV** 5.5%
Producer Shmaltz Brewing Company **Price** $$$$
Packaging 12oz/355ml bottle
Characteristics Bitter, hoppy

The Coney Island series of lagers is produced by Shmaltz, the same folks behind He'Brew. This beer is the flagship and features a bewildering eight different malts (two or three is where most brewers stop) and six different hops.

Flavors and aromas Our tasters would forgive you if you thought that this was a pale ale rather than an amber lager. The aromas—bright, citrusy hops (and some diacetyl)—combine with mild caramel on the palate and lead to a lingering bitter finish. We liked this beer, but it really isn't much like any other lager we've tasted. Approach it with caution; if you're in a mood for a basic lager, consider a Sam Adams instead.

Design This label is not for everyone, with the ghoulish carny and his surreal facial tattoos. But you've got to give them credit for doing something different.

Coors

Pale Lager

Country USA (CO) **Style** North American Lager **ABV** 5.0%
Producer Coors Brewing Company **Group** Molson Coors **Price** $
Packaging 12oz/355ml, 40oz/1.18L bottle; 12oz/355ml can
Characteristics Refreshing

Coors is produced in the world's largest brewery facility, located in Golden, CO, where the brand's marketing machine works to remind us of its high altitude and proximity to the Rockies. If you watch much television, Coors' alpine provenance is probably embedded in your cerebral cortex for life. But this was just a modest regional beer when, in 1977, it took its star turn as a load of alcoholic contraband in the film Smokey and the Bandit.

Flavors and aromas A light sweet nose smells vaguely of white wine, but who swirls and sniffs Coors? This beer has a light mouthfeel, with low malt presence, and if there are hops, they're very subtle. There's enough carbonation and just a pinch of bitterness, which gives the finish some crispness, but sweetness dominates.

Design The retro design is actually kind of classy, but cold-activated cans are a little too Sharper Image for our tastes.

Coors Light

Pale Lager

Country USA (CO) **Style** Light Beer **ABV** 4.2%
Producer Coors Brewing Company **Group** Molson Coors **Price** $
Packaging 12oz/355ml bottle; 12oz/355ml, 16oz/473ml can
Characteristics Bland

Despite operating the world's largest brewery and having a history that dates back to 1874, Coors has only been distributing its beer across the whole United States since the early 1990s. But that hasn't prevented Coors Light from becoming the fourth-bestselling beer in the country.

Flavors and aromas The best American light beers are refreshing and dry, with minimal malt character and no bitterness. Here, there's a light, sweet character in the aroma (described by one taster as "cidery;" another was reminded of Chardonnay) that seemed out of place. Still, it's unlikely that anyone consuming this beer from an ice-cold can would notice.

Design Calling yourself "the Silver Bullet" certainly limits your design space. But the extent to which Coors Light shares elements (like snow-covered mountains) with dozens of other brands is probably more a function of its success than a desire to follow.

Corona Extra

Pale Lager

Country Mexico **Style** North American Lager **ABV** 4.6%
Producer Grupo Modelo **Price** $$
Packaging 7oz/207ml, 12oz/355ml, 24oz/710ml bottle;
12oz/355ml can **Characteristics** Bland

The best-selling—and most consistently skunky—imported beer in the United States, Corona has aggressively marketed its beer to evoke images of vacations on tropical beaches. Surprisingly, the beer has only been regularly imported to the United States since 1981. Barbecues and Cinco de Mayo parties haven't been the same since.

Flavors and aromas It's hard to get past the fact that Corona Extra is the all-star captain of Team Skunky Beer. But we were surprised to discover that there were hints of hop bitterness and malt here. There's also a touch of astringency. If this were a clean bottle, we might be inclined to call this a fine lawnmower beer.

Design Frankly, we're sufficiently incensed by the resolute refusal to package the beer in a bottle that won't lead to instant and permanent damage of the contents that we don't really care what's on the outside.

Corona Light

Pale Lager

Country Mexico **Style** Light Beer **ABV** 4.1%
Producer Grupo Modelo **Price** $
Packaging 12oz/355ml bottle
Characteristics Bland

Corona Light is Grupo Modelo's first foray into light beer, and it currently stands as the most popular imported light beer in North America, beating out Amstel Light. While the beer market in the US has been fairly flat over the last decade, Corona Light has grown steadily. Never underestimate the power of beach-vacation marketing.

Flavors and aromas Every bit as skunky as you'd expect from a Corona product, this light offering is nearly devoid of beer character. "Overcarbonated water," opined one taster, and another was moved to imagine beer-flavored ChapStick. But mostly this was just skunky.

Design They insist on using clear glass, and we insist that a better name would be "Corona Lightstruck." It would be funny if it wasn't sad.

Czechvar

Pale Lager

Country Czech Republic **Style** Continental Lager **ABV** 5.0%
Producer Ceske Budejovice Brewery **Group** Budweiser Budvar
Price $$$ **Packaging** 12oz/355ml bottle
Characteristics Hoppy, refreshing

When, in the late 19th century, Anheuser-Busch named its "Budweiser" after the town of Ceské Budejovice (Budweis)— where beer had been brewed since the 13th century—it spawned a century's worth of legal battles. In recent years, the companies have begun cooperating, and AB now distributes this age-old Czech pilsner under the Czechvar name. Still, the trademark dispute is still not resolved.

Flavors and aromas A fresh nose has pleasant, somewhat sweet malt and nice noble hop character, with a touch of cooked corn. Light bitterness, crackery malt, and good carbonation are a promising, and there is a touch of sweetness that is balanced by the crisp bitterness. The finish is more dry and bitter, with a lingering hop flavor that makes this a decent Continental lager.

Design Lovely use of almost-white space. It would go great with some brown glass bottles. Really.

Dale's Pale Ale

Pale Ale

Country USA (CO) **Style** American Pale Ale **ABV** 6.5%
Producer Oskar Blues **Price** $$
Packaging 12oz/355ml can
Characteristics Bitter, hoppy

"Dale" here is Dale Katechis, founder of Oskar Blues. To us, it kind of seems like they're all Dale's beers, but no matter. This was the first of the Oskar Blues line to get the canning treatment, starting in 2002. It's part of an incipient movement to sell craft beer in cans—a great idea, as far as we're concerned.

Flavors and aromas Aroma hops give this beer a lemony, floral aroma that verges on cleaning-product smell. The carbonation is on the high side, which helps show off the pleasant hop flavor and mild caramel. There's also intense bitterness, which is crisp and well executed, but strong enough to push things out of balance. Still, the hop choice makes this a nice alternative to super-citrusy pale ales. This is a beer for hopheads only.

Design Did someone forget to design the back of the can? It's just a random collection of small logos.

Delirium Tremens

Belgian Ale

Country Belgium **Style** Pale Belgian Ale **ABV** 8.5%
Producer Brouwerij Huyghe **Price** $$$$
Packaging 22oz/650ml, 25.4oz/750ml
Characteristics Strong, unusual, yeasty

For most of the last century, Huyghe produced pilsner-style beers. Only in the 1980s did they switch to big, essentially Belgian brews. Delirium Tremens was launched in late 1989, and it has garnered fame for its unmistakable pink elephant logo, its intense flavor profile, and its sky-high alcohol level.

Flavors and aromas Everyone seemed to find something a little different, but all agreed that it was a tasty, complex beer. The nose shows big yeast and spice character, with some pear and bitter orange. In the mouth, there's lightly fruity sweetness and tangy tart notes, followed by a dry and slightly bitter finish. The complexity makes this a nice beer for slow, lingering drinking.

Design The ceramic gray bottle—one of the only ones with zero transparency—is quite distinctive, but your Delirium memories will likely be dominated by the still-more-distinctive pink elephants.

Deschutes Black Butte Porter

Dark Ale

Country USA (OR) **Style** Porter **ABV** 5.2%
Producer Deschutes Brewery **Price** $$
Packaging 12oz/355ml bottle
Characteristics Malty, roasty

Hailing from the Pacific Northwest—a part of the world that's known for exceptionally hoppy beers—Deschutes has done quite well with its Black Butte Porter. While the market for porters is small, that hasn't stopped this from becoming one of the bestselling craft beers in the country.

Flavors and aromas A grainy, roasty nose suggests coffee, with chocolate emerging as the beer warms. In the mouth, there's some richness to the body, and ample, well-defined roast character. Bitterness is well matched to the malt and roast character, and good carbonation keeps things lively. The finish is clean and slightly bitter. It's a straightforward example of the style that hits all the important notes.

Design An uncluttered variation of the conventional oval label design format with an interestingly stylized depiction of the beer's namesake. It makes good sense.

Deschutes Green Lake Organic Ale

Pale Ale

Country USA (OR) **Style** American Amber Ale **ABV** 5.2%
Producer Deschutes Brewery **Price** $$
Packaging 12oz/355ml bottle
Characteristics Bitter, hoppy, malty

This is the only Deschutes beer to be labeled as organic, and it's priced the same as their other year-round seasonals. We like the idea of using Salmon-Safe certified hops—we hope they'll end up in all of their beers.

Flavors and aromas Striking balance is the hallmark of this beer, beginning with a nose that splits evenly between citrus-tangerine hops and caramel. In the mouth, we registered bright citrus hops alongside caramel malt and lurking bitterness—providing a suggestion of unsweetened cola. It's slightly sweet on the tongue for a moment, before the bitterness gently grabs the palate and glides up in intensity, when balance—but not drinkability—fades somewhat.

Design This label stands out from the other Deschutes offerings through its center-oval image, which spills out into the rest of the label. It's still distinctly Deschutes, though.

Deschutes Mirror Pond Pale Ale

rating
7

Pale Ale

Country USA (OR) **Style** American Pale Ale **ABV** 5.0%
Producer Deschutes Brewery **Price** $$
Packaging 12oz/355ml bottle
Characteristics Hoppy, refreshing

Most craft breweries that make it to a near-national scale have a beer whose reputation precedes them into new states—Sierra Nevada's Pale Ale, New Belgium's Fat Tire. In Deschutes' case, Black Butte Porter and Mirror Pond Pale Ale seem to be filling that role.

Flavors and aromas Mirror Pond has the typical citrusy character that comes from the use of the Cascade variety of hops, but it also has pleasantly grassy and floral notes, which we suspect are the result of adding hops after fermentation (dry-hopping). The beer is light-bodied, with a focus on hop bitterness and a background of pale and caramel malt. This is a well-balanced, easy introduction to the world of American pale ales.

Design This appealing bottle has the same clean design as the rest of Deschutes' regulars, with simple shapes and a rendering of the namesake Mirror Pond.

Deschutes Obsidian Stout

rating
9

Dark Ale

Country USA (OR) **Style** Stout **ABV** 6.4%
Producer Deschutes Brewery **Price** $$
Packaging 12oz/355ml bottle
Characteristics Roasty

Bend, Oregon's Deschutes Brewery receives a lot of attention these days for limited-edition Imperial porters and stouts (particularly the oak-aged Abyss) but they've been cranking out top-flight dark beers in the IPA-obsessed Pacific Northwest for over twenty years.

Flavors and aromas Obsidian Stout is a no-nonsense beer. It's moderately austere; there's no sweet soda quality here. The malt character is intensely roasted and dry. This is less bitter than straight espresso, but it shares much of the same language, with some acidity from the roast grains. Out of a bottle, the mouthfeel is creamy and smooth, but if you can find this on nitro in a pub, it's well worth your time. This is a superb stout.

Design The label here is just fine, we suppose, with clean lines and attractive design. But the older, dark blue design seemed more appropriate for a very dark beer called "Obsidian."

Dogfish Head 60 Minute IPA

India Pale Ale

Country USA (DE) **ABV** 6.0%
Producer Dogfish Head Craft Brewery **Price** $$$
Packaging 12oz/355ml bottle
Characteristics Bitter, hoppy

rating
8

Dogfish Head makes a line of IPAs that take their names seriously. The 60 Minute is so called because it's boiled for 60 minutes, and has 60 IBUs that come from 60 hop additions. At 6.0% ABV, this is one consistent beer. You can probably guess how the 90 Minute is put together...

Flavors and aromas A bright, firm bouquet with lemon/citrus notes is zesty and exciting. We got a bit of toasty malt, too. The palate is light-bodied, perhaps even slightly thin, but there is some Munich-malt character along with plenty of lemon and orange-peel hop flavor. The bitterness outweighs the malt, but is still restrained by IPA (and Dogfish Head) standards. This is a nice beer that one could drink in multiples—which can get dangerous.

Design Dogfish Head's crazy, unique beers often end up with long, elaborate descriptions on the label. We like the text on this one, which gets right to the point.

Dogfish Head 90 Minute IPA

Strong Beer

Country USA (DE) **Style** Imperial IPA **ABV** 9.0%
Producer Dogfish Head Craft Brewery **Price** $$$$
Packaging 12oz/355ml bottle
Characteristics Hoppy, strong

Dogfish Head's Sam Caligione seems incapable of producing a beer that can be casually consumed. Each brew—and 90 Minute IPA is no exception—demands attention. Calling this an IPA is a bit misleading; at 9% alcohol, it's clearly pushing into "Imperial" territory. But more to the point, this doesn't really come off as an IPA so much as a strong ale or light barleywine.

Flavors and aromas There are plenty of hops in the nose, and the IBU numbers are nothing to scoff at, but the bitterness is subdued in the face of an onslaught of malty sweetness and a thick, full body. We like this beer, even if we probably couldn't drink more than one or two in an evening.

Design The font is hard to read, and it's hard to tell the Dogfish Head beers apart without reading closely, but we still find a certain charm to these labels.

Dogfish Head World Wide Stout

rating
3

Strong Beer

Country USA (DE) **Style** Imperial Stout **ABV** 18.0%
Producer Dogfish Head Craft Brewery **Price** $$$$$
Packaging 12oz/355ml bottle
Characteristics Strong

This high-alcohol beer (varying by release; the current is labeled at 18% ABV) cements Dogfish Head's status one of the most fiercely independent, freewheeling breweries in the United States. The World Wide Stout is described by the brewer as having "more in common with a port than a cheap mass-market beer."

Flavors and aromas We found World Wide Stout to have more in common with moonshine than either port or mass-market beer. Hot, spicy alcohol rode roughshod over all beer character. Yes, there were dark molasses, prunes, and minor roasted grain notes to be found here, but they couldn't prevent us from vivid flashbacks to our earliest encounters with cheap vodka.

Design A standard Dogfish Head bottle and label give little hint to the volatile fumes inside. We could have used a stronger warning.

Don de Dieu

Belgian Ale

Country Canada (QC) **Style** Pale Belgian Ale **ABV** 9.0%
Producer Unibroue **Group** Sapporo **Price** $$$$
Packaging 12oz/355ml, 22oz/650ml bottle
Characteristics Sour, strong, unusual, yeasty

rating
8

This beer from Canada's Unibroue offers the most specific beer-pairing we've ever seen: "Enjoy Don de Dieu with...aged cheese and dried sausage at a riverside picnic while watching sailboats and race boats...during summer regattas."

Flavors and aromas The distinctive Unibroue ester profile is apparent here, with some attractive tart notes of sour cherry and pears. The body is sweet but well balanced by tartness in the mouth; some tasters noticed spicy pepper and clove notes.

Design The Don de Dieu seems unassuming—until you get the back story. It was named after the boat of Samuel de Champlain, who, according to the Unibroue website, was "commissioned by the King of France to pursue, by way of the great Canadian waterway, the exploration of the vast and inhospitable land called 'America.'" Summer regatta indeed.

Dos Equis Special Lager

rating
5

Pale Lager

Country Mexico **Style** North American Lager **ABV** 4.5%
Producer Cuauhtémoc Moctezuma **Price** $$
Packaging 12oz/355ml, 22oz/650ml bottle
Characteristics Refreshing

This Mexican beer has risen in visibility recently, partly on the strength of the Wes-Anderson-meets-Chuck-Norris-one-liners ad campaign, "The Most Interesting Man in the World." But the beer has been in production for over a century, and unlike its even-more-ubiquitous compatriot Corona, Mexicans really drink Dos Equis.

Flavors and aromas A fairly faint nose with low aromas of cooked corn and minimal hops is all there is to be found. The palate is similarly empty; there are crackers and malt in the palate, hints of green apple, and no hops to speak of. Despite fairly substantial carbonation, there's a dull, flat quality to this beer, which lacks bitterness that might brighten it up.

Design The name is literally a description of what is printed on the bottle: the letter X, twice, on cheaply shiny paper against green glass.

Duchesse de Bourgogne

rating
9

Sour Beer

Country Belgium **Style** Flanders Red Ale **ABV** 6.2%
Producer Brouwerij Verhaeghe **Price** $$$$
Packaging 11.2oz/330ml, 25.4oz/750ml bottle
Characteristics Malty, sour, unusual, yeasty

This intense beer is named for the 15th-century Mary of Burgundy, who ruled that region and much of the Low Countries until she fell off a horse while hunting. The beer is aged in enormous oak vats, where it gets its balsamic character, and like most soured beers, it's a blend of older and younger beer.

Flavors and aromas An epic, complex affair, this beer has an earthy nose, with aromas of cider vinegar, mild fruitiness, and nuts. In the mouth, there are pronounced sherry notes, and the vinegar component is more balsamic than cider. There's mild sweetness, lots of soft nutty character, and the whole package is strikingly drinkable for all of its unusual, nontraditional flavors.

Design How much more Flemish could this label be? The answer is "none." None more Flemish.

Duvel

Belgian Ale

Country Belgium **Style** Pale Belgian Ale **ABV** 8.5%
Producer Brouwerij Duvel Moortgat **Price** $$$$
Packaging 11.2oz/330ml, 25.4oz/750ml bottle
Characteristics Unusual, yeasty

Belgian beers frequently distinguish themselves from their peers through the use of proprietary house yeast strains. Duvel's yeast traces its roots to Scotland; proprietor Albert Moortgat purchased it on a visit shortly after World War I. No less formidable than the yeast is Duvel's marketing—the brand rivals Chimay in strong-Belgian-ale dominance around the world.

Flavors and aromas Duvel has a restrained, subtle nose, with mild esters and intriguing dry spices. The carbonation was very high for the dry palate, which appealed to some tasters and turned off others. There are some sharp edges here; tasters mentioned pepper and sulfur, and the finish is dry, intensifying a bitterness that would seem mild in a beer with more malt.

Design The simple white label and Gothic font are pretty neutral, but the curiously shaped bottle is kind of cute. We like it.

Eel River Organic IPA

India Pale Ale

Country USA (CA) **ABV** 7.0%
Producer Eel River Brewing Company **Price** $$$
Packaging 12oz/355ml, 22oz/650ml bottle
Characteristics Bitter, unusual

Eel River, in coastal northern California, was the first all-organic brewery in the United States, and their beers can be found across the western part of the country, as well as at their taproom and grill in Fortuna.

Flavors and aromas What seemed at first to be a promising, light-bodied IPA turned out to be a problematic beer, as our tasters observed a metallic off-flavor that reminded them of some of the less-stellar homebrews they'd experienced over the years. Re-tasting confirmed this impression. Light citrus-peel aroma and flavor hops mingle with a pleasantly spicy bitterness before the briny metal shows up and things turn south.

Design Eel River's labels are visually kind of muddy, but the IPA label is the cleanest of the lot. The fields of grain are a nice idea, and we like the hops bursting out of the logo.

Eel River Organic Porter

rating
7

Dark Ale

Country USA (CA) **Style** Porter **ABV** 5.8%
Producer Eel River Brewing Company **Price** $$$
Packaging 12oz/355ml, 22oz/650ml bottle
Characteristics Bitter, malty, roasty, strong

Eel River's motto, according to their website, is "Be Natural; Drink Naked"—something easier done in the redwood forests of northern California than most places, we imagine.

Flavors and aromas Two of our tasters noted that, after the aromas of heavy malt, dark caramel, molasses, and spices, they were expecting a "syrupy" palate. Pleasantly, that doesn't materialize—this beer has the flavor intensity of an Imperial porter without the heft or alcohol. It's a minor miracle that this beer winds up balanced, with heavy caramels, strong roast flavors, and some acidity and bitterness to even things out.

Design Is that a moon setting over a field? It looks like the Apocalypse. Or at least some kind of bad time.

Erdinger Hefe-Weizen

rating
5

Wheat Beer

Country Germany **Style** Bavarian Hefeweizen **ABV** 5.3%
Producer Erdinger Weissbräu **Price** $$$
Packaging 11.2oz/330ml, 16.9oz/500ml bottle
Characteristics Malty

Erdinger is not old-school by
German standards, dating only to
the late 19th century, but the
brewery does a brisk business
today, calling itself "the world's
biggest wheat beer brewery."

Flavors and aromas Not only did
we fail to identify this Bavarian
hefeweizen assuch, we didn't even
register it as a wheat beer in the
blind tasting. The expected clove
and banana yeast character was
entirely absent, and the only nod
to wheat was a full, bready malt
palate. The beer is slightly sweet in
the nose and the palate, and
finishes short and mildly malty. It
doesn't taste bad, but it lacks any
real character or charm.

Design Looks a lot like a Paulaner
label. Too bad it doesn't taste like
a Paulaner wheat beer.

Fin du Monde

Belgian Ale

Country Canada (QC) **Style** Pale Belgian Ale **ABV** 8.0%
Producer Unibroue **Group** Sapporo **Price** $$$$
Packaging 12oz/355ml, 22oz/650ml bottle
Characteristics Strong, yeasty

We love Unibroue's Québécois take on Belgian Abbey ales, particularly given that they're often half the price of the real thing. Le Fin Du Monde is as good a place to start with their lineup as any.

Flavors and aromas If you feel that we've done a poor job of explaining what "ester" flavors are, don't sweat it. Just find a bottle of Le Fin du Monde, chill it to about 50°F, and carefully pour yourself a glass. The beautiful dancing aromas of bananas, strawberry, and pear—the byproduct of Unibroue's particular house yeast—let you know immediately that this is not the pale, golden beer you grew up with. This is a textbook Belgian Tripel, although it's sweeter than some of the original Trappist versions of the style.

Design You'll never have any trouble picking a big, bold Unibroue beer out of a shelf-full. This is a good thing, because these beers taste as good as they look.

Flying Dog Gonzo Porter

Strong Beer

Country USA (CO) **Style** Imperial Porter **ABV** 7.8%
Producer Flying Dog Brewery **Price** $$$
Packaging 12oz/355ml bottle
Characteristics Malty, roasty, strong

A generation ago, the Imperial porter style was basically nonexistent. Today it's on the front lines for craft breweries looking to make names for themselves with big, flashy beers.

Flavors and aromas Dark malts, coffee, and alcohol are all prominently featured in the nose here, preparing you for big intensity. That intensity is there, as is the alcohol. Our tasters split between those who found this to be simply big, dark, and hot, and those who enjoyed the interplay of alcohol, dark roasts, and malt, describing it in terms that wouldn't be out of place in a doppelbock description. This was one of the most polarizing beers we tasted for The Beer Trials.

Design We're not sure the beers have nearly the connection to the spirit of Hunter S. Thompson that the brewers claim, but a label with a Ralph Steadman illustration of the Good Doctor isn't going to make that easy to prove.

Flying Dog Snake Dog IPA

India Pale Ale

Country USA (CO) **ABV** 7.1%
Producer Flying Dog Brewery **Price** $$
Packaging 12oz/355ml bottle
Characteristics Bitter

Flying Dog seems determined to live up to its name—the Aspen-based brewpub moved beer production to Denver in the mid-1990s, then from Denver to Maryland in 2006. At some point that pub closed, but there's now one in Denver near Flying Dog's headquarters, which remain in Colorado. Confused? Wait until you see the labels.

Flavors and aromas Snake Dog IPA turned out to be a troublesome beer. A light nose of mostly pale malt had modest floral and lemony hop aromas, but once we sipped the beer, we were surprised to find the mouthfeel dominated by some harsh bitterness. Hop character in the finish had some interesting notes—mint and lemon peel—but in the end this beer came across as unbalanced.

Design Messy, graphic, brash, and confusing. This must be a Ralph Steadman label. But what does it all mean?

Foster's Lager

Pale Lager

Country Australia **Style** North American Lager **ABV** 4.9%
Producer Foster's Group **Price** $$
Packaging 12oz/355ml, 25.4oz/750ml bottle; 12.7oz/375ml,
25.4oz/750ml can **Characteristics** Refreshing

Many Aussies are embarrassed by Foster's—not only because of the big, dumb, in-your-face "Australian for beer" campaign and the big, dumb, in-your-face cans, but also because they feel that the only widely available Australian beer in North America represents their homeland poorly. And they're right. The irony is that Foster's is not especially popular Down Under. But such are the vagaries of globalization.

Flavors and aromas This big can of fake Australia is pretty darn American, with no real hop profile to speak of and minimal bitterness. But for a clean, light lager, this was pretty decent, and could serve as a nice thirst quencher on a hot day. No rough edges showed up to put us off.

Design The oversized 375ml can with giant lettering is goofy, but the even-more-oversized 750ml can is even goofier. Still, it's classier for sidewalk-strutting than malt liquor.

Franziskaner Hefe-Weisse

Wheat Beer

Country Germany **Style** Bavarian Hefeweizen **ABV** 5.0%
Producer Spaten-Franziskaner-Bräu **Group** InBev **Price** $$
Packaging 12oz/355ml, 18.6oz/500ml bottle
Characteristics Refreshing, yeasty

"Franziskaner" is the German name for a Franciscan monk, but unlike the monastic Paulaner brewery, this brewery was named for its location across the street from a Franciscan abbey. Operations were merged with Spaten in 1922.

Flavors and aromas Distinct banana, pear, and bubble-gum esters, along with mild clove aromas, mark this as a classic Bavarian hefeweizen. The fruitiness of the palate is complemented by mild wheat—less noticeable than in other Bavarian wheat beers we tasted—and a light and dry finish. The slight prominence of the esters over the clove flavors here give this a hint of a Belgian feel, which was not a problem. This is a fresh, attractive beer.

Design That is one satisfied monk. But why is he so happy? His stein is empty!

Full Sail Amber

Pale Ale

Country USA (OR) **Style** American Amber Ale **ABV** 5.5%
Producer Full Sail Brewing Company **Price** $$
Packaging 12oz/355ml bottle
Characteristics Hoppy

Full Sail's Amber ale, according to the brewery, was the first bottled craft beer in Oregon, after they bought and installed an aging Italian bottling line named Mimi.

Flavors and aromas This beer is definitely on the lighter end of the pale ale spectrum in aroma and flavors. Most of our panelists found it thin and lacking, although there's a certain easygoing delicateness to the beer that might appeal to the flavor-timid. Light caramel flavors, soft bitterness, and a hop profile that's not 100% American give it a slight English-ale tinge.

Design Full Sail's labels are on the busy side, but somehow still manage to come across as clean, and they are readily recognizable on a shelf. We like the use of the not-quite-geometric figures and the logo-is-the-white-space motif.

Full Sail Pale Ale

Pale Ale

Country USA (OR) **Style** American Amber Ale **ABV** 5.4%
Producer Full Sail Brewing Company **Price** $$
Packaging 12oz/355ml bottle
Characteristics Hoppy

Full Sail Brewing Company takes pride in being employee-owned; that fact appears at the top of every bottle label. The brewery's main facility is located on the Columbia River Gorge east of Portland, which is widely considered to be the windsurfing capital of the world.

Flavors and aromas Mild citrus and lemon peel hop aromas mingle with some fruity esters, giving this just a touch of a sweetened kid's cereal quality in the nose. But the palate is unmistakably ale, with peppy carbonation and commingling malt and flavor hops. The bitterness is low, and can't quite keep this from being caramel-malt sweet, but not so much as to make it cloying.

Design It seems like Full Sail has been through more label redesigns than most breweries, but we hope this one sticks. The wood-panel background is unusual but nice.

Fuller's 1845

Strong Beer

Country England **Style** Strong Ale **ABV** 6.3%
Producer Fuller Smith & Turner **Price** $$$$
Packaging 16.9oz/500ml bottle
Characteristics Bitter, hoppy, malty

Fuller's 1845 Celebration Ale
commemorates the 150th
anniversary of the company's
incorporation. It's a "strong ale" in
English parlance, but at 6.3% ABV,
it's not overwhelmingly high in
alcohol by American craft ale
standards.

Flavors and aromas A bright,
complex nose offers biscuity malt,
spices, and hints of cider vinegar
and pear. In the mouth there is
light but interesting English malt
character and full-bodied hop
flavor, along with a pleasantly
complex and lingering bitterness.
Green apple character comes
forward as this warms, but seems
to add complexity and interest
rather than distracting. Mild
oxidative notes detracted for
some, but others thought this was
nearly perfect.

Design A distinctively old-
fashioned bottle with subtle
embossing is nice. We wonder if
the brewmaster ever pulls the beer
after 99 days, though. Or 101.

Genesee Cream Ale

rating
7

Pale Lager

Country USA (NY) **Style** Cream Ale **ABV** 5.1%
Producer High Falls Brewing Company **Price** $
Packaging 12oz/355ml bottle; 12oz/355ml can
Characteristics Malty, refreshing

Don't let the name confuse you—the cream ale style has much more in common with mainstream lagers than ales. Introduced in 1960, Genesee in 1964 adopted the slogan, "The Male Ale." The brand peaked in the mid-1970s and hangs on a throwback. Based on our tasting, Genny Cream deserves better.

Flavors and aromas A faintly hoppy beer—in hop character, it's somewhere between Budweiser and Heineken—Genny Cream offers a nice nose and a mouth of clean, bready malt. Our tasters were willing to guess that this was an all-malt brew that finishes light and clean, with just a hint of fruitiness nodding to the use of ale yeast in this lager-styled beer.

Design The cursive font used here gives off a vibe that's more cream soda than cream ale. That seems suboptimal.

Goose Island Honker's Ale

Pale Ale

Country USA (IL) **Style** English Bitter **ABV** 4.2%
Producer Goose Island Beer Company **Group** Craft Brewers
Alliance **Price** $$ **Packaging** 12oz/355ml bottle
Characteristics Hoppy, malty

Chicago's Goose Island seems
keen to make styles that are similar
to, but generally less common
than, those offered in most craft-
beer lineups. Honker's Ale, for
instance, is an English-style bitter,
whereas most breweries in these
parts would instead offer an
American-style pale ale.

Flavors and aromas A toasty,
bready nose has some leafy,
verdant hop character. The palate
has more toasted grains, light
caramel, and low bitterness and
woody hops. The modest
carbonation supports a creamy
mouthfeel, but low bitterness
doesn't quite find balance with the
malt. Our tasters found this
acceptably tasty, smooth and
drinkable, but not especially
complex or interesting.

Design Thank goodness for the
goose on this label—otherwise it
would be all honked up, and we'd
be confused.

Goose Island IPA

India Pale Ale

Country USA (IL) **ABV** 5.9%
Producer Goose Island Beer Company **Group** Craft Brewers
Alliance **Price** $$ **Packaging** 12oz/355ml bottle
Characteristics Hoppy, refreshing

Goose Island, pride of Chicago, was founded as the Clybourn Brewpub in 1988, which it still operates. The brewery, now part of the Redhook-Widmer-Kona Craft Brewers Alliance, turns out dozens of beers every year.

Flavors and aromas This IPA made several of our tasters intensely eager for the reveal. Big, forward dry-hop aromas are fresh and eager, with grassy orange and lemon components, but rather than a shift to potent bitterness, the hop flavor keeps coming. There is quiet, smooth malt, and soft, mild bitterness, but the focus here stays on the hop flavor to the end. A "perfect summer IPA," claimed one taster, and no one seemed inclined to disagree.

Design All of Goose Island's regular beer labels, this one included, remind us of Christmas. Every time. We suppose the most wonderful time of the year is when you have a beer in front of you.

Great Divide Hoss Rye Lager

Amber Lager

Country USA (CO) **Style** Oktoberfest **ABV** 6.2%
Producer Great Divide Brewing Company **Price** $$$
Packaging 12oz/355ml bottle
Characteristics Bitter, malty, refreshing

"Hoss"—at least as we know and love the word—is a way friends sometimes address each other in the South, originally derived from the word "horse," and roughly translated as "dude," as in: "What's up, hoss?" This is Great Divide's first lager. Introduced as a seasonal beer in August 2009, it was inducted into the year-round ranks almost immediately.

Flavors and aromas Nobody identified this as a märzen, despite a deeper color than the other beers. A somewhat perfumey nose suggests hops, honey, nuts, and caramel. The palate is sweetish, with light caramel notes, and there is some fruity character. There's also light, clean bitterness that lingers into the sticky-but-not-sweet finish.

Design Two years ago, Great Divide had uniformly goofy labels. Now they have some of the best. It's a shame that every great beer doesn't have a label this distinctive.

Great Divide Yeti

rating 9

Strong Beer

Country USA (CO) **Style** Imperial Stout **ABV** 9.5%
Producer Great Divide Brewing Company **Price** $$$$
Packaging 12oz/355ml bottle
Characteristics Bitter, malty, roasty, strong

Great Divide's Imperial stout comes in a number of limited-release variations, mostly involving oak aging and additional dark ingredients like chocolate or espresso. We tasted the basic bottling—if it's fair to call a big, complex beer "basic."

Flavors and aromas Yeti was a big winner with our tasters, starting with the roasty, rich, spicy nose, and following through to the big, dense palate and lingering, pleasant aftertaste. In the mouth there are lightly smoky notes and more intense roast flavors alongside bittersweet espresso and chocolate—though burnt or ashy notes aren't in evidence here. The lingering finish is full enough to be warmly satisfying.

Design "Untamed" and "imposing," notes the label, but that yeti silhouette is looking rather petite in the shadow of that lettering.

Grolsch Premium Lager

Pale Lager

Country Netherlands **Style** Continental Lager **ABV** 5.0%
Producer Grolsch **Group** SABMiller **Price** $$ **Packaging**
16oz/473ml, 16.9oz/500ml, 50.7oz/1.5 l swingtop bottle;
8.45oz/250ml, 11.2oz/330ml, 12oz/355ml, 24oz/710ml bottle;
11.2oz/330ml, 16.9oz/500ml can **Characteristics** Malty, refreshing

Grolsch is an old brand—nearly four centuries old. The pale lager style we associate with the brand (and with that unmistakable glass bottle with the swing-cap and rubber stopper) was still more than 200 years away from being developed. Today, Grolsch is owned by MillerCoors. Call us luddites, but we find this fact sort of sad.

Flavors and aromas This is an inoffensive but fairly generic European lager, a decent drink that doesn't warrant or hold much of your attention. The balance of flavor here is clean light malt, with low hop character and light bitterness. Smooth mouthfeel and suitable carbonation round things out. We'd be totally satisfied to drink this at a party or a concert.

Design The swing-cap enclosure is—pardon the pun—tops. We wish there were more of these, particularly for large bottles of strong beers. Of course, we wish the Grolsch glass were brown.

Guinness Draught

Dark Ale

rating
5

Country Ireland **Style** Stout **ABV** 4.3%
Producer Guinness **Group** Diageo **Price** $$$
Packaging 11.2oz/330ml bottle; 14.9oz/441ml can
Characteristics Roasty

It's hard to think of a beer brand that commands a more universal respect than Guinness, which is spoken of in reverent tones from Dublin to Dubai. Even those drinkers who lack the fortitude to drink it pay an honest, ungrudging respect. This version emulates the creamines of a nitro pour with a widget. And yet…

Flavors and aromas Other than its opaque color, nearly every aspect of the Guinness mythos comes across as overstated. The famously heavy, filling beer is actually light, both in flavor and alcoholic content; the should-be-powerful roast flavors are meek and watery, and the overall impression is one of half a dark beer stretched to fill a full bottle's portion.

Design A well-poured Guinness in an imperial pint glass is pretty to look at. But the Guinness Draught cans and bottles come off as cheap and gimmicky.

Guinness Extra Stout

Dark Ale

Country Ireland **Style** Stout **ABV** 5.0%
Producer Guinness **Group** Diageo **Price** $$
Packaging 12oz/355ml, 22oz/650ml bottle; 16oz/473ml can
Characteristics Bitter, roasty, sour

Prior to the invention of the new-fangled "nitro widget," this was the face of take-home Guinness. It's noticeably carbonated, unlike draught Guinness, and it's a bit stronger. Some countries instead get Guinness Foreign Extra Stout, which can hit 8% ABV.

Flavors and aromas Our tasters found buttery notes in the nose, along with some spicy character. The palate here is dominated by a sharp roast acidity and matching roast flavors. The acidity of the grains—or perhaps a touch of yeast character—comes across in the mouth as slightly fruity, but the dominant element is roast character that is both bitter and acidic. The mouthfeel suffers more than the flavor. One of our tasters loved this beer, but it's certainly not for everyone.

Design While it's a fairly small part of their business, it's a testament to the power of the brand that even the Guinness Extra Stout label is instantly recognizable.

Hacker-Pschorr Weisse

Wheat Beer

Country Germany **Style** Bavarian Hefeweizen **ABV** 5.5%
Producer Hacker-Pschorr Bräu **Price** $$$
Packaging 12oz/355ml, 16.9oz/500ml bottle
Characteristics Malty, refreshing, yeasty

Traditionalist Munich brewery Hacker-Pschorr, one of the stars of the Oktoberfest constellation, traces its origins to 1417; the brewery was split into the separate Hacker and Pschorr breweries a couple hundred years ago, and it was not until 1972 that they were reunited.

Flavors and aromas Spicy cloves, banana, and plenty of wheaty malt fill the unmistakably Bavarian nose of this beer. The estery character is muted until the glass is swirled, then jumps right out. The palate is lightly lemony, with plenty more of the elements of the nose, though the spice tends to outshine the banana character a bit. There's a hint of chalk in the mouthfeel, and the finish is a bit soft, but this is generally a winner.

Design This is a distinctive label, featuring the portrait of a natty gentleman whose name you will struggle to pronounce. It's dignified and exotic at the same time.

Hamm's

rating
4

Pale Lager

Country USA (WI) **Style** North American Lager **ABV** 4.7%
Producer Hamm's Brewery **Group** SABMiller **Price** $
Packaging 12oz/355ml bottle; 12oz/355ml can
Characteristics Bland

Ah, Hamm's. Just the mention of the name takes us back to the days when the Hamm's bear would dance away to the famous jingle ("From the land of sky blue waters...") between morning cartoons. Those ads ran from the early 1950s until the mid-1980s, but nowadays, the popularity of this beer amongst the college-party set probably owes more to the bargain-bin price and the lack of any striking beer quality (our translation of "drinkability").

Flavors and aromas The beer itself is rather less memorable than the ads. Our panel was struck by the lack of hop aroma, malt character, hop bitterness, or hop flavor. Served cold enough, though, it's probably indistinguishable from most other ice-cold, adjunct-heavy pale lagers.

Design Is it childish of us to wish that the can featured the dancing bear?

Harp Lager

Pale Lager

Country Ireland **Style** North American Lager **ABV** 5.0%
Producer Diageo **Price** $
Packaging 11.2oz/330ml, 16.9oz/500ml bottle
Characteristics Refreshing

This second-most-recognizable Irish brand is frequently co-marketed in the US with Guinness—US packaging employs the same harp logo for both, and the two are often combined in the same glass to form a Black and Tan. But the beer was originally produced in the 1960s by an odd consortium of British brewers, including Guinness, Bass, and Scottish & Newcastle.

Flavors and aromas Bitterness is more present here than in American-styled lagers, but the low malt presence and strong carbonation (and what is likely a fairly high mineral content in the water) make this an effervescent, seltzer-ish take on lager.

Design A straightforward label offers the Harp logo, and the name of the beer. This isn't particularly distinctive, or original, but it communicates the basic idea with a minimum of fuss. There's a certain elegance to it all.

Harpoon IPA

rating
5

India Pale Ale

Country USA (MA) **ABV** 5.9%
Producer Harpoon Brewery **Price** $$
Packaging 12oz/355ml, 22oz/650ml bottle
Characteristics Bitter, hoppy

Harpoon is Boston's other craft
brewery; founded in 1986—not
long after Boston Beer—they've
done reasonably well by
themselves, without quite
matching the massive success of
the Samuel Adams brand.
Harpoon owns and operates two
breweries: one on the Boston
waterfront, and one in Windsor,
Vermont.

Flavors and aromas Citrus hops
and sweet malt are joined by some
mild esters in the nose. In the
mouth, there's medium body, with
forward, fairly strong bitterness,
fruity esters, and light caramel.
The moderate carbonation suits
this beer well, but the dry finish
has a lingering bitterness that is
rather harsh, almost acrid. A
cleaner yeast profile and a bit
more supporting malt would put
this beer into a much better spot.

Design A lively, sprightly label,
vaguely nautical, with nice use of
color and a sense of whimsy. It's a
nice bottle to look at.

He'Brew Genesis Ale

Brown Ale

rating 7

Country USA (CA) **ABV** 5.6%
Producer Shmaltz Brewing Company **Price** $$
Packaging 12oz/355ml bottle
Characteristics Bitter, malty, roasty

Shmaltz Brewing Company, founded in 1996, makes kosher ales under the He'Brew label and lagers under the Coney Island Brand. The beers were brewed for several years at Anderson Valley before being taken on by Mendocino.

Flavors and aromas Genesis Ale has a malt-toffee nose with caramel, dark dried fruits, and some alcohol (despite a relatively mild 5.6% ABV). There's some roast grain in the mouth, and more dark sugars and fruits, but also a fair amount of hoppy bitterness. The finish is a bit rough, with alcohol and bitterness competing, and they both outpace the malt. This is still a pretty decent brew that gets away from conventional styles.

Design The festive and cute label is nicely eye-catching; this is a brewery that clearly doesn't take itself too seriously.

He'Brew Messiah Bold

Brown Ale

Country USA (CA) **ABV** 5.6%
Producer Shmaltz Brewing Company **Price** $$
Packaging 12oz/355ml bottle
Characteristics Malty, roasty

There's probably a long, meandering parable about Shmaltz founder Jeremy Cowan's travels across the continent looking for a permanent place to brew his He'Brew ales, but instead we'll just note that every He'Brew beer is, in fact, kosher.

Flavors and aromas Lots of caramel malt and a mild, coffee-evoking roastiness frame this smooth, mildly bitter beer. There's also a touch of smoke to be found here in the roast. Our tasters were fond of Messiah Bold; one suggested a pairing with fish and chips. Perhaps it's debatable whether this is really the Chosen Beer, but don't hesitate to choose it at the store.

Design This is the same label as the Genesis Ale, with a pan-out on the world over which the rabbi is presiding. Still, we'll take it.

Heineken

rating
6

Pale Lager

Country Netherlands **Style** Continental Lager **ABV** 5.0%
Producer Heineken **Price** $$
Packaging 12oz/355ml bottle; 12oz/355ml, 24oz/710ml can
Characteristics Malty

Heineken is the Budweiser of Europe, a megabrand on whom every possible opinion has been levied—it's weak, it's flavorful, it's the best of its kind, it's the worst of its kind. It's highly unlikely that you do not already have your own strong opinion about this beer, but here's ours: it's so frequently skunked that it's never worth ordering in the bottle. On tap, it's a different matter entirely.

Flavors and aromas Our tasters found skunky (lightstruck) notes in the nose of every sample, along with some noble aroma hops and crackery malt. The flavor is malt-focused and sweet, with a low hop character, and bitterness doesn't really make a distinct appearance until the sweetish aftertaste.

Design This could be the king of the oval labels. It's readable, clean, and both recognizable and, apparently, recognized. It's also slapped on a green bottle, which contributes to the skunk.

Hennepin

Belgian Ale

Country USA (NY) **Style** Saison **ABV** 7.7%
Producer Brewery Ommegang **Group** Duvel Moortgat **Price** $$$
Packaging 12oz/355ml, 25.6oz/750ml bottle
Characteristics Refreshing, unusual, yeasty

Perhaps it isn't fair to hold up Hennepin as an example of how American breweries are helping revive the saison style and breathe new life into it, since Ommegang is owned (and occasionally assisted) by the Belgian brewery Duvel. But this is life, where a lot of things aren't fair, so we'll do it anyway.

Flavors and aromas Banana esters and floral notes make up the light nose here. The palate is also light—easygoing and refreshing—but there are some odd darker funky notes here, suggesting there's a bit of Brettanomyces character (see the style guide for more on this term) in play. There's a complex interplay of flavors that are challenging to unpack, but probably worth the effort.

Design Clean text meshes well with bright colors, but we wish it were a little easier to tell what kind of beer lurks inside.

Henry Weinhard's Blue Boar

Pale Ale

Country USA (OR) **Style** American Pale Ale **ABV** 4.6%
Producer Blitz-Weinhard Brewing Company **Price** $$
Packaging 12oz/355ml bottle
Characteristics Bland

Henry Weinhard's story is a classic one: German brewer emigrates to the US in the mid-19th century, founds a brewery that finds regional success, barely survives Prohibition, and hangs on as a decent regional brand—until consolidation buys the operation and shutters the brewery.

Flavors and aromas Apparently, Henry's boars are domesticated. Our bottles had a skunky nose with mild, woody aroma hops, and a light, tame palate with a bit of sweetness that is balanced with medium bitterness. There's not much hop character here; in fact, there's not much character at all. One would have no trouble selling this as a pale lager. We'd stick to Weinhard's Private Reserve.

Design There's a very basic, clean label that seems to suggest clearly the positioning of Henry Weinhard's as a sort of upscale-cheap.

Henry Weinhard's Hefeweizen

rating **5**

Wheat Beer

Country USA (WI) **Style** American Hefeweizen **ABV** 4.9%
Producer Blitz-Weinhard Brewing Company **Price** $$
Packaging 12oz/355ml bottle
Characteristics Malty, refreshing

The Henry Weinhard's brand produces two wheat beers: a Belgian-style wheat beer and this hefeweizen. This beer is "honey-brewed," which we think means that honey is an ingredient.

Flavors and aromas There are very mild hints of the Bavarian weizen yeast character—clove and banana—but overall it's more in the mold of a sweet American-style wheat beer. There's some citrus zest here, and black pepper, but the wheat character comes off as bland cereal. There are things to like about this beer, but the individual pieces never quite find harmony with each other.

Design Normally we like labels with minimal text. But this one frustrates us. What does "honey-brewed" mean?

Henry Weinhard's Private Reserve

Pale Lager

Country USA (WI) **Style** Continental Lager **ABV** 4.8%
Producer Blitz-Weinhard Brewing Company **Price** $$
Packaging 12oz/355ml bottle
Characteristics Hoppy, refreshing

Weinhard's was a staple of our college drinking days, and it seems like the relationship we had to the beer was not new—in 1887, Henry Weinhard offered to fill the new Skidmore Fountain in downtown Portland with beer for its inauguration.

Flavors and aromas The Private Reserve, a pale American lager that had a lot more character than we expected of it, was one of the pleasant surprises of our blind tastings. While this beer has the light sweetness and low bitterness of many of its peers, it's got a fair whack of hop character, both in flavor and aroma, and a crisp, fresh finish. Was this beer this good back when we were drinking it in college? We can only speculate.

Design It's simple, direct, and unpretentious. We don't love it, but it suits the contents well.

Heegaarden

Wheat Beer

Country Belgium **Style** Witbier **ABV** 5.0%
Producer Hoegaarden Brewery **Group** InBev **Price** $$$
Packaging 11.2oz/330ml bottle
Characteristics Malty, refreshing, unusual, yeasty

Spiced with coriander and bitter orange peel, Hoegaarden—produced in the city of the same name—is generally regarded as the standard measure for the Belgian witbier style ("white beer," a category of wheat beer). The brewery makes several beers, but this is the best-known and most widely available.

Flavors and aromas There's lots of banana (and other fruity esters) in the nose of this beer, plus some clove, which means this has a vaguely Bavarian hefeweizen atmosphere at first. But there's more sweetness here, with floral, herbal notes building on the complex nose, and the palate yielding complex spices like subtle coriander. The mouthfeel is excellent, and the finish comes dry and light, making this a refreshing, invigorating beer.

Design In a perfect world, nobody would know about Coors Light, and we'd be free to call Hoegaarden "The Silver Bullet."

Hop Ottin' IPA

India Pale Ale

Country USA (CA) **ABV** 7.0%
Producer Anderson Valley Brewing Company **Price** $$$
Packaging 12oz/355ml bottle
Characteristics Bitter, hoppy

Anderson Valley, better known for Boont Amber than for this beer, hails from Mendocino County, California. They've got a quintessentially northern California brewing operation set on a rural ranch just outside of the farming community of Boonville, complete with a vintage-styled Bavarian brewhouse and 18-hole disc golf course.

Flavors and aromas An aroma of dusty dry hops was appealing, but there was little more to this beer beyond the nice nose and then a significant wall of bitterness. If you're looking for a full-strength, American rendition of English best bitters, with long, lingering bitterness, give this a shot, but for our money, there are better options out there. We're also left wondering what exactly it means to be "Ottin'," too.

Design We do like that pastoral scenery, but there's one distracting point here: the Haight called—they want their font back.

Hop Rod Rye

rating
9

India Pale Ale

Country USA (CA) **ABV** 8.0%
Producer Bear Republic Brewing Company **Price** $$$$
Packaging 12oz/355ml, 22oz/650ml bottle
Characteristics Bitter, hoppy, unusual

Rye as a brewing ingredient suffered a major setback in 1516, when a municipality in Bavaria passed the first version of the Reinheitsgebot, which prevented brewers from competing with bakers to buy wheat and rye. But it's making a gradual comeback, and brewers like Bear Republic have created a new niche for rye in hoppy, IPA-styled beers like this.

Flavors and aromas It would be natural to think that big flavors and subtle complexity are an either/or proposition, but Hop Rod Rye puts the lie to that. Yes, this is a big, citrusy hop bomb, no doubt. But it has layers of intriguing spices—tasters noted allspice, gingerbread, and other herbs—tied together in a beautiful package with a big, firm head. This was one of our very favorites.

Design We'd snap this up in any packaging, but the vintage hot rod and flames are stylish, compelling, and complement the spicy intensity of the brew.

Icehouse

Pale Lager

Country USA (WI) **Style** North American Lager **ABV** 5.5%
Producer SABMiller **Price** $
Packaging 12oz/355ml bottle; 12oz/355ml, 16oz/473ml can
Characteristics Bland

"Icehouse is brewed below freezing for a never watered down taste," claims Miller's Icehouse website (that's also nearly the complete text of the site). That's a typical jumble of confusing claims, but the basic idea behind Icehouse is the same as other ice beers: instead of pasteurizing the beer, they chill it, so that tiny ice crystals form on proteins, yeast, and bacteria, after which they can be removed with a normal filter.

Flavors and aromas Light and thin, with cooked corn aromas and crackery malt, it's got nothing going on. The high carbonation is the most interesting thing here. Consume Icehouse to appreciate how cheap it can be to get drunk.

Design The message we get from Icehouse cans, with their big lettering, above-average ABV (for mass-market American pale lagers, anyway), and little else, is "The price and alcohol content is what sells this beer."

Iron City Beer

rating
6

Pale Lager

Country USA (PA) **Style** North American Lager **ABV** 4.5%
Producer Iron City Brewing Company **Price** $
Packaging 12oz/355ml, 16oz/473ml bottle; 12oz/355ml can
Characteristics Refreshing

Iron City is, unsurprisingly, a
Pittsburgh beer, though
production has recently been
moved to the old Rolling Rock
brewery in Latrobe. Iron City
Brewing produces a significant
number of inexpensive regional
brands (like the appealingly named
Totally Dirt Cheap Beer), but the
flagship brand, nearly 150 years
old, endures.

Flavors and aromas Iron City Beer
has all the hallmarks of an
American-style pale lager: it's
lightly hopped, lacking in
bitterness, and fairly sweet. Our
panel found it to be an acceptable
drink, if undistinguished. The
distinctive glass bottle might tip us
to this over similarly priced
offerings, but we wouldn't
particularly bother seeking it out.

Design The 16-ounce bottle shape
is distinctive and catchy, a sort of
hulking cousin to the classic
"stubby" bottle. The logo is nice
and clean, too. We'll pass on the
aluminum bottles, though.

Keystone Light

rating
4

Pale Lager

Country USA (CO) **Style** Light Beer **ABV** 4.2%
Producer Molson Coors **Price** $
Packaging 12oz/355ml, 16oz/473ml can
Characteristics Bland

Budget Coors brand Keystone ran a memorable series of ads promoting their product as an antidote to "bitter beer face". It remains unclear to us if anyone actually knows what this is, but the cartoonishly puckered faces haunt us to this day.

Flavors and aromas Our tasting panel sampled 15 light beers. The best were refreshing and clean and managed to be light without being watery. The rest were insipid and thin, and to call them watery is to deny how refreshing and tasty water can be. Keystone Light is from the latter group. Flavorless, flat, and somehow heavy despite itself, this is a beer to avoid.

Design The standard Generic American Beer template is applied here. Big vertical lettering, snow-capped mountains, blue and white color scheme. Rinse, repeat.

Kingfisher Premium

rating
6

Pale Lager

Country India **Style** North American Lager **ABV** 4.8%
Producer United Breweries **Price** $$
Packaging 12oz/355ml, 22oz/650ml bottle
Characteristics Refreshing

The UB Group is an Indian company with many branches and businesses, including a large volume of spirits and even Kingfisher Airlines—the only airline-beer conglomerate we know of. Perplexingly, Kingfisher also owns the California craft brewery Mendocino. This beer and Taj Mahal are the two most commonly found beers at Indian restaurants outside India.

Flavors and aromas Floral hops and English pale malt character give this a clean, nice nose. There's low carbonation, and mild bitterness, giving the palate some heft to it, but there's hop character that gives some brighter notes, and the finish is dry, with woodier hops. We'd like to see a bit more bitterness and hop character, but this is a decent enough lager.

Design The eponymous kingfisher enlivens an otherwise bland and uninteresting design. Our advice: double the size of the bird and scrap the rest.

Kirin Ichiban

Pale Lager

Country Japan **Style** Japanese Lager **ABV** 5.0%
Producer Kirin Brewery **Price** $$
Packaging 12oz/355ml, 22oz/650ml bottle; 12oz/355ml,
24oz/710ml can **Characteristics** Refreshing

"Ichiban Shibori" means "first pressings," and reflects a process where less effort is put into extracting sugars from the grain. This requires more grain, but Kirin claims it results in a "smoother" taste. Kirin also switched in 2009 to an all-malt formulation.

Flavors and aromas Japanese lagers, with their ultra-light profiles, are some of the most sensitive beers around when it comes to showing off flaws, which is probably why we were able to detect a skunky note even though this beer is packaged in sensible brown glass. Past that, Kirin Ichiban is quintessentially Japanese: a very light nose leads into a palate of very light, delicate malt, with just a hint of bitterness, and a dry finish. Despite the lightness, it's not watery.

Design The Kirin logo is half deer and half dragon, which is awesome enough to make us want to break out the old D&D books and loot some orcs.

Kokanee Glacier Beer

Pale Lager

Country Canada (BC) **Style** North American Lager **ABV** 5.0%
Producer Columbia Brewery **Group** InBev **Price** $
Packaging 12oz/355ml bottle; 12oz/355ml, 16oz/473ml can
Characteristics Refreshing

Kokanee doesn't have much presence in the eastern or southern US, but it's a popular upmarket lager in Canada and can be found in the western US. The beer was launched in the 1950s and acquired by Labatt in 1974.

Flavors and aromas Lemony, floral hops are faint but detectable in the nose, along with some cooked corn. This American-style lager has medium body, and comes off a little bit lacking in carbonation. There's crackery malt, and more of the floral hop character from the nose, plus bitterness that—with the hop flavors—elevates this above a randomly selected American lager. The finish is crisp enough, with some lingering malt, and in the end this strikes us as decently refreshing.

Design If you insist on showing a mountain on your lager label, you might as well show some serious, craggy, dangerous peaks.

Kona Fire Rock Pale Ale

Pale Ale

Country USA (HI) **Style** American Pale Ale **ABV** 5.9%
Producer Kona Brewing **Group** Craft Brewers Alliance **Price** $$
Packaging 12oz/355ml, 22oz/650ml bottle
Characteristics Bitter, hoppy, malty

Fire Rock, introduced in 1995, was one of Kona's first two beers, along with Big Wave Golden Ale. Kona is now the most popular craft beer in Hawaii, and it's one of the only American craft beers to see distribution in Japan.

Flavors and aromas If you're expecting beer from Hawaii to be unremarkable, expect again: we loved this balanced, full-bodied ale, with malty sweetness and full-bore West Coast hoppiness. The bitterness here comes on slowly but catches up to the malt. Seek this one out.

Design It's slightly kitschy, with retro fonts and tiki-themed graphics—everything you'd expect from a Hawaii-based beer, and more.

Kona Longboard Lager

rating
5

Pale Lager

Country USA (HI) **Style** North American Lager **ABV** 4.6%
Producer Kona Brewing **Group** Craft Brewers Alliance **Price** $$
Packaging 12oz/355ml bottle
Characteristics Refreshing

Kona's Longboard Lager and Fire Rock Pale Ale are ubiquitous in Hawaii, but thanks to the brewery's partnership with Widmer and Redhook, its beers are starting to make appearances on the mainland.

Flavors and aromas A light nose smells strikingly of sugar and corn. The flavor here is thin, slightly sweet, with more of the corn character. (For a premium-priced craft lager, that's a poor sign.) There are some noble hops in the nose here, but if you're going to pony up for a high-end lager, we suggest you look elsewhere. If you're going to go Hawaiian, go Fire Rock, not Longboard.

Design They've absolutely nailed the color palette of a Hawaiian shirt. Aloha.

La Chouffe

Belgian Ale

Country Belgium **Style** Pale Belgian Ale **ABV** 8.0%
Producer Brasserie d'Achouffe **Group** Duvel Moortgat **Price** $$$$
Packaging 11.2oz/330ml, 25.4oz/750ml, 50.7oz/1.5L bottle
Characteristics Refreshing, strong, unusual, yeasty

Brasserie d'Achouffe's was started as a hobby in 1982, but La Chouffe (French for "the gnome") won fans and acclaim from the start. And this beer-enthusiast's Belgian is seen almost only at high-end beer-nerd bars here on this side of the pond.

Flavors and aromas Ample fruity esters—pear, strawberry, and banana—dominate the nose here. The palate is dry and fruity, and you can't help but notice the generous carbonations as this fizzes in your mouth. The finish is crisp and dry in a way that suggests Champagne, and as this warms a bit, it develops some mineral water flavors that intensify the comparison to fine sparkling wine.

Design As expected, the label prominently features their rendition of a gnome. His "what have we here?" posture mirrors the feeling we have when we discover a bottle of this in the fridge.

Labatt Blue

rating
5

Pale Lager

Country Canada (ON) **Style** North American Lager **ABV** 5.0%
Producer Labatt Brewing Company **Group** InBev **Price** $
Packaging 12oz/355ml, 40oz/1.18L bottle; 12/355ml, 24oz/710ml,
25.4 oz/750ml can **Characteristics** Bland

Labatt Blue is the flagship brand of
the Labatt Brewery (though
Budweiser, produced by Labatt for
the Canadian market, is the top-
selling beer in Canada). Labatt
Blue and Molson Canadian have a
long rivalry for the title of best-
selling Canadian beer. But Labatt
has a special place in the heart of
many a Canadian—and for good
reason. Even if this beer isn't
sophisticated, it's fun, easy
drinking.

Flavors and aromas It was
nothing special. But isn't there a
place for nostalgia? Our tasters
uniformly panned this beer as
weak, lacking in flavor, and
watered down. The thin aroma
was particularly singled out as
lacking in charm. But, in a pinch,
it'll get the job done.

Design Labatt Blue is named
because the label is blue, which is
reasonable enough. But Labatt
Blue Light has a silver label. What
gives?

Lagunitas Censored Copper Ale

rating 7

Pale Ale

Country USA (CA) **Style** American Amber Ale **ABV** 5.9%
Producer Lagunitas Brewing Company **Price** $$
Packaging 12oz/355ml bottle
Characteristics Bitter, hoppy, malty

The unsubstantiated story about this beer's name that floats around is that the original name was inspired by the resinous hop aroma of the beer, which reminded the brewers of a certain smokable herb. The name didn't fly with government regulators, and thus, "Censored."

Flavors and aromas Despite the supposed origins of the beer's name, we found the nose to be on the fruity side of the citrus spectrum (one taster noted pineapple) rather than the sappy side. The medium-full body of this beer has pronounced caramel character, and the bitterness is apparent but lags slightly behind the malt.

Design Lagunitas has a bold, forward style (and a doggy!), but the "obscured name" device on this label is one of the most irritating graphical elements of any beer in the book.

Lagunitas IPA

India Pale Ale

Country USA (CA) **ABV** 5.7%
Producer Lagunitas Brewing Company **Price** $$
Packaging 12oz/355ml, 22oz/650ml bottle
Characteristics Bitter, hoppy

Despite being smack in the middle of Sonoma's wine country, Lagunitas has probably done as much as anyone to put their hometown of Petaluma on the map. And what fun a visit to this facility is: it starts with a tasting of their beers, then leads into a hazy tour.

Flavors and aromas A powerful, hop-driven IPA that makes up in volume what it lacks in subtlety. Big, pungent, slightly resinous hops lead into a beer that is crisp at first, with ample bitterness, but the palate-coating body gets a little sticky after a few sips. There's always the potential for this kind of beer to come off as unbalanced, and some of our tasters wanted more dry malt character, while others thought this was a fantastic IPA.

Design It's no trouble at all to spot the Lagunitas beer on the shelf, but like the contents, the package can seem a little bit assaulting.

Lagunitas Pils

Pale Lager

Country USA (CA) **Style** Pilsner **ABV** 5.3%
Producer Lagunitas Brewing Company **Price** $$
Packaging 12oz/355ml bottle
Characteristics Bitter, hoppy, malty, refreshing

Lagunitas makes only one lager—
this old-school pilsner—and the
quality here is high enough that
we wouldn't mind seeing more.

Flavors and aromas There is corn
in the nose here—not unusual for
a pilsner—along with light and
sweet grain flavors, and some
"hoppy snap," as one taster put it.
Malt dominates at first, and
bitterness starts slowly but builds,
gradually moving from softly
American to Bohemian levels and
edging into German lager territory.
Floral flavor hops carry things
along nicely throughout.

Design Nothing screams "PILS"
like a label with giant letters that
say "PILS." Subtlety not really in
evidence here.

Leffe Blonde

Belgian Ale

Country Belgium **Style** Pale Belgian Ale **ABV** 6.6%
Producer InBev **Price** $$$
Packaging 11.2oz/330ml, 12oz/355ml bottle
Characteristics Malty, yeasty

Leffe Blonde is a very ubiquitous Belgian, often the only one available (along with Hoegaarden, of course) at bars with limited scope. It bears the name of the Leffe Abbey, but the beers are brewed by InBev at the Stella Artois brewery.

Flavors and aromas Leffe Blonde starts off with great enthusiasm: bright esters and a spicy, pepper/clove note in the nose. The beer is beautiful, too, with a big, dense rocky head. In the mouth, things slow down a bit. There's lots of fruit, and a nice, well-integrated hint of bitterness, but this beer is well on the sweet side. Like beers dominated by hop bitterness, this will appeal to some drinkers, but in our opinion, a slightly less sweet version of this beer would be an improvement.

Design The stained glass window is colorful and attractive, but the faux-burned-parchment background seems forced and awkward.

Lindemans Cassis

Sour Beer

Country Belgium **Style** Lambic **ABV** 4.0%
Producer Brouwerij Lindemans **Price** $$$$
Packaging 12oz/355ml, 25.4oz/750ml bottle
Characteristics Sour, unusual

Lambic beers are made with wild fermentation; the breweries have slatted roofs that can be opened to allow the local airborne bacteria to drop into the open fermenter. The result is a dry, tart beer with intense and unusual yeast flavors. This lambic has black currants added to make it more palatable.

Flavors and aromas Unlike the other two Lindeman's we tasted, this one has more apparent lambic mustiness to it, which was a plus to some tasters and a minus for others. Nobody successfully identified the cassis element blind, but there is clear fruit character in the beer, along with definite acidity. Significantly less sugar here, too.

Design The swirling lines here have an elegant, Art Nouveau feel, like a casual Mucha doodle.

Lindemans Framboise

Sour Beer

Country Belgium **Style** Lambic **ABV** 4.0%
Producer Brouwerij Lindemans **Price** $$$$
Packaging 12oz/355ml, 25.4oz/750ml bottle
Characteristics Sour, unusual

To make sour lambic ales more palatable, they're frequently mixed with fruits. Sour cherries are the most traditional, but raspberries (framboise, in French) are not uncommon, and cassis, pear, and peach can also be found.

Flavors and aromas We'll say this about Lindeman's Framboise: there's no mistaking it for anything other than a raspberry beer. A nice big pink head and massive raspberry nose leads into a tangy-sweet palate. The tartness is nice and mouthwatering, but the overall effect is cartoonish. This presents more as a raspberry soda than a sour beer employing raspberries to take the edge off. It is, to be fair, a darn tasty raspberry soda.

Design Lindemans appears to be going for the champagne market with these elegant bottles, which lack only mushroom corks and wire cages to complete the effect.

Lindemans Kriek

Sour Beer

Country Belgium **Style** Lambic **ABV** 4.0%
Producer Brouwerij Lindemans **Price** $$$$
Packaging 12oz/355ml, 25.4oz/750ml bottle
Characteristics Sour, unusual

Kriek (Flemish for cherry) is an iconic style of beer from Belgium. Sour cherries are added after initial fermentation, and the sugar in the cherries ferments out. But some producers—including Lindemans—add sugar to take the edge off of the intense, dry tartness. If you like this style, you'll like this beer. But this is a very divisive beer that you also just might hate. For people who don't like fruity beer this could be a revelation that it doesn't have to be sweet. But some still might find the cherry cloying or synthetic.

Flavors and aromas Everyone found "cherry candy." Big synthetic tart-candy flavors develop into cough-syrup cherry. There's sourness here, but not nearly enough to find balance with the intense sweetness.

Design Lindemans has apparently decided on a "don't fix it if it's not broken approach"—these labels are identical but for the name and image of the fruit.

Löwenbräu Original

rating
7

Pale Lager

Country Germany **Style** Continental Lager **ABV** 5.2%
Producer Löwenbräu **Group** InBev **Price** $$
Packaging 12oz/355ml, 16.9oz/500ml bottle; 12oz/355ml can
Characteristics Bitter, malty, refreshing

Löwenbräu, or "Lion's Brew," is the most widely avilable Bavarian beer in America, but it's the least respected of the six major Munich breweries amongst Bavarians. It was ubiquitous in the United States during the 1980s, but that was under the regional production of Miller. In recent years, the Löwenbräu in North America has been exported from Munich.

Flavors and aromas This beer shows some sweet-smelling pilsner malt in the nose, along with a bit of skunkiness and very mild noble hops. The palate finds a reasonable balance of mild grainy malt and slightly spicy hops, with a bitterness that softly lingers into the finish. As this warms in the glass, the graininess of the malt and the bitterness of the hops become more pronounced.

Design If you need any convincing that Europeans don't really believe in green glass, the clash between the slightly teal label and the bottle color should settle things.

Magic Hat #9

Pale Ale

Country USA (VT) **Style** American Pale Ale **ABV** 5.1%
Producer Magic Hat Brewing Company **Price** $$
Packaging 12oz/355ml, 22oz/650ml bottle
Characteristics Refreshing, unusual

rating
5

Burlington, Vermont's Magic Hat Brewing, founded in 1994, has seen steady expansion and currently serves most of the East Coast, with a focus on light ales with low bitterness, like their flagship "not quite pale ale" #9.

Flavors and aromas This exceptionally light pale ale has more in common with some of the pale lagers we tasted than most of the pale ales, with minimal hop character and low bitterness in a very light palate, but the real crux of the matter here is that there is an apricot flavor which, given the light profile, has ample room to charm or annoy you. This is an introduction to hops for soda drinkers who crave that sweetness.

Design The label is the perfect meeting point between the psychedelic poster art of the late 1960s, and a colorblindness test at the optometrist's office.

Maredsous Brune

Belgian Ale

Country Belgium **Style** Dark Belgian Ale **ABV** 8.0%
Producer Duvel Moortgat **Price** $$$$
Packaging 11.2oz/330ml, 25.4oz/750ml bottle
Characteristics Malty, strong, yeasty

Maredsous is a Benedictine order in Belgium known—like Chimay—for beer and cheese. The cheeses are made at the abbey, but the beer is brewed by Duvel Moortgat under a 1963 arrangement.

Flavors and aromas The mahogany color of this beer suits the flavor profile, from the sherry, allspice, and warm dark caramel nose to the mild smoky roasted grain notes in the palate and dark dried fruits. There are hints of tobacco and wood and a soft background sourness, with moderately low carbonation for a Belgian-style ale. Drying alcohol and an oiliness to the mouthfeel kept this from really grabbing us.

Design The elegant hexagonal label is cool, in much the same way as Westmalle's new label. Are all the Belgians moving to classic geometric forms?

Maredsous Tripel

rating **8**

Belgian Ale

Country Belgium **Style** Pale Belgian Ale **ABV** 10.0%
Producer Duvel Moortgat **Price** $$$$
Packaging 11.2oz/330ml, 25.4oz/750ml bottle
Characteristics Malty, strong, unusual, yeasty

Maredsous's beers have recently been renamed. This tripel was formerly known as Maredsous 10—many Belgian abbey breweries use numbering systems of varying sorts; here it's the ABV of the beer—and the Brune was Maredsous 8.

Flavors and aromas Modest esters on the nose share space with a floral-spice perfume. The palate has mild cider vinegar, fruity flavors, and some alcoholic heat, before dry spices (allspice, perhaps) and mild bitterness clean things up. Not entirely typical, but the flavors come together in interesting, subtle ways, and our tasters were pleased.

Design If that bottle shape looks familiar, it's probably because it's the same distinctive bottle used for Duvel.

Maudite

Belgian Ale

Country Canada (QC) **Style** Dark Belgian Ale **ABV** 9.0%
Producer Unibroue **Group** Sapporo **Price** $$$$
Packaging 12oz/355ml, 22oz/650ml bottle
Characteristics Malty, sour, strong, unusual, yeasty

Maudite ("the Damned") was the second Unibroue beer produced. It pitches itself as one of the strongest beers in the world. We don't know how many people drink it for that reason, but we found more than just the alcohol.

Flavors and aromas Big mixed fruity esters are the primary notes here with some spiciness as well. This isn't nearly as dark as the color suggests, but it's very well balanced and less sweet than Fin du Monde or Don de Dieu. One taster not generally crazy about Belgians demanded a plate of mussels and fries to go with this, declaring this beer "crisp, classic, and perfect." We didn't all hold it at that level, but clearly Unibroue is on to something here.

Design The vaguely hellish scene depicted on the bottle represents the Québécois Legend of the Flying Canoe, a story about the perils of invoking the devil when you miss your family.

Mendocino Red Tail Ale

Pale Ale

Country USA (CA) **Style** American Pale Ale **ABV** 6.0%
Producer Mendocino Brewing Company **Group** United Breweries
Group **Price** $$ **Packaging** 12oz/355ml, 22oz/650ml bottle
Characteristics Hoppy

Mendocino Brewing, under its original name (Hopland), was the country's second post-Prohibition brewpub. Their flagship Red Tail Ale has been a brewery staple since they opened, though early bottlings were limited to 1.5L bottles. Nowadays, Mendocino Brewing is holding up its image as the champion for alternative lifestyles: we once saw the brewer pouring draught beer at Burning Man.

Flavors and aromas Our tasters were split between those who liked the piney hops and mild bitterness of this light-bodied ale, and those who found it to lack substance and heft. It's worth a try just for a taste of craft beer history, though.

Design We like the concept here, but the hawk image is busy and visually confusing.

Michelob AmberBock

Amber Lager

Country USA (MO) **Style** American Bock **ABV** 5.2%
Producer Anheuser-Busch **Price** $
Packaging 7oz/207ml, 12oz/355ml, 24oz/710ml bottle;
12oz/355ml, 16oz/473ml can **Characteristics** Malty, refreshing

Michelob drinkers comprise the most sophisticated segment that Anheuser-Busch has ever tried to appeal to. Many current offerings are "ultra-light", like Michelob Ultra and Michelob Ultra Light, but Michelob makes more traditional styles and some ales, as well, with AmberBock being the most widely available of these.

Flavors and aromas Pale lager fans have little to fear here; while AmberBock is darker than most of its sibling beers, it's through a very small addition of black patent malt that contributes almost no flavor. There's a wee hint of caramel, but mostly this is a clean, fresh lager, with very low hop character. Our panel, while not unanimous, generally liked it.

Design The retro-styled label here is a touch generic, but it's appropriate (the brand dates back to 1896) and we like it. Plus they've used brown glass, a rare treat for large-production domestics.

Michelob Light

Pale Lager

Country USA (MO) **Style** Light Beer **ABV** 4.3%
Producer Anheuser-Busch **Price** $
Packaging 12oz/355ml bottle; 12oz/355ml, 16oz/473ml can
Characteristics Bland

Anheuser-Busch's Michelob Light was introduced in 1978, the second response to the huge success of Miller Lite (after 1977's Natural Light). Bud Light came later, in 1982, when it became clear that the other brands were not having the desired effect on the market.

Flavors and aromas Producers of light beer (and near-beer) are faced with a difficult decision: to try to emulate full-strength beers, or to try to create a product that goes its own minimalist way. Neither approach is easy. Our panelists approved of Bud Light for taking the latter approach, but were less thrilled with Michelob Light, which aspires to taste like a full-strength lager, but comes across as a weak wannabe. Bland and uninspired.

Design The modern Michelob "teardrop" bottle is a pale imitation of the lava-lamp-shaped 1970s version, and we're not impressed.

Michelob Original Lager

Pale Lager

Country USA (MO) **Style** Continental Lager **ABV** 5.0%
Producer Anheuser-Busch **Price** $
Packaging 7oz/207ml, 12oz/355ml bottle; 12oz/355ml can
Characteristics Refreshing

Anheuser-Busch makes a tremendous number of lagers that are variations on the same few themes, but Michelob stands out by virtue of its all-barley grain bill. This is also the label under which AB brewers make a number of almost-craft ales and lagers.

Flavors and aromas It might be some work to convince our panel that this beer truly is "ultra-premium," but that's not to say that it was without appeal. A light nose is slightly sweet, as is the palate, but gentle carbonation and mild hop bitterness elevate this into a pleasant state of balance. It's a surprisingly subtle brew that has more in common with Czechvar than Budweiser.

Design The current label is a bit on the generic-craft-beer side, but we're really not sad to see the disappearance of the old teardrop-shaped bottles, which remind us of fizzy wine coolers.

Michelob Ultra

Pale Lager

Country USA (MO) **Style** Light Beer **ABV** 4.2%
Producer Anheuser-Busch **Price** $
Packaging 12oz/355ml, 16oz/473ml bottle; 10oz/296ml,
12oz/355ml, 16oz/473ml, 24oz/710ml can; 16oz/473ml aluminum
bottle **Characteristics** Refreshing

Michelob Ultra, a "low-carb" light lager, is everywhere these days, with high profile commercials featuring Tour de France winner Lance Armstrong. The irony here is that pro cyclists are usually looking for all the carbs they can get.

Flavors and aromas A very, very light beer, with a paper-thin aroma of green-apple acetaldehyde and essentially nothing else. The mouthfeel is strikingly similar to seltzer water, and fails to keep this from coming off as flat and dull. There are no hops here, and the malt has been completely consumed by yeast, leaving a dry, spritzy beverage with a faint resemblance to beer.

Design Ultra-low calories, ultra-low carbs, ultra-generic bottle. The big surprise here is the employment of brown glass, which is a plus.

Mickey's

Pale Lager

Country USA (WI) **Style** Malt Liquor **ABV** 5.6%
Producer SABMiller **Price** $
Packaging 12oz/355ml bottle; 16oz/473ml, 24oz/710ml,
32oz/946ml, 40oz/1.18L can **Characteristics** Malty

The "Green Hornet"—the 24oz
bottle offering of Mickey's—was a
popular and inexpensive drink
choice in our college days, but for
those who want a streamlined
drink, try the widemouth "Green
Grenade" 12oz bottle. Don't
forget to look for the rebus under
the cap.

Flavors and aromas Clearly
aimed at the post-high-school set,
Mickey's has a sweet nose, a sweet
aroma, and a sweet finish. There
does seem to be some evidence of
flavor hops, but bitterness is low,
carbonation is high, and there's a
slight graininess to the palate that
lingers into the finish and almost—
almost—outweighs the sweet
flavors.

Design You mostly see this in cans
these days, which don't carry quite
the elegance of the classic
Mickey's 40oz bottle.

Miller Chill

Pale Lager

Country USA (WI) **Style** Light Beer **ABV** 4.2%
Producer Miller Brewing Company **Group** SABMiller **Price** $
Packaging 12oz/355ml bottle
Characteristics Unusual

Miller introduced this chelada-flavored (lime and salt) light beer in 2007, but where Bud Light Lime was an immediate and lasting success, Miller Chill started strong before falling off. The formulation was revamped in 2009 to try to regain momentum.

Flavors and aromas Our tasters, experienced as they are in styles from around the world, were totally caught off-guard by this artificial-lime-flavored beer. The flavoring suggests lime more than actually resembling lime—two tasters noted that it smelled like Froot Loops—but the biggest criticism here is that it doesn't much resemble beer. It is, however, dry and crisp, with refreshing, lively carbonation.

Design The label looks like a lime. Too bad the beer doesn't particularly taste like lime.

Miller Genuine Draft

rating 6

Pale Lager

Country USA (WI) **Style** North American Lager **ABV** 4.7%
Producer Miller Brewing Company **Group** SABMiller **Price** $
Packaging 12oz/355ml, 22oz/650ml, 40oz/1.18L bottle;
12oz/355ml, 16oz/473ml can **Characteristics** Refreshing

MGD is a cold-filtered (rather than heat-pasteurized) version of Miller's High Life beer, developed in the mid-1980s as Miller started to lose its market edge with Miller Lite. A number of other breweries have produced "genuine draft" products, usually in cans aping Miller's, but none have achieved much success.

Flavors and aromas An airy, light nose has hints of cidery sweetness and little else. A faint corn flavor and graham cracker sweetness make up the bulk of this light, soft palate, with medium carbonation. This is bland and inoffensive, with no signs of hop bitterness or flavor. Tasters slightly preferred this beer from can than bottle, but they were not terribly different.

Design Miller's beer is theoretically unskunkable, allowing us to forgive them slightly for the use of clear glass. But we still don't think it looks good.

Miller High Life

Pale Lager

rating 5

Country USA (WI) **Style** North American Lager **ABV** 5.0%
Producer Miller Brewing Company **Group** SABMiller **Price** $
Packaging 12oz/355ml bottle; 12oz/355ml, 16oz/473ml can
Characteristics Bland

The Champagne of Beers is an epic, evocative slogan—certainly better than the more literal A Gassy, Carbonated Beer. Introduced in 1903, High Life was consigned for the last few decades to the nostalgia beer bin, during which Miller Lite rose to become one of the country's best-selling beers, but the recent "Take Back the High Life" campaign has reestablished the brand.

Flavors and aromas It seems that this beer would best live on in reprints of old advertisements, forever young, fresh, and Champagne-esque. We found it to be flat and lifeless, with the merest hint of citrus/lemon hop character differentiating it from an army of less-expensive budget lagers.

Design The packaging here is stuck in the 1950s—though we're pleased that it includes the most joyously silly slogan in the industry—which seems fitting, since the bland flavor seems to come from the same era.

Miller Lite

rating
4

Pale Lager

Country USA (WI) **Style** Light Beer **ABV** 4.2%
Producer Miller Brewing Company **Group** SABMiller **Price** $
Packaging 7oz/207ml, 12oz/355ml, 16oz/473ml, 40oz/1.18L
bottle; 12oz/355ml, 16oz/473ml can **Characteristics** Bland

Miller Lite was the first light-as-in-low-calories beer, and ushered us all into a new world where drinking thin, low-calorie beers was a sign of macho virility—an age that continues to this day, if the Super Bowl is any indication. While you may have mixed feelings about the conscious misspelling of the name, you'll probably admit that it's better than the original: Gablinger's Diet Beer.

Flavors and aromas Yeast esters dominate what little there is to the nose of this beer—one taster identified bubblegum, another banana—in an otherwise unremarkable light lager with a slight touch of bitterness. In a style that's all about showing off clean and refreshing flavors, the esters were out of place and off-putting.

Design It's sort of surreal that any company can own a common misspelling to the degree that Miller owns "Lite". They've built the label around it. Strunk and White would be appalled.

Modelo Especial

Pale Lager

Country Mexico **Style** North American Lager **ABV** 4.4%
Producer Grupo Modelo **Price** $
Packaging 12oz/355ml bottle; 12oz/355ml, 24oz/710ml can
Characteristics Bland

The pale sibling of dark lager Negra Modelo is the third-best-selling import in the US (behind Heineken and Corona Extra). And it's the unsung champion of Mexican beers, especially in Mexico, where it's more popular than Corona and on equal footing with Dos Equis. It's the workhorse of the Mexican beer industry.

Flavors and aromas Our panel found Modelo Especial to be less than totally Especial. A very light nose of almost nothing at all leads into a light palate, faintly sweet, with some corn flavor to the malt. Bitterness is nearly undetectable. At the back of the tongue we were left with a slight numbing tingle that suggests a touch of chlorophenol. But mostly there's an exaggerated lack of of flavor here.

Design An intriguing bottle shape holds our attention, and the label is interesting, but as always, clear glass is a major turnoff to fresh beer lovers.

Molson Canadian

Pale Lager

Country Canada (ON) **Style** North American Lager **ABV** 5.0%
Producer Molson Coors **Price** $
Packaging 12oz/355ml bottle; 12oz/355ml can
Characteristics Refreshing

Montreal's Molson is the oldest brewery in North America, founded in 1786. Flagship brand Molson Canadian has tried to define itself as the quintessential Canadian beer, and in 2009, Molson family members bought the Montreal Canadiens hockey team.

Flavors and aromas The nose is light and airy, with mild hops and clean pilsner malt. The flavor is sweet, with pleasant corn flavors, bright carbonation, and low hop character. The finish is lightly floral and dry, and the whole thing is fresh and bright. There are no evident flaws here, and Molson Canadian might be the best domestic-style lager we tasted. It's all about light, sweet malt and carbon dioxide lift, and nothing in this beer intrudes.

Design The alternating colors are decidedly circusy, but there's a good old-fashioned Canadian earnestness that we can't help but like.

Moretti

Pale Lager

Country Italy **Style** Continental Lager **ABV** 4.6%
Producer Birra Moretti **Group** Heineken **Price** $$
Packaging 11.2oz/330ml, 22.3oz/660ml bottle; 11.2oz/330ml can
Characteristics Malty, refreshing

Italian beer has a bad rap, but the basic profile of standard Italian imports makes some sense—light, German-styled lagers that tone down malt intensity fit the warmer climate of Mediterranean Italy. Moretti, interestingly, is not commonly found in Italy; it's way more prevalent in the US.

Flavors and aromas Birra Moretti went over well with our tasters, with its full-bodied nose of malt and light caramel, and a light, refreshingly crisp palate that features just enough bitterness to keep it clean and dry. There's no soda sweetness here, and it would be easy to drink several of these without getting palate fatigue.

Design The label is fairly German in its restrained, uncluttered approach. We wonder if the gentleman depicted is supposed to be Italian, Bavarian, or just a dude with a beer.

Murphy's Stout

Dark Ale

Country Ireland **Style** Stout **ABV** 4.0%
Producer Murphy's Brewery **Group** Heineken **Price** $$
Packaging 12oz bottle; 16oz/473ml can
Characteristics Roasty

Murphy's Irish Stout has been around since 1856. The Murphy's Brewery was largely a regional brewer before being bought by Heineken in 1983. Cans read "Murphy's Stout," and we suspect the omission of the word "Irish" is because the beer was actually brewed in Scotland.

Flavors and aromas Two cans yielded strikingly different results. The first was fiercely smoky, in both the nose and palate. The second tempered that to diacetyl and ashy, burnt coffee notes in the nose. In both samples, a light, thin palate was roasty, dry, and notably watery. The roast flavor lingers on into the finish. While the absence of smoke in the second can was a relief, this still struck us as a beer with issues.

Design A simple and clean design, with lots of nice white space, and an excellent, subtle, parabolic swoop of a separator.

Natural Ice

rating 4

Pale Lager

Country USA (MO) **Style** North American Lager **ABV** 5.9%
Producer Anheuser-Busch **Price** $
Packaging 12oz/355ml, 22oz/650ml, 32oz/946ml bottle; 12oz,
16oz, 24oz, 40oz can **Characteristics** Bland

1995 saw Anheuser-Busch fully commit to the ice beer phenomenon, following up Bud Ice and Bud Light Ice with both of their value brands: Natural Ice and Busch Ice.

Flavors and aromas A thin, estery nose reminded one taster of white wine. The palate is lightly grainy, but doesn't have much more flavor. There's a tiny hint of bitterness, which doesn't really go anywhere, and a total lack of flavor hops. The carbonation leads to an impression of beer-flavored mineral water, and at least one taster was convinced that this was light beer. We'd avoid it.

Design Most of the elements of the label are made of ice, but you can't really tell it apart from stone. Could "stone beer" be the next fad beer?

Natural Light

Pale Lager

Country USA (MO) **Style** Light Beer **ABV** 4.2%
Producer Anheuser-Busch **Price** $
Packaging 12oz/355ml, 22oz/650ml, 32oz/946ml bottle; 12oz,
16oz, 24oz can **Characteristics** Refreshing

Natural Light is the best-selling sub-premium (read: cheap) beer in the United States, but you're probably more likely to end up with one in hand if you ask for it by its frat-party nickname, Natty Light. Natural Ice's distinction is that it's the beer most commonly seen in the US in a 24-pack being hauled out of a package store with a lenient carding policy by a college freshman.

Flavors and aromas This had more flavor than we expected. There's graham-cracker malt, and a faint touch of aroma hops. It's not great, but at this price point, we're not sure that matters—as long as you're comfortable being spotted as a Natty Light drinker.

Design The abstract double-swoosh logo and the italic text swirling up the bottle seem to suggest something in a state of high velocity. Are they implying that this beer should be consumed quickly? We have little doubt that it often is.

Negra Modelo

Amber Lager

Country Mexico **Style** Vienna Lager **ABV** 5.4%
Producer Grupo Modelo **Price** $$
Packaging 12oz/355ml bottle
Characteristics Malty

This is often the favorite or most prestigious beer according to Mexican-beer snobs in the US, but we think Mexico executes better on its classic pale lager style than on dark beer; if you want something in the style of Negra Modelo, there are many better beers. And "Vienna Lager"? It's an increasingly rare style developed in Austria in the mid-19th century and brought to Mexico by German immigrants.

Flavors and aromas This beer stands out among its Mexican peers, with its full body of caramel and slight roasted notes and light bitterness. But the aromas and flavors here are probably too light to appeal to ale drinkers accustomed to full-bodied dark beers. Still, we appreciate that this is not another pale German lager.

Design The gold foil is rather liberally applied here, but the bottle shape is distinctive and nice, and they've chosen the correct glass for packaging beer.

New Belgium 1554

Dark Belgian Ale

Country USA (CO) **ABV** 5.5%
Producer New Belgium Brewing **Price** $$
Packaging 12oz/355ml, 22oz/650ml bottle
Characteristics Malty, roasty, unusual

NB's website claims that this "enlightened black ale" is brewed with a "light lager yeast," so we're unsure why it's called an ale. It's based on an antiquated recipe, and it's worth remembering that most of what we think of today as Belgian-beer character is the product of the last century of brewing.

Flavors and aromas This beer has "black" character in the form of bright roast coffee, but low esters and minimal hop character mean there's little balance for an intense sweetness akin to a milk stout. At lower temperatures, the sweet character is probably less pronounced, giving this beer a good shot at seeming full-bodied and flavorful even at refrigerator temperatures.

Design Is this black ale "enlightened" because it's reading a book? It seems like that's what is being portrayed here. Or perhaps it's reading a book because it's enlightened.

New Belgium Abbey Ale

rating
7

Belgian Ale

Country USA (CO) **Style** Dark Belgian Ale **ABV** 7.0%
Producer New Belgium Brewing **Price** $$
Packaging 12oz/355ml bottle
Characteristics Bitter, roasty, unusual, yeasty

New Belgium's Abbey Ale is, like Fat Tire, based on one of founder Jeff Lebesch's homebrew recipes, though these days the brewhouse is helmed by authentic Belgian Peter Bouckaert.

Flavors and aromas New Belgium's Abbey Ale is Belgian-lite, with subtle banana esters as the main nod to Old World monasteries. Roast grains offer coffee notes and there's perceptible hop bitterness. The end result is a beer that's adequately drinkable, but that reads more like an American brown ale with some extra yeast-influenced kick.

Design A new design for Abbey ale hit shelves at press time. The new labels are clean, bold, and look nothing like the bottles we sampled.

New Belgium Fat Tire

rating
4

Pale Ale

Country USA (CO) **Style** American Amber Ale **ABV** 5.2%
Producer New Belgium Brewing **Price** $$
Packaging 12oz/355ml, 22oz/650ml bottle; 12oz/355ml can
Characteristics Malty

Colorado is home to dozens of breweries, most notably Coors and Fort Collins' bicycle-obsessed New Belgium, which will be a familiar sight to any reader cruising the micros section of the local grocery store.

Flavors and aromas New Belgium is clearly capable of producing some fine, unique beers, but we found their flagship Fat Tire, with its intense hop character of sharp grapefruit and pineapple, to be charmless and thin. Stick to the smaller-production offerings to find the charm and potential that New Belgium has to offer.

Design Our favorite part of this beer, without a doubt, is the classic cruiser, lovingly parked on a path in the woods. Beer picnic?

Newcastle Brown Ale

Brown Ale

Country England **ABV** 4.7%
Producer Heineken **Price** $$
Packaging 12oz/355ml, 18.6oz/550ml, 20oz/590ml bottle
Characteristics Malty, refreshing

Newcastle Brown seems to serve as every college student's first introduction to British beer. It's not our favorite version of the style—it's thinner than English ale at its best. But whatever they're doing business-wise, it seems to be working.

Flavors and aromas Light caramel and toasted malt form the centerpiece of this somewhat divisive beer, which split tasters between those who found this to be a light, pleasant beer and those who thought it thin and empty. One pleasantly missing item was a skunky aroma, which used to plague Newcastle's clear bottles. This beer may fall into the same too-light-for-some-too-heavy-for-others hole as Negra Modelo.

Design The distinctive blue-star logo and embossed glass bottle ("The One and Only") make this easy to spot on store shelves and bar signs, though there are many, many imitators out there.

North Coast Old Rasputin

rating
9

Strong Beer

Country USA (CA) **Style** Imperial Stout **ABV** 9.0%
Producer North Coast Brewing Company **Price** $$$
Packaging 12oz/355ml bottle
Characteristics Bitter, malty, roasty, strong

No doubt it's the water that makes Mendocino County home to a host of fine breweries, but we can't help but wonder if there's something else to it.

Flavors and aromas Our tasters raved about this beer, particularly the nose, with its warm sweet balance of roasty and caramel elements. The complex interplay of aromas is matched by the palate, which is velvety and smooth. The high alcohol content is surprisingly well hidden, but make no mistake: Old Rasputin packs a wallop.

Design This beer is hypnotic, dark, and deep, and the name and package reflect that almost perfectly. Just looking at this beer makes us feel a bit wobbly.

North Coast Old Stock Ale

Strong Beer

Country USA (CA) **Style** Strong Ale **ABV** 12.5%
Producer North Coast Brewing Company **Price** $$$$
Packaging 12oz/355ml bottle
Characteristics Bitter, malty, strong, unusual

This beer is vintage dated (ours were from 2009) to reflect North Coast's desire that they be aged— a growing trend that has both support and opposition in the beer world. In our experience, some beers really do improve with age, but as with wine, it's not a given.

Flavors and aromas This high-complexity ale got good marks from our tasters even though some of them found flavors and aromas that they didn't like. Spicy cola or sassafras and dark fruits lead into earthy flavors and sweet, syrupy notes in the palate balanced with subtle bitterness and alcohol. Tasters were least pleased by the aftertaste, which they found unappealing. North Coast recommends aging this beer; if the sweetness died down, this could be really special.

Design A nicely minimalist label shows off the pertinent info: the name of the beer, the vintage date, and North Coast's attractive logo.

O'Doul's

rating
5

Pale Lager

Country USA (MO) **Style** Non-alcoholic **ABV** 0.5%
Producer Anheuser-Busch **Price** $
Packaging 12oz/355ml bottle; 12oz/355ml can
Characteristics Refreshing

Nonalcoholic beer has never taken off in the US and Canada in the way it has in Europe, but Anheuser-Busch's O'Douls still seems to be going strong. There's also an amber version.

Flavors and aromas O'Douls is clearly in the mode of a light American lager, but it's not a bad one at that, and none of our tasters guessed that it was non-alcoholic. Faint hops and malt behind mild skunkiness lead into a typically thin, dry palate. Lightly bready, crisp and dry, with faint floral notes, this finishes with a touch of astringency, but it's basically a clean, refreshing, light lager.

Design A blandly green label and a boringly conventional oval label help encourage others to politely ignore the bottle in your hand.

Old Speckled Hen

Pale Ale

rating
7

Country England **Style** English Pale Ale **ABV** 5.2%
Producer Greene King **Price** $$
Packaging 12oz/355ml bottle; 14.9oz/440ml can
Characteristics Bitter, malty

Old Speckled Hen's recipe and octagonal label are a 1979 tribute to the MG auto factory in Abingdon, England, which was celebrating its 50th birthday. After the auto factory moved away the next year, the brand nearly died off, but today it's in wide distribution.

Flavors and aromas A creamy nitro pour and unmistakable English malt nose set the stage for a light-bodied, slightly thin beer with ample hop bitterness. Some of our tasters enjoyed this, while others were put off by the buttery diacetyl aroma common to northern English yeast strains. This might be a good beer to test your diacetyl sensitivity on—one in five drinkers cannot sense low or moderate levels of diacetyl.

Design The octagonal label on glass bottles is really attractive, but it's disconcerting to see a beer of this color in clear glass. The can design is busier and less appealing.

222   **THE BEER TRIALS**

Olde English 800

Pale Lager

Country USA (WI) **Style** North American Lager **ABV** 5.9%-8%
Producer SABMiller **Price** $
Packaging 22oz/650ml, 32oz/946ml, 40oz/1.18L bottle;
12oz/355ml, 16oz/473ml, 24oz/710ml can **Characteristics** Strong

Miller's high-gravity lager may be the most famous malt liquor out there. It comes in a variety of strengths, including, improbably, a 4.2% ABV version for states with strict limits on beer alcohol content. It's best drunk out of a brown paper bag.

Flavors and aromas A dense malt nose with corn and grainy aromas comes across as sweet and slightly musty. The palate is more open, but this is full-bodied and a bit heavy in the mouth. That's softened some by bright carbonation, but the full, sweet beer finishes heavy and with a hint of alcoholic bitterness. As this warms, the sweetness intensifies; it's hard to imagine drinking a lot of this, but with the high alcohol content, you wouldn't need to.

Design This label is like a worn-down rattrap of a casino in downtown Vegas, miles away from the strip, untouched since some cut-rate designer went to work on it in 1973.

Olympia

Pale Lager

Country USA (WI) **Style** North American Lager **ABV** 4.7%
Producer Pabst Brewing Company **Price** $
Packaging 12oz/355ml bottle; 12oz/355ml, 16oz/473ml can
Characteristics Refreshing

While they've retained the 1902 slogan "It's the Water," the sale of the brewery and its subsequent closure means that Olympia is no longer brewed with the water they were talking about—though to be fair, it does still seem to be mostly water.

Flavors and aromas This is an almost perfectly neutral American lager, with little flavor to recommend it, and little in the way of flaws to detract. A hint of skunkiness in the nose, some sweet malt, and modest carbonation describe nearly the entirety of the beer. The finish is dry, and clean, and if you have important things to do while you drink, you'll find that nothing here—save your increasing blood-alcohol content—will distract you from your task.

Design Vintage Olympia memorabilia suggests that this design hasn't changed much over the decades, and it retains an unforced, stately air.

Ommegang Abbey Ale

Belgian Ale

Country USA (NY) **Style** Dark Belgian Ale **ABV** 8.5%
Producer Brewery Ommegang **Group** Duvel Moortgat **Price** $$$
Packaging 12oz/355ml, 25.6oz/750ml bottle
Characteristics Malty, strong, unusual, yeasty

Ommegang was founded in 1997 on a former hop farm outside Cooperstown, New York—home of the baseball hall of fame—brewing Belgian-style ales. Just six years later, they were purchased by the Belgian brewery Duvel Moortgat, which strikes us as the highest compliment a Belgian brewer can pay to an American.

Flavors and aromas Our tasters pulled cider, licorice, English-character malt, and alcohol out of the nose. Esters are restrained. The palate is full and fruity, with dark caramelized sugars, prune and raisin notes, and a hint of port wine. Mild bitterness and alcohol keep the lingering finish dry. One taster wrote that it "smells like the set of a Peter Greenway film."

Design We're unclear about what makes a Belgian Abbey ale "burgundian." Though, now that we think of it, a glass of Burgundy sounds lovely.

Oskar Blues Mama's Little Yella

rating
7

Pale Lager

Country USA (CO) **Style** Pilsner **ABV** 5.3%
Producer Oskar Blues **Price** $$
Packaging 12oz/355ml can
Characteristics Bitter, refreshing

Oskar Blues was originally a brewpub and blues club—well, it still is—and we wonder how they got by until 2009 serving barbecue without an easy-drinking pilsner to seal the deal.

Flavors and aromas This starts off promising, with good hop aroma and light malt, but there's a touch of skunkiness that in theory has no place in a canned beer. A smooth mouthfeel, slightly creamy, has a light body with a bit of hop flavor and modest bitterness that lingers into the finish. In short, it's a domestic lager—in a can, no less—that aspires to European ideals without pushing too hard.

Design The name of this beer is the kind of pun that makes us grit our teeth a little, but the beer inside helps ease the pain.

Oskar Blues Old Chub

rating 8

Pale Ale

Country USA (CO) **Style** Scottish Ale **ABV** 8.0%
Producer Oskar Blues **Price** $$
Packaging 12oz/355ml can
Characteristics Malty, roasty, strong, unusual, yeasty

Oskar Blues is pushing the envelope of canned beer—while the number of canned craft beers seems to be accelerating, we're not aware of other brewers who are canning strong beers like the Old Chub or the 10.5% ABV Ten Fiddy Imperial stout.

Flavors and aromas A complex sassafras and cinnamon nose has lightly roasted grain notes. Bright flavors here include lively fruitiness and acidity, as well as toasted and roasty notes. Medium full body is malty; some tasters found it sweet. Carbonation is low, which bothered some, but the alcohol and moderate hop bitterness (too much to be authentically Scottish) tame the malt in the finish.

Design All of Oskar Blues' cans have essentially the same design, with a different set of bright, high contrast colors.

Otter Creek Copper Ale

Pale Ale

Country USA (VT) **Style** Alt **ABV** 5.4%
Producer Otter Creek Brewing **Price** $$
Packaging 12oz/355ml bottle
Characteristics Refreshing

Otter Creek Copper Ale was the brewery's first beer in 1991. The Vermont microbrewery's alt-style ale uses a surprising six different malts, and still serves as their flagship beer.

Flavors and aromas Mild malt, low hop aroma, and some fruity esters show up in the aroma of this beer. The palate is fruity, slightly sweet, and has a bit of a beer-seltzer effervescence to it. Bitterness is low, and the product as a whole lacks definition or interest. Our first bottle of this was significantly oxidized; we didn't notice a stale character to this one, but it would be nice to discover that there's more here than what we found.

Design Giant lettering accentuated with a drop shadow nearly obscures a pretty nice little drawing of a brewery on a waterfall. It's like they don't want us looking at the picture.

Pabst Blue Ribbon

Pale Lager

Country USA (IL) **Style** North American Lager **ABV** 4.7%
Producer Pabst Brewing Company **Price** $
Packaging 12oz/355ml, 40oz/1.18L bottle; 12oz/355ml,
16oz/473ml, 24oz/710ml can **Characteristics** Refreshing

Pabst is a classic example of a beer that through clever marketing managed to convert itself from a down-and-out US brand to the lifestyle drink of urban hipsters. The revolution seems to have started at Portland's Lutz Tavern in the early 2000s. For more on the retro-chic revivial of Pabst, read Edward McClelland's excellent article on salon.com.

Flavors and aromas We don't see this beer winning many more World's Fair prizes, but as a budget lager it holds its own in its price class, with perhaps a touch more hop character than similar offerings. It will doubtless remain a staple of "Dollar Pounder Nights" for years to come.

Design An iconic label, suitably simple, if a bit literal. The PBR label has changed little over the decades, but we're waiting for the reintroduction of the actual blue ribbon around the neck of each bottle.

Pacifico

Pale Lager

Country Mexico **Style** North American Lager **ABV** 4.4%
Producer Grupo Modelo **Price** $$
Packaging 12oz/355ml, 24oz/710ml bottle
Characteristics Refreshing

For the last 50 years, Pacifico has been brewed by Grupo Modelo, but a century ago it took its name from the ocean on which its hometown of Mazatlán—where it remains über popular—is located. It's the pride and joy of Sinaloa.

Flavors and aromas There was evidence that this beer was lightstruck, which speaks rather poorly to its provenance given that it's packaged in brown glass. There are also lemony noble hop flavors, nice bitterness, and a tinge of bitterness, leading to a soft, refreshing finish.

Design This is what Corona should look like. This is what every Mexican beer should look like, in fact. We approve.

Paulaner Hefe-Weizen

Wheat Beer

Country Germany **Style** Bavarian Hefeweizen **ABV** 5.5%
Producer Paulaner **Price** $$$
Packaging 16.9oz/500ml bottle
Characteristics Refreshing, yeasty

Paulaner's pale hefeweizen is its top-selling beer, out of about a dozen different bottlings. As is the norm with the major Munich breweries, they make beers in essentially every style associated with Bavaria.

Flavors and aromas A classic Bavarian hefeweizen, Paulaner Hefe showcases all of the yeast-produced flavors absent in the American rendition of the style. Clove and banana are big and forward in the nose, there's also lemon and bubblegum, and the palate is full, round, and soft, with clove spice and wheat suggesting spice cookies. The palate and finish are fairly dry, with beautifully lingering clove and other baking spice notes.

Design The monk in Paulaner's logo is looking kind of smug. We might, too, if we could make beer this good.

Paulaner Oktoberfest

Amber Lager

Country Germany **Style** Oktoberfest **ABV** 5.8%
Producer Paulaner **Price** $$
Packaging 12oz/355ml, 16.9oz/500ml bottle
Characteristics Malty, refreshing

Paulaner's export Oktoberfest is not the same as the one they serve in Munich at the 'fest itself. Ours is amber-colored (and labeled as such), while the native version follows the trend of increasingly golden Oktoberfest beers.

Flavors and aromas The clean, malty nose has fruitiness and nutty notes along with a hint of baking spices. The mouth features a precise, clean palate with light body. The balance of nutty flavors and fruity Munich malt is more careful here than the other Oktoberfests we tasted, but the intensity is less, as well. The finish has a touch of crisp bitterness and nice malt; some tasters liked it, and others thought it overwhelmed the delicate palate.

Design An army of beer servers, loaded down with the ammunition of their trade, present an inspiring scene here.

Paulaner Premium Pils

Pale Lager

Country Germany **Style** Pilsner **ABV** 4.9%
Producer Paulaner **Price** $$
Packaging 12oz/355ml bottle
Characteristics Bitter, hoppy

Paulaner's Bavarian pils is a classic example of the style, and the brewery wants to remind you that while pilsner was first brewed in Bohemia, it was a Bavarian brewer—Josef Groll—at the helm.

Flavors and aromas This intensely bitter pale lager is striking; there are very few out there that put so much emphasis on bitterness. There are also noble hops to be found here in the nose and the mouth, and some sweet malt. But mostly this beer offers bitterness, early and often. We suspect that more craft beer fans would drink lagers if they all tasted like this. We also suspect that many Bud Light fans would give up beer altogether if that were the case.

Design This is like some weird alcoholic mullet: stern German lettering on top and faux-classy Burgundy script on the bottom.

Paulaner Salvator

rating
8

Strong Beer

Country Germany **Style** Doppelbock **ABV** 7.9%
Producer Paulaner **Price** $$$
Packaging 12oz/355ml, 16.9oz/500ml bottle
Characteristics Malty, strong, unusual

Before doppelbock was thought of and named as a double-strength version of bock beer, the style was called Salvator, after the original version developed by the Paulaner monks nearly 400 years ago to be a filling, nourishing beer to consume during religious fasting.

Flavors and aromas One of our two samples of Salvator seems to have undergone some oxidation, with honey and sake notes. A second bottle was much fresher, showing lots of spices, dried fruits, and alcohol in the nose. The heart of this beer, though, is the deep, dark fruit/caramel notes which have both a density and a clarity that points to the single-minded approach to doppelbock flavor—long boils to caramelize and reduce a lot of light grain to a dark, dense beer.

Design There's something deeply licentious about the scene depicted here. We'll say no more.

Peroni Nastro Azzurro

Pale Lager

Country Italy **Style** Continental Lager **ABV** 5.1%
Producer Birra Peroni **Group** SABMiller **Price** $$
Packaging 12oz/355ml bottle
Characteristics Bitter, refreshing

"Nastro Azzurro" is Italian for "blue ribbon," and this lager is the premium product of Italy's largest brewery, though the regular Peroni Lager sells more beer in Italy. In 2005 Peroni became part of the SABMiller empire.

Flavors and aromas Peroni is built like a warm-climate German pilsner, from the noble hops, light cooked-corn malt, and, yes, slight skunkiness of the nose, to the palate, which starts out with light-bodied malt and bitterness that starts crisp and grows increasingly focused. Here, however, the light body is hard-pressed to take the edge off the hops, and there's a harshness that can register as astringent or metallic.

Design Points for the simple, bold color scheme and pared-down text. Not so much for the green glass.

Pike Kilt Lifter

Pale Ale

Country USA (WA) **Style** Scottish Ale **ABV** 6.5%
Producer Pike Brewing Company **Price** $$
Packaging 12oz/355ml, 22oz/650ml bottle
Characteristics Malty, unusual

In Scotland, beers are sometimes brewed with water that has been filtered through peat, giving it a hint of peat not unlike that found in some Scotch whisky. Other brewers sometimes simulate this with a small measure of barley kilned over a peat fire—like Seattle's Pike Kilt Lifter.

Flavors and aromas Our first sample of Kilt Lifter was loaded with peaty phenolics, which one taster (not knowing that he was tasting a Scottish ale) took to be Brett spoilage. A second bottle was much tamer, and more to our liking—a little peat goes a long way. There's rich caramel here, a little on the dark side, and more bitterness than is probably typical in Edinburgh, but not enough to upset the balance.

Design If you've seen one Pike Street label, you've seen them all, but who cares? This is one of the best faux-retro designs in the book—lively, without being busy.

Pike Pale

Pale Ale

Country USA (WA) **Style** English Pale Ale **ABV** 5.0%
Producer Pike Brewing Company **Price** $$
Packaging 12oz/355ml, 22oz/650ml bottle
Characteristics Bitter, malty

Pike Pale is a "heritage amber ale," which we read as code for "somewhat English in style." That's a fair description of the beer to us.

Flavors and aromas A rich malty nose and low, effervescent carbonation hint that this beer is from England, but there are some resiny hops in there as well. The palate is malty and crisp, with a bubbly bitterness that sneaks just past being balanced. It's a well-built ESB that straddles two brewing traditions with ease and grace.

Design The subtle way the rays break out of the center diamond and into the background is an elegant touch in a fine design.

Pilsner Urquell

rating
6

Pale Lager

Country Czech Republic **Style** Pilsner **ABV** 4.4%
Producer Plzensky Prazdroj **Group** SABMiller **Price** $$
Packaging 12oz/355ml bottle; 12oz/355ml can
Characteristics Bitter, refreshing

Pilsner Urquell—Czech for "original pilsner"—was first brewed in 1842, and the beer world hasn't been the same since. Judging by world production, the novelty of pale, clean, light beers still hasn't quite worn off.

Flavors and aromas The traditional light-skunk/noble hop combo came out here, giving this a generally bright nose, with some milder cooked corn notes. The palate has lightstruck notes, with very mild malt sweetness, and crisp hops are stronger than standard Continental lagers like Becks or Heineken without quite reaching the intensity of a Bavarian pils. Finish is lingeringly bitter and our tasters felt it overwhelmed the malt.

Design Okay, we admit it. The green glass looks very nice here, with the clean white space and red seal device. But we can't enjoy liking it.

Pyramid Haywire

Wheat Beer

Country USA (WA) **Style** American Wheat Beer **ABV** 5.2%
Producer Pyramid Brewery **Group** Magic Hat Brewing **Price** $$
Packaging 12oz/355ml bottle
Characteristics Refreshing

Pyramid isn't the flashiest craft
brewery around these days, but it
is one of the largest. The Brewer's
Association estimated that in
2009, Pyramid was the 5th largest
craft brewery in the US. That's a lot
of hefeweizen.

Flavors and aromas We won't
mistake this for a traditional
hefeweizen anytime soon, but
there's some charm here. Light
wheat and floral aromas with a
hint of fresh cider or lemon juice
introduce a light-bodied, slightly
fruity ale with a slightly grainy
texture. Carbonation is relatively
low for a wheat beer, but the
mouthfeel is nice. The finish has
mild fruitiness and wheat and
seems slightly sweet. Drink cool on
a hot day to maximize enjoyment.

Design So the blue guy is rock
climbing, and there's San Francisco
in the background, and a runner...
no, sorry, we don't get it either.
Reject label for a sports drink?

Pyramid Thunderhead IPA

India Pale Ale

Country USA (WA) **ABV** 6.7%
Producer Pyramid Brewery **Group** Magic Hat Brewing **Price** $$
Packaging 12oz/355ml, 22oz/650ml bottle
Characteristics Bitter, unusual, yeasty

Pyramid's origins are in small town Washington state, where they came to prominence with Apricot Ale, but today they operate pubs from Seattle to Sacramento.

Flavors and aromas Yeast character is a rare player in American presentations of beer. But when it does show up, it's less often a sign of enlightenment or appeals to tradition as a sign of unanticipated hot fermentations. We were unclear which was the case with our sample of Pyramid Thunderhead IPA, with a nose dominated by fruity esters. In the mouth, this beer showed a lingering bitterness and low malt character, along with more yeast flavors. Our panel split on whether this was an intriguing evolution or a less-than-stellar development.

Design The recent redesign of Pyramid's brands features quasi-extreme sports (like downhill skiing) performed against a backdrop of Egyptian pyramids. Odd.

Rainier Beer

Pale Lager

Country USA (IL) **Style** North American Lager **ABV** 4.7%
Producer Pabst Brewing Company **Price** $
Packaging 16oz/473ml can
Characteristics Refreshing

In the 1970s and '80s—generally a fairly lowbrow era for beer advertising, all things considered—Rainier had quirky, surreal spots, featuring herds of longneck bottles roaming the Northwest, or lonely motorcycles singing the brand name. Now it's another dying brand in the Pabst stable.

Flavors and aromas A generically off-brand lager profile was what our panel found. Light, sweet malt, with mild fruity esters in the nose and no evident hops resolve into a blandly inoffensive palate and a short, reasonably dry finish. Nothing to get terribly bothered about except the lack of anything to get excited about.

Design There's a lot of nostalgia bound up in that big stylized "R", and the use of the mountain is nicely subtle. One of the better cheap beer designs.

Red Seal Ale

Pale Ale

rating
8

Country USA (CA) **Style** American Amber Ale **ABV** 5.5%
Producer North Coast Brewing Company **Price** $$$
Packaging 12oz/355ml bottle
Characteristics Bitter, hoppy, refreshing

Mendocino County, California, has fewer than 100,000 residents, but boasts three microbreweries of international stature: Mendocino Brewing, Anderson Valley, and North Coast. In our view, any county would be fortunate to have one of those fine establishments.

Flavors and aromas Our tasters were torn. Was Red Seal Ale good? Or was it excellent? You'll have to play decision-maker here, but with ample hops in the nose and body, the malt has plenty of room to play. The citrusy hops have a fresh, almost minty character, and all tasters agreed that this was refreshing, complete beer. We doubt you'll find your task to be arduous.

Design The label features a seal, which is unmistakably red. How could we find fault here?

Red Stripe

Pale Lager

Country Jamaica **Style** North American Lager **ABV** 4.7%
Producer Desnoes & Geddes **Group** Diageo **Price** $
Packaging 12oz/355ml, 24oz/710ml bottle; 16.4oz/485ml can
Characteristics Refreshing

Red Stripe Lager—likely the only
Jamaican beer you've ever heard
of—has been around since the
1950s, but only achieved
significant popularity in the US in
the last two decades, after
Guinness purchased the brand.

Flavors and aromas Our first
bottle of Red Stripe showed
butterscotch in the nose—a
serious flaw in a pale lager—but
the second was clear of it. What
both bottles were also clear of was
much in the way of other flavors.
Tasters identified subtle esters, a
slightly sweet palate, and a total
lack of hop character. This isn't
exactly watery, and might qualify
as refreshing in the right
circumstances, but there's very
little in the way of character or
flavor.

Design It's clean, it's iconic, and it
reminds us of that series of
literalist interpretations of old
music videos on YouTube.

Redhook ESB

Pale Ale

rating 7

Country USA (WA) **Style** American ESB **ABV** 5.8%
Producer Redhook Ale Brewery **Group** Craft Brewers Alliance
Price $$ **Packaging** 12oz/355ml bottle
Characteristics Bitter, malty

Redhook was founded in 1981 in the quirky Seattle neighborhood of Fremont, but its first efforts—estery, Belgian-influenced beers—didn't get it very far. It wasn't until 1987 that Redhook ESB was introduced, and it's now their best-selling beer.

Flavors and aromas Mild honey and nutty notes with ample caramel frame the nose. In the mouth, this beer is lively, with good carbonation, mild yeasty fruitiness, citrusy flavor hops, and a mild body. Bitterness isn't strong, but it's definitely there, giving this easy-drinking beer definition. A nice beer, but perhaps not more than that.

Design The low contrast between Redhook's signature-red colored label and the brown glass makes the two-part label less striking than that on the Long Hammer IPA.

Redhook Long Hammer IPA

rating
7

India Pale Ale

Country USA (WA) **ABV** 6.5%
Producer Redhook Ale Brewery **Group** Craft Brewers Alliance
Price $$ **Packaging** 12oz/355ml bottle
Characteristics Bitter, hoppy

Redhook has been the face of craft brewing in Seattle since forever—1981, actually—and Long Hammer is a recent rebranding of their Redhook IPA, originally known as 1984's Ballard Bitter. That's a long run for a modern craft beer.

Flavors and aromas Plenty of hops emerge from the nose of this beer: orange peel and pine character plus some complexity that one taster identified as rosemary. The palate is on the light side of medium, but there are darkish caramel notes to go with the assertively bitter hoppiness. The finish is dry and rather bitter. There's a touch of harshness, but hop lovers will find this enjoyable and well-constructed.

Design The new longneck bottles feature a two-piece label that surrounds a raised-glass barley feature right in the middle. The would-be designer in us sighs and blushes a bit.

Rochefort 6

Belgian Ale

Country Belgium **Style** Dark Belgian Ale **ABV** 7.5%
Producer Brasserie de Rochefort **Price** $$$$$
Packaging 11.2oz/330ml bottle
Characteristics Malty, strong, unusual, yeasty

Rochefort, one of the smaller Trappist producers, produces only three beers—6, 8, and 10—and this is the lightest of the three both in color and alcohol. It's no golden ale, though. It's a 7.5% ABV beer with a rich brown color.

Flavors and aromas As with the Rochefort 8, we struggled to find a fresh bottle of this—perplexing, since generally these beers should have the stuffing to age. One bottle was entirely dead. The other had hints of oxidation, but fared reasonably well, with rich caramel and rock candy in the nose, plus spicy esters (one taster mentioned gingerbread, and a complex palate of caramelized sugars and alcohol that reminded tasters of dark rum, orange liqueur, and spices.

Design The shape of the Rochefort bottle is elfin and graceful, and looks smaller than it is. A clean label design plays a nice supporting role.

Rochefort 8

Belgian Ale

Country Belgium **Style** Dark Belgian Ale **ABV** 9.2%
Producer Brasserie de Rochefort **Price** $$$$
Packaging 11.2oz/330ml, 25.4oz/750ml bottle
Characteristics Bitter, strong, unusual, yeasty

Belgian brewers seem to love bottle caps. Rochefort uses a different cap color for each beer (this is the green cap; Rochefort 6 is red). Ultra-rare Westvleteren does away with labels entirely, using caps as the sole source of external information.

Flavors and aromas This is a difficult beer to assess, with two of three bottles exhibiting a deep, sour funk—our third bottle finally showed some of the dark sugars and spices one might expect from a traditional dark Belgian ale. Dark caramels, sassafras, and light fruity esters mingle with moderately apparent alcohol and very mild cider vinegar notes. The finish is a bit hot and has a touch of sweetness not present in the palate. Spices outweigh esters here, and this is an intensely warming beer.

Design A simple concept cluttered up with a lot of little elements. We suggest following in the footsteps of Westmalle.

Rodenbach

Sour Beer

Country Belgium **Style** Flanders Red Ale **ABV** 5.2%
Producer Brouwerij Rodenbach **Group** Palm Breweries
Price $$$$ **Packaging** 25.4oz/750ml bottle
Characteristics Refreshing, sour, unusual

Sour beer producers nearly always blend their beers—the microbes that produce sour character aren't known for consistency—and like the Grand Cru bottling, this Flemish beer is a mix of young and aged beers.

Flavors and aromas Rodenbach's regular offering is very dry compared to other sour beers we tasted, and some tasters felt like it was lacking intensity. There's lots of interesting stuff here, though, from a sour, tangy nose with savory umami notes to an edgy palate that is more acidic than tart. The dry finish is crisp, with some apple character, and is a bit austere, but if you like geuze or other dry sour styles, this is worth a try. If you're not sure about sour beers, stick to the Grand Cru, which is more forgiving.

Design This simple design is sufficiently minimal to come across as eye-catching and bold.

Rodenbach Grand Cru

Sour Beer

Country Belgium **Style** Flanders Red Ale **ABV** 6.0%
Producer Brouwerij Rodenbach **Group** Palm Breweries
Price $$$$ **Packaging** 25.4oz/750ml bottle
Characteristics Malty, sour, strong, unusual

Rodenbach has been in operation since 1821, though barrel-aging—the hallmark of their famous sour beers—didn't start for another sixty years. The remarkable complexity of their Grand Cru is compounded by a relatively low alcohol content.

Flavors and aromas "Insanely complex" wrote one taster, and notes consisted of long lists like "vinegar, molasses, leather...tart, tangy, drying, sweet, fruity." Somewhere in the oak barrel room at Rodenbach, someone is doing something right. In a nutshell, apple cider vinegar flavors sing harmonies with multilayered malt and just enough sweetness to take the edge off the acidic character. We weren't perfectly unanimous; the sole voice of dissent in our group characterized it as full of "unripe pear, unripe lemon, unripe persimmon."

Design Clearly intended to evoke the world of Champagne. The barrel-room-portal logo is nice.

Rogue Dead Guy

rating 7

Pale Ale

Country USA (OR) **Style** Alt **ABV** 6.5%
Producer Rogue Ales Brewery **Price** $$$
Packaging 12oz/355ml, 22oz/650ml, 64oz/1.89L bottle
Characteristics Bitter, malty

Rogue calls this beer a maibock—a light version of the hearty German bock lager—but they ferment it with their house ale yeast (known as "Pacman"). The Dusseldorf alt-style beer is also an amber, malty beer made like a lager with top-fermenting yeast, which seems more like what you get here, so we call Dead Guy an alt.

Flavors and aromas Mild woody hops and light caramel make up the nose here. The palate is mildly malty and low-intensity, with minimal hop character or bitterness. This is more like a mild amber lager than an American-style amber ale. One taster found it a refreshing, food-friendly beer, but the rest wanted more flavor intensity, whether it be flavor hops, bitterness, or malt character.

Design We wish all of Rogue's labels had this kind of character. The Day of the Dead-styled skeleton is iconic and memorable, and it's easy to remember "Dead Guy" when you're at the store.

Rogue Old Crustacean

Strong Beer

Country USA (OR) **Style** Barleywine **ABV** 11.5%
Producer Rogue Ales Brewery **Price** $$$$$
Packaging 7oz/207ml bottle
Characteristics Bitter, hoppy, malty, strong

At 11.5% ABV, Old Crustacean was the third-booziest beer we tasted, behind the Dogfish Head World Wide Stout and North Coast's Old Stock Ale. Like densely packed wines, these beers are built to last and may require time to really seem drinkable.

Flavors and aromas "This one goes to 11." Every aspect of this barleywine seems to be in overdrive, from the spicy, malty nose to the intensely bitter and malty palate, which overflows with spices and citrus hop character. For all the intensity of the bitterness, this still sweet at the same time, which is unusual. The huge finish is thick, bitter, long, and complex. It's hard to imagine drinking more than a few ounces of this. Buyer beware.

Design We haven't seen it yet, but Rogue's XS line of high-gravity beers are moving from 750ml bottles to 7oz bottles, which probably suits the huge alcohol content.

Rogue Shakespeare Oatmeal Stout

rating **8**

Dark Ale

Country USA (OR) **Style** Stout **ABV** 6.0%
Producer Rogue Ales Brewery **Price** $$$$
Packaging 22oz/650ml bottle
Characteristics Roasty

The Rogue website offers a creed and a mission statement; both suggest a proletarian, everyman spirit which is at odds with their pricing, which tends to be high by West Coast craft brew standards. But the quality here is generally high and Rogue has had little trouble expanding significantly up and down the coastal states.

Flavors and aromas We wouldn't have guessed that this beer was an oatmeal stout. This isn't a creamy, soft beer, but it does have a prominent roast barley aroma and flavor that makes it much like a full-flavor version of Guinness Draught. There's clean iced coffee flavors, chocolate, slightly grassy hops, and a long, satisfyingly dry finish.

Design Rogue makes a lot out of their packaging at any price, and the silk screened bottles are a nice touch, but the hippie-brewpub-styled bottle drawings don't really fit with the revolutionary-styled Rogue logo.

Rolling Rock

Pale Lager

Country USA (MO) **Style** North American Lager **ABV** 4.6%
Producer Anheuser-Busch **Price** $$
Packaging 7oz/207ml, 12oz/355ml bottle; 12oz/355ml,
16oz/473ml can **Characteristics** Malty, refreshing

Once a symbol of working class Pennsylvania, Rolling Rock has spent the last decade switching owners, and the Latrobe brewery has gone the way of so many other regional breweries (though the facility is now employed to produce Iron City beers). Currently owned by InBev, the brand is reputedly on the market again.

Flavors and aromas We might quibble with claims that this is a premium lager, but it's not half bad as an American-style lager. There's plenty of sweetness in the malt, a hint of hops, light but contained skunkiness, and lively carbonation. You're not going to find anything revelatory, but this could easily be the best option in a cooler at a barbecue near you.

Design The famous quality pledge is here, and it's a little overwrought, frankly. We like the silk screened bottles, and the green glass looks nice, but as usual, we're disappointed by the off-flavors it invites.

Russian River Pliny the Elder

rating
9

Strong Beer

Country USA (CA) **Style** Imperial IPA **ABV** 8.0%
Producer Russian River Brewing Company **Price** $$$$
Packaging 16.9oz/500ml bottle
Characteristics Bitter, hoppy, strong

Russian River brews a triple version of this double IPA, known as Pliny the Younger, and it's one of the cult beers of 2010, with kegs in Portland going dry in hours. Appropriate enough for a beer from the heart of California wine country.

Flavors and aromas An intense nose of resiny citrus and floral hops is attention-grabbing and impressive. The palate has a good, full body, less thick than the Dogfish Head 90 Minute IPA, and while bitterness outpaces malt, the flavor hops are the center of attention here—grassy, citrus, and herbal flavors are intricate and complex. The bitterness hangs into the finish, but it's not gripping or harsh.

Design The design is great, but the passionate exhortations about how to treat and consume the beer are even better.

Saison Dupont

Belgian Ale

Country Belgium **Style** Saison **ABV** 6.5%
Producer Brasserie Dupont **Price** $$$$
Packaging 11.2oz/330ml, 12.7oz/375ml, 25.4oz/750ml bottle
Characteristics Bitter, refreshing, unusual, yeasty

There's great diversity in the world of saisons, also known as farmhouse ales. One particular source of variety is yeast character. Saison Dupont's yeast is perhaps the most highly prized, and it's used by many American breweries looking to dabble in the style.

Flavors and aromas A big, fluffy, long-lasting head introduces this dry, fruity, complex beer. The nose is lightly estery and full of peppery, spicy phenolic notes. It's calm and restrained, but the palate is bursting with dry, spicy flavors, complex yeast character, and rich hop bitterness. The finish is dry, perhaps a touch astringent, but the overall effect here is beguiling and fresh, and flavors shift and dance around with each sip.

Design This attractive bottle evokes nice Burgundy, but carries a little more pizzazz than your typical French wine.

Sam Adams Light

Pale Lager

Country USA (MA) **Style** Light Beer **ABV** 5.4%
Producer Boston Beer Company **Price** $$
Packaging 12oz/355ml bottle
Characteristics Refreshing

Sam Adams Light—the only Boston Beer product to use the casual form of Mr. Adams' name—is definitely lighter than standard lagers, but it's not nearly as low in calories as most light lagers, weighing in at 125 where most are in the 100-110 range.

Flavors and aromas Where other light beers only point, Samuel Adams Light dares to tread. The only light beer in our tasting that multiple tasters mistook for a full-calorie beer, this whiskey-colored beer has light aroma hops, mild caramel, bready malt in the palate, and most surprising, a medium-bodied mouthfeel. This would be on the thin end of the spectrum, for a regular beer, but for a light beer, it's almost magical.

Design Mr. Adams is nearly buried by the heft of his name above, and the horizontal lines look like they're borrowed from some optical illusion.

Samuel Adams Boston Lager

Amber Lager

Country USA (MA) **Style** American Amber Lager **ABV** 4.9%
Producer Boston Beer Company **Price** $$
Packaging 12oz/355ml bottle
Characteristics Refreshing

Launched in 1985, this beer was a tweak of a family recipe that founder Jim Koch updated with help from Miller Lite creator Joseph Owades. Today, it's the flagship beer of the largest American-owned brewery.

Flavors and aromas This amber lager is somewhat more full-bodied than most of the pale lagers we tasted; it also contains flavor hops and perceptible bitterness, which give it a crisp, snappy finish. Good carbonation leaves a lingering head, and caramel fills out the palate. One taster thought the body was too heavy for the flavor profile, but almost all thought this was pretty good.

Design The front of this label is remarkably restrained, with barely more than a dozen words of text. Thumbs up for that.

Samuel Adams Cherry Wheat

rating
3

Wheat Beer

Country USA (MA) **Style** American Wheat Beer **ABV** 4.1%
Producer Boston Beer Company **Price** $$
Packaging 12oz/355ml bottle
Characteristics Bitter, unusual

The Boston Beer Company has spent much of its existence as a contract brewer, hiring others to produce beers to their specifications and recipes. Today, they brew a third of their beer, but the rest is still brewed offsite.

Flavors and aromas Cherry is evident in this beer from the first sniff, overwhelming any malt or hop character, but the aroma is acceptable. In the mouth, though, the synthetic-tasting cherry (which comes from real Michigan cherries, apparently) runs headlong into unexpected and striking bitterness, leaving a strikingly medicinal, NyQuil taste moderated only by the lack of heft in the body. Wheat character emerges in the end, but can't really help.

Design Unlike the other bottles, Mr. Adams gets a color image here, which gives him a nice healthy glow that works well with other colors here.

Samuel Smith India Ale

India Pale Ale

Country England **ABV** 5.0%
Producer Samuel Smith Brewery **Price** $$$$
Packaging 12oz/355ml, 18.7oz/553ml bottle
Characteristics Bitter, malty, yeasty

The heart and soul of English IPA is in Burton-on-Trent, but there's not a lot of it sold in North America. While we had some frustration trying to get fresh samples, tasting the difference between English and American IPAs is worth it.

Flavors and aromas This is a challenging ale to evaluate—as are many of Samuel Smith's products—because it is hard to know whether the samples we taste are representative of the brewery's output. It does show the facets we expect of an English IPA: strong English malt character, palpable bitterness, and perhaps some diacetyl. If you're not bothered by overt butterscotch character and some green apple as well, you'll like this. But freshness dating and bottle-conditioning would likely make this a much more reliable product.

Design This label is hyper-busy, but pulls it off well. An attractive use of strong, bold colors.

Samuel Smith Oatmeal Stout

rating
6

Dark Ale

Country England **Style** Stout **ABV** 5.0%
Producer Samuel Smith Brewery **Price** $$$$
Packaging 12oz/355ml, 18.7oz/553ml bottle
Characteristics Malty, roasty

The buttery diacetyl flavors in Samuel Smith's beer are the byproduct of their traditional yeasts. Complex systems were developed over the years to help ensure full fermentation, but to some extent, these flavors are just part of the style.

Flavors and aromas A nose with chocolate, diacetyl, toasty malt, and a whiff of acetaldehyde or cider vinegar didn't excite our tasters, but things improved somewhat in the palate, where we found mild roast character, baking chocolate, malt, and good carbonation. The finish is sweet and heavy to the point of being moderately cloying. More dark malt, roast character, or bitterness would be welcome here.

Design With a cleaner label than the India Ale, with the distinctive Samuel Smith bottle shape and strong, yellow background, this one's never tough to spot.

Samuel Smith Pale Ale

Pale Ale

Country England **Style** English Pale Ale **ABV** 5.0%
Producer Samuel Smith Brewery **Price** $$$$
Packaging 12oz/355ml, 18.7oz/553ml bottle
Characteristics Malty

Samuel Smith is an old operation. Founded in 1758, it's the oldest brewery in Yorkshire. That brewery—the Old Brewery—is the namesake for this English pale ale.

Flavors and aromas Mild diacetyl butterscotch and complex English malt make this a warm, soft smelling beer. That malt is the clear backbone of the palate here, though it's a little thin, with carbonation that's a bit above the norm for an English ale. There's soft bitterness here, which can't cover up the malt, and some tasters wanted more of it. The finish is malty, not dry, and features some green hop flavors.

Design After looking at the India Ale and the Oatmeal Stout, the Old Brewery Pale Ale label is a disappointment, particularly since it's almost identical to the Nut Brown Ale label.

Sapporo Premium

Pale Lager

Country Japan **Style** Japanese Lager **ABV** 4.9%
Producer Sapporo Breweries **Price** $$
Packaging 12oz/355ml, 16oz/473ml, 20.3oz/600ml bottle;
12oz/355ml, 22oz/650ml can **Characteristics** Refreshing

Sapporo made headlines in 2009 when it announced plans to brew beer from barley seeds that had spent five months in space. A lottery system gave lucky folks the opportunity to buy the beer at about $19 a bottle. A spokesman said the beer would taste the same as regular Sapporo.

Flavors and aromas Sapporo has a light nose that gives up a bit of malt and a suggestion of bitterness. The palate benefits from good carbonation, which presents the light malt and modest bitterness in a good light. We didn't love this beer, but it has a sense of being essentially beer, which doesn't hold for many of the lightly flavored beers we tried. In this style, however, we preferred Kirin Ichiban.

Design Sapporo's gold star and black background is attractive, and seems to promise something a little more bold than what is contained within.

Saranac Adirondack Lager

Pale Lager

Country USA (NY) **Style** North American Lager **ABV** 5.5%
Producer Matt Brewing Company **Price** $
Packaging 12oz/355ml bottle
Characteristics Bitter, refreshing

Saranac's Adirondack is an amber lager that slips through the cracks of established style a bit. But for us, that's not a drawback. Beer style is a shorthand for us to talk about things we already know about. Shouldn't we be putting more effort into discovering things we don't know about?

Flavors and aromas A nose of mild, woody hops and nutty malt lead into a palate that is relatively full-bodied and flavorful for an American lager. There's mild bitterness to balance, and this seems like it has potential, but an astringent, harsh note hits the back of the mouth in the finish and drags this back to the realm of the merely ordinary. Still not a bad tipple, ultimately.

Design Our research assistant, who hails from New England, was perplexed. She thought for sure this beer would show an Adirondack chair. It doesn't.

Saranac IPA

India Pale Ale

rating 8

Country USA (NY) **ABV** 5.8%
Producer Matt Brewing Company **Price** $
Packaging 12oz/355ml bottle
Characteristics Bitter

Saranac beers are brewed at F.X. Matt Brewery in Utica, New York. F.X. Matt produces a dizzying array of beers—there have been more than forty beers released under the Saranac name.

Flavors and aromas Citrusy, West Coast-style hops in the nose share space with mild malt and a touch of diacetyl. The palate jumps with bright carbonation and sparkling bitterness, while malt character is low—just present enough to keep things interesting. While the hop flavor in the mouth is also low, bitterness crescendos over several sips to become the dominant key. Our tasters were pretty fond of this.

Design A green label frames a tranquil waterfall painting. Oh, and there's some barley. It's like the subject of the label had just stepped out of frame when they took the photo.

Saranac Pale Ale

Pale Ale

Country USA (NY) **Style** American Pale Ale **ABV** 5.5%
Producer Matt Brewing Company **Price** $
Packaging 12oz/355ml bottle
Characteristics Bitter

Prior to the Saranac line of beers introduced in 1985, F.X. Matt Brewery produced a number of American-style lagers, competing with large national breweries. Miller Lite inventor Joseph Owades was a regular consultant on the Saranac product line.

Flavors and aromas There's a faint citrus nose (or perhaps it's pine). The medium-full body has a light flavor profile, with minimal malt character, a bit of hop flavor, and moderate bitterness that seems almost obtrusive by comparison. The bitterness lingers into the finish, where this takes a slight turn for the worse: an oily mouthfeel that lingers. Not a terrible beer, but we imagine that there will generally be more exciting options available.

Design Nice clean label, but that lake could really use a jumping trout or a drooling moose to liven it up a bit.

Schlenkerla Helles

Smoke Beer

Country Germany **ABV** 4.3%
Producer Brauerei Heller-Trum **Group** Aecht Schlenkerla
Price $$$$ **Packaging** 16.9oz/500ml bottle
Characteristics Malty, unusual

Schlenkerla Helles is not produced with smoke malt, but the brewery is so infused with the stuff that while they don't call it a rauchbier, they have no illusions about the impact of using the same yeasts, storage, and brewing equipment. This is secondhand smoke beer.

Flavors and aromas Heavy hot cereal and corn flavors fill the nose of this unusual beer. Mild smoke character plays a backseat role. In the palate, there are still strong corn notes, but the weightiness of the nose gives way to more focused smoke character, mildly sweet malt, and spices. The finish, for all that, is remarkably mild and pleasant. Tasters had mixed opinions about the aroma but generally found this to be surprisingly drinkable.

Design The pale blue-diamond background is elegant, but with the stylized Gothic font, it's not exactly a paragon of readability.

Schlenkerla Rauchbier Märzen

Smoke Beer

Country Germany **ABV** 5.1%
Producer Brauerei Heller-Trum **Group** Aecht Schlenkerla
Price $$$$ **Packaging** 16.9oz/500ml bottle
Characteristics Malty, unusual

The smoke quality in these beers is as much a nod to tradition as a question of style. Historically, barley was frequently dried over open fires, so smoked malt was the rule, rather than the exception. Bamberg is the home of Germany's living rauchbier tradition.

Flavors and aromas Intense, fresh campfire smoke jumps out of the glass, making this an immediately polarizing beer. In the mouth, there's more smokiness, as well as some definite fruity malt character pulling this towards balance. Other than the smoke, this gives a definite impression of clean character, but it's not for the faint of heart.

Design No one can accuse the folks at Schlenkerla of gussying up their label for the export market. It's relentlessly German.

Schneider Weisse

Wheat Beer

Country Germany **Style** Bavarian Hefeweizen **ABV** 5.2%
Producer G. Schneider & Sohn **Price** $$$$
Packaging 16.9oz/500ml bottle
Characteristics Refreshing, yeasty

Formed in 1872, the G. Schneider & Sohn brewing concern is currently on its sixth Georg Schneider. The Schneiders make wheat beers exclusively, in a wide variety of traditional Bavarian styles. This is one of the more widely available of the authentic Bavarian hefeweizens.

Flavors and aromas Darker than most of the wheat beers we tasted, this has definite Bavarian character in the nose, with the spice component coming across as earthy and muted. Despite some slightly tart character, the palate is flat, with carbonation not supporting the malt as much as usual, and there are some bitter elements to the finish. Panelists agreed that this was acceptably drinkable, but there are better examples of this style.

Design Somebody had to fill all that white space, and they had a perfectly good company crest laying around. It's not rocket science.

Session Premium Lager

Pale Lager

Country USA (OR) **Style** North American Lager **ABV** 5.1%
Producer Full Sail Brewing Company **Price** $
Packaging 11oz/325ml bottle
Characteristics Refreshing

In an odd reversal of marketing, Session (a Full Sail product) is an all-malt lager marketed, essentially, as a cheap beer—or at least a beer to drink when you might have been otherwise inclined to drink a cheap beer.

Flavors and aromas Lemony hops lead off, with light malt and some cooked corn aromas. There's good carbonation making this lively at first, but malt flavors are corn-like and somewhat flat in the mouth. Low bitterness fails to offer much support, and the finish has a cornflakes character to it. An average pale domestic lager.

Design The adorable "stubby" bottle serves double duty: it charms with style, and prevents you from trying to smell this beer.

Sheaf Stout

Dark Ale

Country Australia **Style** Stout **ABV** 5.7%
Producer Carlton & United Breweries **Group** Fosters Group
Price $$$ **Packaging** 12.7oz/375ml, 22oz/650ml, 25.6oz/750ml
bottle **Characteristics** Malty, roasty, yeasty

Originally brewed by Tooth and Company, Tooth's Sheaf Stout is now part of the Foster's Group and is simply Sheaf Stout.

Flavors and aromas After one bottle that was badly off, a second offered a combination of nice bittersweet chocolate and harsh sharpie marker on the nose. The palate is similar: pleasant chocolate richness mingling with harsh alcohols. The marker quality subsides in the finish, letting the roast character and chocolate come out. This is a beer with potential, but the hot notes suggest issues with the fermentation.

Design The big yellow and brown label looks nice enough until you realize that most of the space is filled with small print you're not really interested in reading. But the basic idea is sound.

Shiner Bock

Amber Lager

Country USA (TX) **Style** American Bock **ABV** 4.4%
Producer Spoetzl Brewery **Price** $
Packaging 12oz/355ml bottle
Characteristics Refreshing

It's hard to talk to Texans about beer without getting a pitch for Shiner Bock—they really seem to love the stuff. The Spoetzl brewery where it is produced is one of the only pre-Prohibition craft breweries in the US still in operation.

Flavors and aromas Not all bock beers are equal. Shiner Bock is perhaps the best known example of an American bock—it's basically an American pale lager with a touch of grain to color. A light nose with only faint malt betrays none of the rich caramels of German bock, and the palate is malty and slightly sweet. This hits most of the high points of American macro-lager, though. Good clean character, nice carbonation, and light malt make this a refreshing beer that's more brewski than bier.

Design The label has all the elements of a German bock: Gothic fonts, a goat, even a German toast on the neck tag. Yet it still seems essentially Texan.

Sierra Nevada Kellerweis

rating
8

Wheat Beer

Country USA (CA) **Style** Bavarian Hefeweizen **ABV** 4.8%
Producer Sierra Nevada Brewing Company **Price** $$
Packaging 12oz/355ml bottle
Characteristics Refreshing, yeasty

Kellerbier is a hoppy, unfiltered German cask lager—"keller" meaning "cellar" or "basement"—but Sierra Nevada's Kellerweis is not a lager; it's a traditional Bavarian-style hefeweizen.

Flavors and aromas Soft, classic hefeweizen banana and clove tell you from the get-go that this is not your typical American hefeweizen. The palate is exceptionally smooth and creamy for a hefe; there's no grainy texture to be found here, just smooth malt and clove spice. There's a touch of barely metallic hop bitterness in the finish, but this is a wonderfully drinkable hefeweizen.

Design Sierra Nevada takes a one-size-fits-all approach to their labels, but their flagship Pale Ale is ubiquitous enough that even a simple color change is enough to make the bottle feel like a new friend you didn't know you had.

Sierra Nevada Pale Ale

Pale Ale

Country USA (CA) **Style** American Pale Ale **ABV** 5.6%
Producer Sierra Nevada Brewing Company **Price** $$
Packaging 12oz/355ml, 24oz/710ml bottle
Characteristics Bitter, hoppy, refreshing

To many beer historians, Sierra Nevada Pale Ale created and defined the genre of American pale ale, having done more than any other beer to introduce the US to West Coast hop strains. It's also the best-selling craft beer in the country, according to Appellation Beer.

Flavors and aromas The pleasant nose of this beer combines light citrusy hops with warm malt flavors. The palate is deft and light, with floral, green hop character, light caramel malt sweetness, and a nice hop kick to pull things together and give this pale ale firm edges. A dry, tasty finish, with some residual hop character and bitterness, makes this a beer with good repeat potential.

Design These labels strike up a nice balance of high contrast for important elements and low contrast for everything else, which helps give them pop.

Sierra Nevada Porter

Dark Ale

Country USA (CA) **Style** Porter **ABV** 5.6%
Producer Sierra Nevada Brewing Company **Price** $$
Packaging 12oz/355ml bottle
Characteristics Bitter, malty, roasty

Brewing equipment is expensive. Sierra Nevada, founded by a homebrew store owner, got its tanks and vats by following a time-honored microbrewery tradition: they used repurposed dairy equipment.

Flavors and aromas A dry, roasty nose announces this porter, which has an enticingly smooth and creamy mouthfeel. Roast character is more pronounced in the mouth, with bitterness from both the malt and hops, and there's some acidity as well, likely from the darker malts. That acidity lingers with the nearly burnt roast quality into the finish. Overall, a good, straightforward example of the darker side of American porter.

Design Visual elements are good, but the center paintings on these labels are so small as to be nearly indistinguishable.

Sierra Nevada Torpedo

Strong Beer

Country USA (CA) **Style** Imperial IPA **ABV** 7.2%
Producer Sierra Nevada Brewing Company **Price** $$
Packaging 12oz/355ml bottle
Characteristics Bitter, hoppy

For the continent's second-largest craft beer to add a high-octane Imperial IPA to their year-round roster is surprising, but perhaps even more surprising is the choice to downplay the high alcohol by calling it an "Extra IPA." We're curious to see if this sticks.

Flavors and aromas A fresh, citrusy nose emerges from an attractive, dense head, with a light touch of caramel. In the mouth, things open with a touch of sweet malt before intense, focused bitterness steps in and puts a halt to all the rest. The big wall of bitterness isn't harsh or astringent, but it is intensely, powerfully bitter. While the bitterness hangs on, there's a fresh, light wave of caramel with each taste, helping to keep this interesting. With the right pairing, this could be a truly remarkable beer.

Design The dark green border of this label is mellow enough to lower your guard for the kick in the teeth that lurks within.

Singha

Pale Lager

Country Thailand **Style** Continental Lager **ABV** 5.0%
Producer Boon Rawd Brewery **Price** $$
Packaging 11.2oz/330ml, 21.3oz/630ml bottle; 11.2oz/330 ml can
Characteristics Hoppy, malty, refreshing

Thailand is not a country with a long history of brewing, and Singha has seen all of it—it's the nation's first domestic beer. The Boon Rawd brewery was founded in 1933 by Boonrawd Sreshthaputra.

Flavors and aromas We were happy to get non-skunked samples, given that what's served in restaurants is so often skunky. Sweet malt and spicy noble hops pair with light cooked corn in the nose here. The light body of this beer has firm malt and clean character. Bitterness isn't strong, but it's definitely present, shining through in the aftertaste. Good flavor intensity persists into the well-balanced finish, and our tasters noted the nice mouthfeel and good carbonation.

Design The animal on the label—griffon? lion?—combines elements of European heraldry and the intricate abstractness of the Kirin mascot.

Skull Splitter

Strong Beer

Country Scotland **Style** Strong Ale **ABV** 8.5%
Producer Orkney Brewery **Price** $$$$
Packaging 11.2oz/330ml, 16.9oz/500ml bottle
Characteristics Malty, strong, yeasty

This beer from the Orkney brewery is named, apparently, for an Earl of Orkney who lived just before the turn of the first millennium. It's a Scotch "Wee Heavy," the strongest designation for traditional Scottish ale.

Flavors and aromas The nose on this doesn't lack for British character or complexity. We found prunes, cherries, rum, fruity esters, diacetyl, classic English malt, spices, and a fair whack of alcohol. Our tasters were less fond of the heavy, thick palate and alcoholic body, which pushed the many flavor elements apart and out of balance.

Design Beer and vikings. Two of our favorite things, and they go great together.

Smithwick's Red Ale

Pale Ale

Country Ireland **Style** English Pale Ale **ABV** 4.5%
Producer Guinness **Group** Diageo **Price** $$
Packaging 12oz/355ml bottle
Characteristics Malty

Smithwicks (the "w" is silent) is part of the Guinness empire these days, but was originally the product of a brewery established by John Smithwick in 1710. Three hundred years later, Smithwicks still does not have a complete website.

Flavors and aromas The North American version of Smithwicks Irish Ale is significantly stronger than the traditional Irish version, but retains a distinct British Isles character of low carbonation and pronounced maltiness. Fans of the style will appreciate this as a widely available example, but those expecting American assertiveness can do better elsewhere.

Design For Ireland's oldest ale, this beer sure has a bland logo. We're unsure if this can be traced back to Mr. Smithwick or if it rests on the shoulders of Guinness's marketing team.

Sol

Pale Lager

Country Mexico **Style** North American Lager **ABV** 4.5%
Producer Cuauhtémoc Moctezuma **Price** $$
Packaging 12oz/355ml bottle
Characteristics Bland

Sol Beer—introduced in 1899 as "El Sol"—is part of a family of beers, mostly not exported, which includes an amber version, a light beer, and a lime-and-salt beer. It's very popular in Mexico, and quite refreshing when fresh—way better than Corona—but the glass bottles bring it down to Corona's level when it's imported into the US. It's a beer that's best drunk on location. In a michelada.

Flavors and aromas A very thin, empty nose gave us little preview of what this beer had to offer... which isn't too much of a strike against this beer, which doesn't have much more than a thick mouthfeel and a flat palate. The high carbonation gives this lackluster beer a seltzer-like quality, but we'd advise you to just drink seltzer if it's all the same to you.

Design Clear glass aside, the Sol label is beautiful. It's hardly changed in the last century, and we think it should stay that way.

Spaten Oktoberfest

Amber Lager

Country Germany **Style** Oktoberfest **ABV** 5.9%
Producer Spaten-Franziskaner-Bräu **Group** InBev **Price** $$
Packaging 12oz/355ml, 16.9oz/500ml bottle
Characteristics Malty

19th century Spaten brewer Gabriel Sedlmayr may be the single most important figure in modern brewing, having had a role in the creation of most of the modern Bavarian lager styles, including the märzen/Oktoberfest style.

Flavors and aromas A solid example of a German amber lager, this is intensely focused on the malt. Typical Munich malt aromas of nutty, lightly toasted grain, with some of the fruitiness that is often evident in beers with a high Munich content, as well as some caramel. The bitterness here is a little bit higher than we'd expect to find in an Oktoberfest, but it keeps things crisp. The finish is dry, moderately bitter, and yet still shows off the malt.

Design A simple label offers little to get excited about, until you realize that the barrels on the cart are full of sweet, sweet beer.

Spaten Optimator

Strong Beer

Country Germany **Style** Doppelbock **ABV** 7.2%
Producer Spaten-Franziskaner-Bräu **Group** InBev **Price** $$
Packaging 12oz/355ml, 16.9oz/500ml bottle
Characteristics Malty, strong, unusual

Optimator is Spaten's strongest beer, and with a name that drips with deadpan cool, we expect it probably gets more attention than some of the other imported doppelbocks, even if the label is rather plain.

Flavors and aromas A somewhat muted nose suggests sweet malt, medium-dark caramels, and some baking spices and fruit aromas, but generally holds back. This shows much better in the mouth, where it is rich and full-bodied, with restrained alcohol, dark dried fruits. Compared to the standard notion of a doppelbock as a big bruiser of a beer, this is restrained and calm. We liked the complexity of this beer, but there is room for more intensity.

Design All the classic doppelbocks—Salvator, Celebrator—have exciting labels, but Optimator's only deviation from business as usual is a doubled version of the spade logo.

Spaten Premium

Pale Lager

Country Germany **Style** Continental Lager **ABV** 5.2%
Producer Spaten-Franziskaner-Bräu **Group** InBev **Price** $$
Packaging 12oz/355ml, 16.9oz/500ml bottle
Characteristics Hoppy, refreshing

One of Munich's oldest breweries (dating back to the 14th century), Spaten and its sister brand Franziskaner, now part of the InBev empire, produce the full range of traditional Bavarian beer styles, from this soft Helles lager to their powerful Optimator doppelbock.

Flavors and aromas Helles lager was Bavaria's answer to Czech Pilsners, and this is about as traditional a rendition as you'll find on this side of the Atlantic. The full-bodied pale malt is brightened with plenty of pungent noble hops, but without the bitterness many drinkers associate with Continental lagers. It's not the easiest beer to find, but this is a style we imagine a lot of lager drinkers could fall in love with.

Design This label seems strikingly German: lots of white space, clean block lettering, and the not-quite-a-cuddly-dog spade logo. The use of green glass for American bottles is unfortunate but expected.

Speakeasy Prohibition Ale

Pale Ale

Country USA (CA) **Style** American Pale Ale **ABV** 6.1%
Producer Speakeasy Ales and Lagers **Price** $$$
Packaging 12oz/355ml, 22oz/650ml bottle
Characteristics Bitter, malty

San Francisco's Speakeasy may not have the recognition of Anchor, but it's definitely a hometown favorite, available in hundreds of locations around the Bay Area. Its reach has expanded steadily into other western states and Canada.

Flavors and aromas Malt and caramel were the dominant flavors in this beer, which our panel didn't like nearly as much as Speakeasy's Big Daddy IPA. The bitterness comes on late and lingers, giving a slightly harsh finish that comes as a surprise after the mild hop profile in the rest of the beer.

Design It seems like the classy Art Deco movement of the Prohibition era should offer better design ideas than this.

St. Pauli Girl

Pale Lager

rating
7

Country Germany **Style** Continental Lager **ABV** 4.9%
Producer St. Pauli Brauerei **Group** InBev **Price** $
Packaging 12oz/355ml, 24oz/710ml bottle
Characteristics Refreshing

St. Pauli Girl is a northern German beer brand owned, like many international pale lagers, by AB InBev. Despite being notable for the cartoon of a busty beer wench on the label and the annual selection of a real-life model to serve as the St. Pauli Girl in poster campaigns, the brewery in Bremen is about as far as one can get from Oktoberfest without exiting Germany, both physically and stylistically.

Flavors and aromas We liked St. Pauli more than most of the internationally styled light lagers, noting a discernible noble hop character on the nose and a softly lingering bitterness. This beer has malt character without coming across as sweet, which is sadly rare in this style of beer.

Design Either you're the kind of person who likes busty beer wenches on your label, or the kind who doesn't. Any commentary we might make is unlikely to change that.

rating
6

Pale Lager

Country USA (WI) **Style** Malt Liquor **ABV** 8.1%
Producer Steel Brewing Company **Group** SABMiller **Price** $
Packaging 22oz/650ml, 40oz/1.18L bottle; 12oz/355ml,
16oz/473ml, 24oz/710 mL can **Characteristics** Malty, strong

Steel Reserve comes in a dizzying array of sizes and strengths. It doesn't have the cultural cachet of Olde English 800, but there are a series of '90s ad jingles by the Ramones, which are worth seeking out.

Flavors and aromas This was one of the big surprises of the tasting reveal. There's a pleasantly malty nose, slightly sweet, with low hop character: simple, but nice. The mouth has a body that's definitely on the full side, but the fine-bubbled carbonation keeps things fresh and bright. There's a soft bitterness, and a malty finish where we get the only hint of the ample alcohol, in the form of a slight booziness. Overall, this is smooth and round, and has little of the volatile, sweet-flat character of other malt liquors we tasted.

Design Anyone remember Coke's anti-image orange-cola OK Soda? The self-consciously clean/cluttered aesthetic here could almost be a tribute.

Steinlager Classic

Pale Lager

rating
5

Country New Zealand **Style** North American Lager **ABV** 5.0%
Producer Lion Nathan **Price** $$
Packaging 11.2oz/330ml, 25.4oz/750ml bottle
Characteristics Bland

Lion Nathan introduced Steineker—later renamed Steinlager to avoid confusion with Heineken—in response to a government official's challenge in 1957 to cut imports by developing an "international style lager."

Flavors and aromas The skunky aroma of our samples of Steinlager were evident before the steward reached the table. Digging deep under the lightstruck notes, we found some hop and malt character. Bitterness is low, with a moderately light palate of crackery malt, and nice carbonation takes the edge off some mild sweetness, lending with a nicely dry finish. We'd like to try this fresh; for drinkers who really don't mind skunkiness, this seems to have more interesting character lurking.

Design Apparently, Lion Nathan set out to create a generic European lager with a generic European lager label. They seem to have succeeded.

Stella Artois

Pale Lager

Country Belgium **Style** Continental Lager **ABV** 5.0%
Producer Stella Artois **Group** InBev **Price** $$
Packaging 12oz/355ml bottle
Characteristics Refreshing

Stella Artois is the best-selling Belgian beer in the world, but it has struggled in recent years with identity issues. Long marketed in the UK under the slogan "Reassuringly Expensive," AB InBev has struggled somewhat to maintain the top-shelf premium lager image effortlessly projected by Heineken.

Flavors and aromas Stella is cut from the same cloth as Heineken: a touch of sweetness, a body dominated by grainy malt and mild corn flavors, and a light but noticeable residual bitterness that sets it apart from North American pale lagers. Our samples were slightly skunky. We might suggest the slogan would be more accurately rendered as "Reassuringly Typical," since that is the real value here.

Design The paper bottle cap cover is a little odd, and the low-contrast background text is hard to read and busy, but the basic element of the label is clear and proud.

Stone IPA

India Pale Ale

Country USA (CA) **ABV** 6.9%
Producer Stone Brewing Company **Price** $$
Packaging 12oz/355ml, 22oz/650ml bottle
Characteristics Bitter, hoppy, yeasty

Stone Brewing—along with a few other, mostly bigger breweries—has done a lot to ensure that the high-intensity, big-hop-character style of pale ale is frequently referred to as "West Coast" in style, rather than "Northwest." This poster boy for hops is generally regarded as one of the best producers of these beers.

Flavors and aromas One of the surprises of our blind tastings was Stone's IPA, which failed to live up to the expectations we have for this generally outstanding brewery. This beer seemed to come up a bit short on every axis: a light nose of lemony hops with some fruity esters led into a light palate with good carbonation and mouthfeel, low malt flavor, and low (by IPA standards) bitterness that nonetheless came off as rough and astringent.

Design It's a simple label that plays down the Stone trademark demon with clean, architectural lines and sturdy fonts.

Stone Levitation Ale

Pale Ale

Country USA (CA) **Style** American Pale Ale **ABV** 4.4%
Producer Stone Brewing Company **Price** $$
Packaging 12oz/355ml bottle
Characteristics Bitter, hoppy, refreshing

Stone Levitation Ale has the distinction of having the lowest alcohol content of any of the regular Stone Brewing offerings, coming in a full percent lower than Stone Pale Ale. They haven't made an concession with hops, though.

Flavors and aromas There's no mistaking the big citrus and resin notes of the nose for anything other than an American pale ale. But the light body prompted one taster to compare this to an English bitter brewed with American hops. Whatever the provenance, this went over well with our tasters, who were won over by this beer. Long lingering hop bitterness in the finish might challenge some drinkers, but we approve.

Design We like the design of Stone's labels, but this one does little to set itself apart from any other Stone brew, save that it is less colorful.

Tecate

Pale Lager

Country Mexico **Style** North American Lager **ABV** 4.5%
Producer Cuauhtémoc Moctezuma **Price** $
Packaging 12oz/355ml, 22oz/650ml bottle; 12oz/355ml,
16oz/473ml, 24oz/710ml can **Characteristics** Malty, refreshing

Tecate's namesake is a small city
on the US-Mexico border a few
miles inland from Tijuana. Tecate
beer is produced today by the
same Heineken subsidiary that
makes Dos Equis, Bohemia, and
Sol.

Flavors and aromas This
American-style pale lager doesn't
inspire a lot of brand loyalty
among either big brand drinkers or
the anti-brand rebels, but we'd be
as happy drinking this as anything
from the competition. Light, sweet
malt in the nose, low hop
bitterness, charming carbonation
all combine to form a refreshing,
clean lager with no flaws. Bring on
the sunshine and light the
barbecue.

Design Everything about this can
screams "Warning! Cheap beer
inside!" which doesn't really do
the product justice. On the upside,
the beer is cheap. If they had a
nicer package it might cost more.

Three Philosophers

Belgian Ale

Country USA (NY) **Style** Dark Belgian Ale **ABV** 9.8%
Producer Brewery Ommegang **Group** Duvel Moortgat
Price $$$$ **Packaging** 25.4oz/750ml, 12oz/355ml bottle
Characteristics Malty, sour, strong, yeasty

This curious beer is an American-Belgian hybrid. Three Philosophers is a Quadrupel-style ale brewed in Cooperstown and then blended with a small portion of Lindemans Kriek, a sour cherry ale from Belgium. This is the only regularly produced, multi-brewery blended beer we are aware of.

Flavors and aromas The cherry quality is nicely subtle, though a couple of our tasters picked up on it. The sour component is more upfront, and mingles with a somewhat English character to the malt, reminding us of apple-cider and malt vinegars. Some tasters were also reminded of port or sherry. Caramel flavors bracket the malt, and the end result is a rich, somewhat viscous brew that tends a bit to the heavy side. Overall, a winner.

Design The vintage-dated neck tag hints at their desire for you to age this beer, but it's pretty good fresh. The label is clean and attractive. A pretty bottle.

Titan IPA

India Pale Ale

Country USA (CO) **ABV** 7.1%
Producer Great Divide Brewing Company **Price** $$$
Packaging 12oz/355ml bottle
Characteristics Bitter, hoppy

The popularity of intensely hoppy IPAs on the West Coast may have been originally related to brewers' proximity to fresh, flavorful hops—hops are notoriously ungraceful agers—but they no longer have a monopoly on the style; it seems like every craft brewer has a big IPA now.

Flavors and aromas A focused nose of resiny, green hops, with a slightly sour tang suggests an herb closely related to hops but not generally legal for brewing practices. Flavor hops and caramel malt show up early on the palate, but you can anticipate the tide of bitterness that arrives and washes it all away, leaving a long lingering bitterness that some tasters felt was overdone or medicinal.

Design The current set of Great Divide labels all have a really keen sense of proportion. Every bit of text has a height and a width that is just dialed in. Nice work, people.

Trumer Pils

Pale Lager

Country USA (CA) **Style** Pilsner **ABV** 4.9%
Producer Trumer Brauerei Berkeley **Price** $$
Packaging 12oz/355ml bottle
Characteristics Bitter, hoppy, refreshing

Trumer is an Austrian-based brewery with facilities in Salzburg and Berkeley. Unlike their Munich- and Pilsen-based peers, they focus on a single brew: German-styled pils.

Flavors and aromas Trumer takes the Bavarian approach to pilsner beer: a much more focused hop bitterness than the rounder Pilsen examples. Our tasters were enthusiastically receptive to the bright, spicy hop nose and the focused bitterness, which was a little less laser-like than some of the pilsners from Munich. The aftertaste was a little harsh, but the opportunity to sample traditionally styled pils in fresh bottles that haven't been subjected to long voyages at sea is worth taking.

Design We like the font, the logo, the subtle texture of the background, and in fact just about everything about this bottle except the seemingly mandatory green glass.

Tsingtao

Pale Lager

Country China **Style** North American Lager **ABV** 4.8%
Producer Tsingtao Brewery **Group** Constellation Brands **Price** $
Packaging 12oz/355ml, 21.6oz/639ml bottle; 12oz/355ml can
Characteristics Bland

China's largest brewery is owned in part by InBev Anheuser-Busch and Japan's Asahi Brewery; its flagship beer is firmly in the mold of American lagers like Budweiser, being lightly hopped and brewed with rice.

Flavors and aromas Tsingtao doesn't stand out among a crowd of American pale lagers. Our bottles were a touch skunky (which is unsurprising given the green packaging) with a bit more body and sweetness than, say, Budweiser. There's very little else to distinguish this beer, other than a hint of butterscotch in the finish.

Design Tsingtao proclaims its Chinese origin in virtually every element of the packaging, from the Buddhist-temple logo to sections of Chinese script. Oh, and the "Beer IMPORTED From China" neck tag.

Victory Hop Devil Ale

India Pale Ale

Country USA (PA) **ABV** 6.7%
Producer Victory Brewing Company **Price** $$$
Packaging 12oz/355ml bottle
Characteristics Bitter, hoppy

Victory Brewing Company was founded in 1996 in a former Pepperidge Farm bakery, and since has grown steadily from a small-town brewpub to a nationally distributed craft brewery. It produces a wide range of American-, Belgian-, and German-styled beers, but the best known are the trio of beers reviewed here.

Flavors and aromas Victory's hop profile is unmistakable; while they claim to use American hops for Hop Devil and Continental hops for Prima Pils, both have a similar—and hard to miss—fresh, dry character to the nose. Balance is clearly not the goal here, but this is a fine example of a successful, powerfully hoppy brew, with ample fresh floral/citrus hops filling in for malt body.

Design Is it likely that most consumers probably take no notice of the big green guy front and center on this label, but we did, and we think it's adorable.

Victory Prima Pils

rating
9

Pale Lager

Country USA (PA) **Style** Continental Lager **ABV** 5.3%
Producer Victory Brewing Company **Price** $$$
Packaging 12oz/355ml bottle
Characteristics Bitter, hoppy

Many craft beer drinkers avoid lagers, having discovered that the light-bodied, low-hops versions of their youth no longer satisfy them. Even if you've become one of those anti-lager snobs, you owe it to yourself to try a hoppy Prima Pils before you swear off pilsners.

Flavors and aromas A dusty, fresh hop nose is fairly intense, well out of the normal range. There's not much malt in the nose, but there is a hint of cooked corn. The hoppy flavor dominates the palate, even past the bright, lingering balance; all of this is accentuated by bright, fresh carbonation. Bitterness dominates the finish, but there's enough body to balance it out. This beer combines traditional Bohemian pilsner flavors with high-energy American nonconformism, and the result is an unusual but tasty lager.

Design That image on the logo is a hop cone. It's big, yeah. It's like they're trying to tell you something...

Victory Storm King

Strong Beer

Country USA (PA) **Style** Imperial Stout **ABV** 9.1%
Producer Victory Brewing Company **Price** $$$
Packaging 12oz/355ml bottle
Characteristics Bitter, malty, strong

While Victory has its roots in a brewpub, Imperial stouts are not really "drinking out" beers in our mind. We'd save this for an after-dinner warmer on a cold winter night.

Flavors and aromas There's a lot going on in this big beer, starting with herbal or minty notes in the nose and a scintillating, lively palate with more herbs—tasters noted mint and licorice—plus bitter chocolate and alcohol. A full, creamy mouthfeel with good carbonation presents all of these flavors well. This is a beer to sip and savor.

Design Apparently, a "Storm King" is a big owl. A dark nightmare of a big owl. This is a big dark nightmare of a beer, so... it works.

Warsteiner Premium

Pale Lager

Country Germany **Style** Pilsner **ABV** 4.8%
Producer Warsteiner Brewery **Price** $$
Packaging 11.2oz/330ml, 16.9oz/500ml bottle, 11.2oz/330ml can
Characteristics Bitter

In the same way that "Budweiser" is Czech for "from Budweis," Warsteiner means "from Warstein." Unlike Budweiser, Warsteiner actually is from Warstein, a Rhine valley city where Warsteiner has been produced since 1753.

Flavors and aromas The aroma is light, with thin, flowery noble hops and pilsner malt, plus some skunkiness. The palate backs off on the malt, bringing a strong bitterness with only mild hop flavors, a profile that carries into the finish. One panelist noted that he was reminded of a Munich pilsner (like Paulaner Pils) but without the rich hop flavors and aromas used in those beers to support the focused bitterness.

Design If you have a hard time reading the Gothic, Germanic font at the center of the label, they've helpfully printed the same information down below in large block letters.

Weihenstephaner Hefe

Wheat Beer

Country Germany **Style** Bavarian Hefeweizen **ABV** 5.4%
Producer Brauerei Weihenstephan **Price** $$$
Packaging 11.2oz/330ml, 16.9oz/500 ml bottle
Characteristics Malty, refreshing, yeasty

Weihenstephan claims (though they're not the only brewery to do so) to be the oldest brewery in the world, marking their founding at a Benedictine abbey in 1040 CE. Today, they're affiliated with (and surrounded by) a technical university.

Flavors and aromas Traditional Bavarian hefeweizen flavors are evident in the nose—clove and banana—but there's also a pleasant lemony/coriander note, as well as wheat malt. The flavor here is smoothly grainy; more hot cereal malt than bread, and it's complemented with clove spiciness and fairly mild banana notes. The low banana character gives this a dryer finish than some of the hefes we tasted, but this was a popular choice.

Design You'll want to buy Weihenstephaner in the 500ml format—the 330ml bottle is barely big enough to contain the brewery's name.

Westmalle Tripel

Belgian Ale

Country Belgium **Style** Pale Belgian Ale **ABV** 9.5%
Producer Brouwerij Westmalle **Price** $$$$$
Packaging 11.2oz/330ml, 25.4oz/750ml bottle
Characteristics Bitter, malty, strong, unusual, yeasty

Many times, we've heard the legend of Trappist ales: ancient brews bubbling out of the depths of hoary cellars. Said cellars can be found in Belgium, sure, but the iconic Trappist style—the tripel—was created at Westmalle in 1934.

Flavors and aromas Half our tasters fairly loved this beer, and half were unenthusiastic. The notes of the latter group suggest that the high alcohol content, which was more present than in other tripels we tasted, may be the culprit. But there are also intriguing spices—cinnamon, clove, nutmeg—along with fruity esters, and the sweetness on the palate is cleaned up into a long finish by dry bitterness, good carbonation, and alcohol. Complex but, perhaps, challenging.

Design The diamond-shaped label is distinctive and clean. We wonder if the logo is a nod to the Freemasons.

Widmer Broken Halo IPA

India Pale Ale

Country USA (OR) **ABV** 6.0%
Producer Widmer Brothers Brewing **Group** Craft Brewers Alliance
Price $$ **Packaging** 12oz/355ml bottle
Characteristics Bitter, hoppy

Widmer is best known for basically inventing the American hefeweizen style in the mid-80s, and recently joined forces with Redhook Goose Island, and Kona Brewing to form the craft beer equivalent of the Traveling Wilburys.

Flavors and aromas Our panel was delighted with the American-styled Broken Halo IPA. What it lacks in in-your-face power, it makes up in impeccable balance, beginning with a complex blend of citrus aromas—our panel listed nearly every citrus fruit grown in North America—before shifting on the tongue to a harmonious blend of hops, bitterness, and supporting malt. The bitterness always leads the malt here, but there are no hard edges to this beer. A wonderfully balanced, calm IPA.

Design There's little cohesion in the naming or label design of Widmer's beers, but we liked the Broken Halo enough to give it a pass.

Widmer Drifter Pale Ale

rating
8

Pale Ale

Country USA (OR) **Style** American Pale Ale **ABV** 5.7%
Producer Widmer Brothers Brewing **Group** Craft Brewers Alliance
Price $$ **Packaging** 12oz/355ml, 22oz/650ml bottle
Characteristics Hoppy, refreshing

Widmer's most recent addition to their year-round bottled beer line is apparently a hit—it quickly rose to become the company's second best-selling beer behind the ubiquitous hefeweizen. Unusual hop character is due in part to use of the New Zealand "Nelson Sauvin" variety.

Flavors and aromas Fresh from the bottle, this shows fairly intense citrusy, resiny hops. But these mellow quickly into a lighter hop-driven nose that's more orange blossom than orange reduction. The palate is smooth, mild, and refreshing, with more floral/light-citrus character. This is a light-bodied beer, but it has clear, well-defined flavors, and all of the parts are nicely balanced. A very nice summer ale.

Design It's easy to miss, but if you really look at the label here, it's remarkably evocative. You can almost hear the seagulls.

Widmer Drop Top Amber

Pale Ale

Country USA (OR) **Style** American Amber Ale **ABV** 5.0%
Producer Widmer Brothers Brewing **Group** Craft Brewers Alliance
Price $$ **Packaging** 12oz/355ml bottle
Characteristics Malty

When Anheuser-Busch took a minority stake in this business and an active role in distribution a decade later, Widmer began to infiltrate pubs and supermarkets formerly the exclusive domain of large breweries.

Flavors and aromas There are beers that seem sweet, and beers that are sweet—Drop Top is in the latter category, having what Widmer describes as "a touch" of lactose (which, like many people, yeast can't digest). We found this to be a perfectly serviceable pale ale but for the distracting and unnecessary sweetness. At typical bar serving temperatures, the sugar probably isn't so noticeable...so why include it?

Design The embossed Widmer crest in the bottle and the color scheme is good, but the casually misaligned name seems like it's trying just a little too hard.

Widmer Hefeweizen

Wheat Beer

rating
5

Country USA (OR) **Style** American Wheat Beer **ABV** 4.9%
Producer Widmer Brothers Brewing **Group** Craft Brewers Alliance
Price $$ **Packaging** 12oz/355ml, 22oz/650ml bottle
Characteristics Refreshing

Kurt and Rob Widmer have been familiar faces in the brewing world since the mid-1980s, when they single-handedly (double-handedly?) created the market for American hefeweizens with this beer. They're also strong supporters of the Portland homebrew scene.

Flavors and aromas Hints of pepper and a tangy note (lemon or buttermilk) are about all that emerge in the very light aroma of this beer. A thin, crackery palate has little of the healthful body of better examples. This is generally very clean, and, other than a light pepper note that persists through the finish, lacking in character and definition.

Design We'll just say this: the label is definitely less boring than the beer inside. Yes, definitely slightly less boring.

Wolaver's Organic IPA

India Pale Ale

Country USA (VT) **ABV** 6.5%
Producer Otter Creek Brewing **Price** $$
Packaging 12oz/355ml bottle
Characteristics Bitter, hoppy

Vermont's organic Wolaver's beers were contract brewed by Otter Creek starting in 1998. The Wolaver family was so happy with the results that in 2002 they bought Otter Creek and merged the companies. The Wolaver's lineup continues to be all-organic.

Flavors and aromas The nose has citrusy hops and toasty malt, which is an odd combination. The first impression of this beer in the mouth is one of sweet, grainy malt and flavor hops, but bitterness marches in at its own pace and gradually takes over, building into a gripping, somewhat astringent center for the beer. Our tasters felt that this IPA lacked complexity, but they generally liked it. If you're nervous about bitterness in beer, this is probably a beer to leave on the shelf.

Design The square framing and bright border color help Wolaver's catch the eye. The odd, British-sounding name helps , too.

Young's Double Chocolate Stout

Dark Ale

rating
6

Country England **Style** Stout **ABV** 5.2%
Producer Wells & Young's **Price** $$$$
Packaging 14.9oz/440ml pub can (nitro); 16.9oz/500ml,
11.2oz/330ml bottle **Characteristics** Malty, unusual, yeasty

London-based Young's is perhaps best-known in its homeland for traditional, low-alcohol beers that are unlikely to see export across the Atlantic, but a handful of their bottled offerings have crossover appeal, like this Double Chocolate Stout (which contains both chocolate malt barley and actual dark chocolate).

Flavors and aromas Our tasters were a little put off by a potent butterscotch aroma in this beer. After that blew off, though, there was plenty to appreciate here. The chocolate shows through in a soft, full mouthfeel and a finish that resembles nothing so much as brownies. The butterscotch aroma/flavor would actually fit in well here if it were toned down a bit. We're sure that some readers will love this beer, while others will want to stay away.

Design We're indifferent to the oddly shaped bottle, but we'd pay extra for the addition of some kind of freshness date here.

Yuengling Light Beer

Pale Lager

Country USA (PA) **Style** Light Beer **ABV** 3.8%
Producer Yuengling Brewery **Price** $
Packaging 12oz/355ml bottle; 12oz/355ml can
Characteristics Bland

Confusingly, Yuengling offers both a "Light Beer," which is a light version of their Yuengling Premium pale lager, and a "Light Lager," which is based on their amber Traditional Lager. We suspect that most drinkers of either don't worry much about which one they're getting.

Flavors and aromas Light malt competes with cooked corn and a slight rubbery note, as well as a hint of skunkiness. The full mouthfeel isn't backed up by nearly enough flavor to balance; there's grainy, bready malt, but not much of it, and hop flavors are absent, with bitterness hovering just on the edge of perceptible. There's a hint of sweetness to the finish that is uncharacteristic of a light lager. Drink cold, or not at all.

Design The blue on this label is an odd contrast to the color scheme of the rest of Yuengling's red, brown, and black palette.

Yuengling Original Black and Tan

Dark Ale

Country USA (PA) **Style** Blended Beer **ABV** 4.7%
Producer Yuengling Brewery **Price** $
Packaging 12oz/355ml bottle; 12oz/355ml, 16oz/473ml can
Characteristics Bitter, malty, refreshing, roasty

Yuengling Black and Tan is a premixed version of the pub cocktail that turns up from time to time, mixing light and dark beers. This version combines Yuengling Premium with Yuengling Dark-Brewed Porter.

Flavors and aromas Our tasters responded well to this porter-and-lager hybrid. Aromas of mild chocolate and roast grains, with hints of sassafras, are fresh and bright. The palate is clean, with sweet malt and chocolate and roast flavors, with mild floral hops and gentle bitterness. The body is light, flavor intensity is lower than we're accustomed to, and in the end this comes off exactly as we suspect it is intended: a refreshing, summer version of dark beer.

Design All of that angled text makes us imagine a designer convinced that there just wasn't room for standard horizontal text. We're pretty sure it would fit, though.

Yuengling Traditional Lager

Amber Lager

Country USA (PA) **Style** Vienna Lager **ABV** 4.4%
Producer Yuengling Brewery **Price** $
Packaging 12oz/355ml, 22oz/650ml, 32oz/946ml bottle,
12oz/355ml, 16oz/473ml can **Characteristics** Refreshing

Once the world was full of regional beers that you had to seek out but had mystique and allure. Yuengling is one of the rare old-school regionals, and we wish there were more of them.

Flavors and aromas "Better than the average light lager," wrote one taster, and if that isn't damning with faint praise, what is? The light amber-colored beer has a faint nose, and a flat, thin palate that has hints of caramel and a very dry finish. This is a very clean, very light lager, and if that's all you want from your beer, we're sure you'll be very happy here.

Design A few years ago, there was a rumor that Yuengling was actually owned by Anheuser-Busch, no doubt fueled by the large eagle logo. They're not, by the way.

Index

Beers